INFORMATION TECHNOLOGY AND GLOBAL INTERDEPENDENCE

Recent Titles in
Contributions in Economics and Economic History

INFORMATION TECHNOLOGY AND GLOBAL INTERDEPENDENCE

EDITED BY

Meheroo Jussawalla, Tadayuki Okuma, & Toshihiro Araki

Foreword by Kazuo Ogura

Published under the auspices of the East-West Center
and the Japan Institute of International Affairs

CONTRIBUTIONS IN ECONOMICS AND ECONOMIC
HISTORY, NUMBER 83

GREENWOOD PRESS
NEW YORK • WESTPORT, CONNECTICUT • LONDON

Library of Congress Cataloging-in-Publication Data

Information technology and global interdependence / edited by Meheroo
   Jussawalla, Tadayuki Okuma, and Toshihiro Araki ; foreword by Kazuo
Ogura.
            p.   cm. — (Contributions in economics and economic history,
   ISSN 0084-9235 ; no. 83)
         "Published under the auspices of the East-West Center and the
Japan Institute of International Affairs."
      Bibliography: p.
      Includes index.
      ISBN 0-313-26326-4 (lib. bdg. : alk. paper)
      1. Information services industry—Technological innovations.
   2. Telecommunication policy. 3. International economic relations.
   4. Information technology. I. Jussawalla, Meheroo.
   II. Ōkuma, Tadayuki. III. Araki, Toshihiro. IV. East-West Center.
   V. Nihon Kokusai Mondai Kenkyūjo. VI. Series.
   HD9999.I492I54   1989
   338'.06—dc19   88-3128

HD
9999
I492
I54
1989

British Library Cataloguing in Publication Data is available.

Library of Congress Catalog Card Number: 88-3128
ISBN: 0-313-26326-4
ISSN: 0084-9235

First published in 1989

Greenwood Press, Inc.
88 Post Road West, Westport, Connecticut 06881

Printed in the United States of America

The paper used in this book complies with the
Permanent Paper Standard issued by the National
Information Standards Organization (Z39.48–1984).

10 9 8 7 6 5 4 3 2 1

Copyright Acknowledgments
Suzanne Settle's "Telecommunications Policy in the United States" was first delivered
as a speech at the May 1986 TIDE 2000 meeting, Honolulu, Hawaii. The views
expressed are the author's own and do not represent the views of either NTIA or the
United States government.

"Information Society and Democratic Prospects" is taken from Majid Tehranian's
Technologies of Power: Information Technologies and Democratic Prospects (Norwood,
N.J.: Ablex Publishing Corporation, forthcoming).

Contents

PART IV
Legal Issues Emerging from Information Technology

PART V
Sociocultural Issues Related to Information Technology

PART VI
Innovations and Future Trends

PART VII
Telecommunications and Development

PART VIII
Conclusions and Recommendations

Foreword:
Information Technologies and International Relations

Kazuo Ogura

Over the past few years, a number of international conferences have addressed the impact of information technologies (IT) on the economies and societies of industrially developed countries. The major discussions in those meetings have generally centered on the effect of IT on employment, industrial structure, telecommunications systems, and trade in services. Some of those problems, particularly trade-related problems, have been recognized as having international implications. Attention seems to have focused, however, on the impact of IT on each economic unit or region and on domestic policy implications or options for each national government. In other words, most of the past discussions have concentrated on the problems that each economy or society is likely to face in adopting IT and adapting itself to development of IT, without going into a deeper study of the impact of the development on international relations. IT is, however, likely to have international or global implications and repercussions.

COMMON RISKS AND DANGERS

One of the global repercussions of IT will be international concern about the risks and dangers that industrial societies may face in the wide application of IT. One such risk may be found in the process of dehumanization that may accompany the wide diffusion of IT. Some researchers argue that the introduction of robots in factories, although reducing the risks of occupational hazards, has made the jobs of semiskilled workers more standardized so that they may not be able to draw as much self-satisfaction as before from their assignments. Such a process of dehumanization of work and its social and economic consequences may be a problem for all industrialized countries, to varying degrees. If such disenchantment is widespread in one society, it tends to have an echo in other countries, thereby affecting the pace and pattern of application of IT globally.

In an entirely different context, one can cite the danger of a biased direction or misplaced allocation of research and development (R&D) resources: wide applications of IT might result in a shift of R&D resources from long-term, basic research to short-term, development research. Because the diffusion of IT is more a process innovation than a product innovation, IT-related technological research tends to be concentrated on the mode of application rather than on the more basic characteristics of relevant technologies. This problem becomes more widespread as the life cycle of IT-related products is shortened. Coping with such a risk is a task common to all countries.

INTERNATIONAL TENSIONS

A second aspect of the international effect of IT is the possibility of increasing international tensions as a result of the diffusion of IT. An example of such tensions is the unbalanced use and application of IT in different countries and areas. One result of such imbalance may be that the benefits of the application of IT are generated mostly in one country or one region at the expense of other less-innovative economies.

In North-South relations, for example, tension might arise in conjunction with the transfer of technology, so-called brain-transfer. How to mitigate or avoid those tensions should be one of the major topics of discussion in international dialogue about IT.

In a somewhat similar vein is the distinct possibility of tension arising out of the unequal distribution of costs and benefits of IT. Given the fact that development and application of IT is a dynamic process that involves transition costs, then social and economic adjustment are indispensable if a society is to make the best use of IT. If, however, such transition costs are shouldered mostly by a particular group of countries, while benefits accrue to other nations, then the whole adjustment process may give rise to international tension.

THE NEED FOR RESHAPING AND RETHINKING

Let us now turn to the more positive side of the international implications of IT. Due to the synergistic nature of IT, barriers to its diffusion will limit its benefits not only in those economies that create barriers but also in countries that commit themselves to the free flow of IT-related products and services. In many cases, internationally concerted actions are likely to be called for to reduce those barriers.

In this connection, we should not forget that the development of IT is likely to affect the pattern and composition of international trade. One notes, for instance, the increasing importance of services, in contrast to manufactured products, in the national incomes of developed economies. Because services are traded less often than goods, whether or not an increasing share of trade is to be realized by newly industrialized countries as a result of the diffusion of IT is open to question.

Another emerging consequence is the tendency to reduce raw material input in manufacturing as a result of the miniaturization of products and computerization of quality-control procedures. Such a trend, if it continues for long, may upset the complementary trade patterns between primary goods producers and suppliers of manufactured products.

Third, the development of computer control and information networks may lead to a more customized marketing of goods and services at lower costs. This may influence location of factories and sales offices and may result in the decentralization of supply bases.

The impact of IT has been felt not only in international trade fields but also in international direct investment. The decreasing labor cost in the total inputs of many electronic products, miniaturization of parts, computerized quality control — all these factors have begun to affect the international direct investment of multinational enterprises that used to invest heavily in developing countries to take advantage of their low labor costs. The rising importance of software and the lack of experts in IT and related technologies in developing countries have also increased the need for foreign investment in human resources; that is, in education or vocational training rather than in the installment of machinery in factories.

All of these factors, which, as a result of the development of IT, are likely to affect international trade relations or investment patterns, are also related to the behavior and strategies of multinational enterprises (MNEs). The synergistic effects of IT and the increasing burden of R&D expenditures tend to highlight the roles of MNEs in the diffusion and application of IT. Small firms and local firms tend to associate themselves with foreign MNEs in order to maintain their competitive positions. Such moves may encourage grouping or affiliation of firms beyond the national boundaries. Affiliation or association has most easily been promoted between parent companies and their interests abroad. In this respect, the large amount of direct investment between the United States and Europe may help facilitate the association of U.S. and European firms.

Grouping or affiliation of firms may, however, result from other motives. Apart from the synergistic effects of IT and large R&D expenditures is the problem of changes in importance of various factors influencing the competitive positions of firms. In addition to the traditional indicators of competitiveness (such as cost of labor or efficiency of management), all of which are internal factors, the level of development of national information networks, the social acceptability of new technologies, and consumers' tastes — that is, factors external to firms — have increased in importance. This trend has urged firms to associate themselves with their competitors to make best use of their mutual information networks and market research techniques. If such groupings or associations are promoted across international borders, then they may have unexpected repercussions in international relations, including the current regulations on restrictive business practices.

Free flow of information and wide diffusion of IT may create new problems in conjunction with sovereignty of national economies. The synergistic nature of IT may result in expansion of information-related industries in the form of multinational conglomerates that can hardly be controlled by national governments. The use of satellite communication might cause similar problems for national control of the flow of information. Harmonizing the traditional concept of sovereignty with the need for the free flow of information could be one of the major problems for discussion among international organizations.

The question of sovereignty is related to the need for standardization of IT and IT-related products or systems. If the emphasis on national sovereignty leads to the lack of international harmonization of standards, then it will reduce the chances for every country to maximize the benefits of IT.

Efforts to secure an environment and conditions better suited to the free flow of information might lead to the rethinking and reshaping of the existing international framework of trade and telecommunications. The increasing importance in our economies of the service sector and its trade implications has begun to lead some to question the validity of some provisions of the General Agreement on Tariffs and Trade, which is based on the conception of trade in goods. In a similar vein, private use of satellites might open for questioning the roles to be played by INTELSAT and related arrangements. Another area that needs rethinking may be intellectual property issues and the existing World Intellectual Property Organization mechanism. The problem of international financial markets for venture capital may become important, too.

All of the international implications that have so far been mentioned in connection with the development of IT orient us to the need for more intense dialogue and closer cooperation among the countries concerned.

I

INTRODUCTION TO INFORMATION TECHNOLOGY

Overview of Thoughts Expressed on Information Technology and Economic Interdependence

MEHEROO JUSSAWALLA

TIDE 2000 stands for Telecommunications, Information, and Interdependent Economies in the year 2000. It represents a project covering three international conferences organized by the Foreign Affairs Ministry of the government of Japan to mark the twentieth anniversary of Japan's accession to the Organization for Economic Cooperation and Development (OECD). All three conferences were focused on the global impact of the technological changes in information and telecommunications networks on economic interdependence, structural adjustments, and sociocultural change. In addition, conferees debated specific issues emerging from innovative technology, such as development of infrastructures in Third World countries, conflicts and trade issues emerging from transborder data flows, and problems of intellectual property rights and copyright laws.

THE CONFERENCES

The first of these three conferences was held in Tokyo in November 1985 and dealt with development issues. Third World representatives addressed the challenges and opportunities arising from a global information economy. The conferees attempted to identify ways in which the industrialized nations might assist developing countries in coming to terms with and taking optimum advantage of sweeping technological changes that challenge their existing industrial structures.

The second conference, held at the East-West Center in Honolulu in May 1986, was focused on the interdependence and integration of markets that information technology has fostered among the OECD member countries. A variety of questions were raised: What are the effects on domestic policies concerning deregulation of telecommunication providers? Why has the natural monopoly concept broken down under pressure from innovative convergent telecommunication networks? Why are European countries continuing to shield their post, telegraph, and telecommunications authorities (PTTs)? Should their domestic policies change in the face of the global integration of networks?

Another issue of significance discussed at the Honolulu conference was international policies for telecommunications. Trade in information services in international financial flows is being changed by the dynamic telecommunications sector, and Europe is responding by setting up both covert and overt barriers to information trade. The conferees responded to the question of whether the General Agreement on Tariff and Trade (GATT) should be used to help solve the services trade issues among OECD countries or whether a new international body should be created to handle the legal aspects and problems of data flow privacy emerging from information trade.

The third conference was held in February 1987 in Fontainebleau, France, at the INSEAD and dealt with current issues of mergers of transnational corporations, their impact on developed countries, the impact of technology on labor organizations, and international competitiveness. This monograph excludes these deliberations and confines itself to the first two TIDE 2000 conferences, both of which were organized by the Japanese Institute of International Affairs. The second conference, held in Honolulu, was cosponsored by the East-West Center's Institute for Culture and Communications.

The Tokyo Conference

This section summarizes the proceedings of the first conference, held in Tokyo under the chairmanship of Dr. Sogo Okamura, Professor Emeritus of Tokyo University. The theme of the conference was the development of advanced information technology and its impact on the interdependence between developed and developing countries. This issue has arisen because the benefits of the Information Revolution were not equally spread; imbalances were created between the North and the South and even among OECD members.

Sir Donald Maitland traced the history of communications from ancient Greece through the Roman Empire to the printing presses of Gutenberg and Caxton. He emphasized the role of the marketplace for ideas and the early innovations of electronic networks. Drawing upon the Maitland Commission's Report, statistics were cited to highlight the disparities in the distribution of telecommunication services. Three-quarters of the 668 million telephones in the world are in eight countries. Developing countries, which account for over 70 percent of the world population and 20 percent of the world's gross domestic product (GDP), use 7 percent of the world's telephones. Tokyo has more telephones than all of Africa. Over the past several years, the United States has added more telephones annually to its system than exist in Africa south of the Sahara. The situation is even worse than these facts make it appear. In many developing countries the telephone system is restricted to the urban areas and beyond these is no system at all.

In the industrialized North, sad to say, this is not the kind of revelation that attracts public attention. Although countries in South and Southeast Asia and Latin America, many of them rich in raw materials, are gaining in influence, international economic activity is still concentrated in North America, Western Europe, and Japan, which between them generate two-thirds of world trade.

The effects of the new technologies on invisible trade — banking, insurance, shipping, aviation, and the like — has also been dramatic. The movement of goods has always been accompanied by an exchange of information. Today, services are available that cannot only shape the routes along which trade flows but can also enable transactions that once took weeks to be completed in a day or even a few minutes. And increases in trade between countries are generally matched by increases in the exchange of information between them. Sir Donald emphasizes that these developments have not proven to be unmitigated blessings. Although developing countries recognized the benefits of new technology, impediments existed in the form of real costs, opportunity costs, and funding for equipment. These impediments accentuated the disparities in the spread of information technology (IT). It is in the mutual interest of the industrialized and developing countries to prevent new gaps from arising by organizing a joint effort to create a world network by the early years of the twenty-first century.

The first session of the first conference dealt with communication systems as infrastructure for development. The key concern was the fact that IT can prove to be either a powerful tool for development or an equally powerful factor for promotion of greater oppression and inequality. To prevent its abuse in application, telecommunications must rapidly be applied to meeting the basic needs of low-income countries.

The second session dealt with the role of transnational corporations as vehicles for technology transfer through their international operations. But such corporations are geared to other goals: seeking resources, markets, and profits in offshore production. Even so, they help by training local technicians, engineers, and managers. The governments of developing countries, however, must foster an environment of collaboration with transnational corporations in order to benefit from technology transfer. Many developing countries view such transfer with suspicion.

Other sessions in the first conference dealt with the development of information services and their importance to economic growth. The globalization of financial services through telecommunication networks was considered useful in the process of development. Regional cooperation through satellite systems was emphasized as a tool for North-South collaboration in information networks. At the same time, developing countries must avoid being overawed by spectacular technologies and find appropriate ones best suited to solve their particular problems. Some participants stressed the need for multilingual communication problems in developing countries. In a multilingual setting, communication systems function as an important social infrastructure.

The Honolulu Conference

The second conference held in Honolulu started out with a look at the need for harmonization of the media revolution, as presented by John Eger, then vice-president of the CBS Broadcasting Group. He cautioned against short-sighted protectionist policies and suggested the acceptance of new technological presumptions that, in turn, require harmonization of tariff policies and laws on privacy and security. The full text of the ideas presented by Dr. Wolfgang Michalski are part of this volume. The economic and social challenges of information technologies were described by Maurice English of the Commission of European Communities' Telecommunications Task Force. Established relationships are being disrupted by IT, yet new opportunities are opening up for all societies, both rich and poor.

The first session dealt with policies, domestic and international, which are undergoing change in consequence of greater interdependence wrought by IT. The main thrust was on deregulation and the future of competition in the telecommunication services industry.

Participants acknowledged the fact that technological developments are placing a strain on existing institutions. The resulting impact of information technology on society makes necessary the introduction of changes in the legal order, which will eventually lead to a "redesigned administrative apparatus." It is no longer possible to distinguish between national and international issues or between economic and political ones. A lively discussion ensued regarding the "obsolescence" of existing international institutions and the "bombshell" effect of this recognition, because it brought into the open a number of hidden weaknesses in existing international organizations. The main thrust of this session was the urgent need for more effective international cooperation to handle the challenge of information technology.

The next session was concerned with the application of IT to society. The interactions between the application of IT and the cultures and traditions of society were discussed at great length, but no conclusive evidence could be cited regarding this interaction. In Europe, institutional adjustments have been called for, and resistance to change has come from ingrained cultural values that needed safeguarding. In general, social institutions have difficulty keeping pace with the rapidly changing information technology. In the context of education, training, and employment, it was conceded that information technology has a significant impact. Training procedures need to be revised.

Participants reviewed carefully the OECD guidelines on trade in information services. In April 1985, the Ministerial Council of OECD adopted the Declaration on Transborder Data Flows, in which member countries declared their intention to promote access to data and information-related services. At that time, the member countries decided to avoid the creation of unjustified barriers to trade, to seek transparency in regulation, to develop common approaches, and, when appropriate, to harmonize solutions and to consider implications for other countries. Ongoing OECD work involves the flow of data that accompanies international trade, which can add up to 11 percent to the cost of products traded internationally.

The challenge to governments in approaching services is to reorient their policies to the future economic environment, to reduce reliance on and related support of old industries, to stop trade nationalism, and to seek international agreements generated by information technology.

A number of overriding questions face the United States government on the eve of trade in services negotiations. Among them are whether to accept the multilateral structure offered by GATT or to pursue more actively bilateral solutions (as with Israel and Canada); where the dividing line should be between GATT and International Telecommunication Union (ITU) responsibilities in telecommunications; whether an umbrella accord should be finished before or at the same time as sectoral agreements; whether or not to include investment issues in the services round; and how end-user oriented the U.S. approach should be. (A consumer bill of rights for corporations is the approach in the Israeli negotiation.)

In the discussion of the legal issues of privacy protection and intellectual property rights emerging from international information flows, the OECD Guidelines on Privacy were debated as a "soft option." The common theme that emerged was the urgent need to find an international institutional framework in which like countries could discuss and develop guidelines or principles to shape domestic law and policy development. The low-level, noncoercive, even "soft" form of international agreement contained in the OECD guidelines had influenced laws developed in many countries, including Japan and Australia. It was suggested that this form of international cooperation and exchange was needed if countries were to cope with the complexity, controversy, and sensitivity of informatics policy questions.

Second-generation privacy and "computer crime" and their impact on the future were debated. The new directions of the OECD's work centered on a recent study of computer crime, which is a serious concern of international scope. The question of how law will address transborder crimes involving informatics was discussed, with full recognition that information transmission knows no fixed place and may pass through several jurisdictions and that, traditionally, criminal law has been developed upon jurisdictional lines.

The results of a study were presented on the operation of European data protection laws and their effect. In some business undertakings, such as electronic funds transfers, there had been a significant impact. On others, including cable television operations, there had been relatively little impact, except on billing practices. The operations of companies involved in transborder flows and informatics generally were affected by tariff policies and intellectual property law restrictions, although it was pointed out that a key provision of the OECD guidelines and most data protection laws was the right of individual access to data.

Papers presented at both sessions have been reviewed and edited for presentation in this volume, although not all papers could be accommodated in consideration of size limitations and restriction of topics.

2

Advanced Information Technologies: Challenges and Opportunities

Wolfgang Michalski

In at least one important respect, information and communications technologies have much in common with other major innovations in the history of mankind: they are set to change dramatically the social and economic fabric of our societies. They are already having far-reaching repercussions on methods of production, employment patterns, and the structures of industry; on the conduct of financial transactions; on the lifestyles of whole communities and entire nations — their patterns of behavior and social contact, their cultural values, and their language. With the further advance and sophistication of information technologies, these changes will continue unabated.

But let it be clear from the outset: information technologies, like all major technical advances, are an integral part of the social and economic systems of industrialized and industrializing nations. This interaction is dynamic and very complicated: just as technological change affects our economic, political, and social structures, so is technological change itself dependent on the resources our economies produce, on the functioning of the political machinery, and most importantly on the capacity of our social and cultural systems both to generate and to absorb new ideas.

It follows from this that the term *information and communication technologies* is used here in its broader sense, to cover all technologies used in the collection, processing, and transmission of information. It includes microelectronic- and optoelectronic-based technologies incorporated in many products and production processes and increasingly used in services. It covers, inter alia, computers, electronic office equipment, telecommunications, industrial robots and computer-controlled machines, electronic components, and software products.

It is my intention in this chapter to offer a broad review of the implications of information and communications technologies for society, the economy, and international relations. It is far from an exhaustive review. The field is too vast and diverse, and much too complex, to attempt such a feat. Rather, I would like to focus on a selection of areas in which information and communications technologies are likely to make a profound impact both within and between countries. I shall endeavor to sketch out in each area the opportunities offered by those new technologies, but also to identify some of the risks that they carry.

IMPLICATIONS FOR SOCIETY

There is an interesting double edge to information and communications technology: although it contributes significantly to the increasing complexities of modern society, it also provides the means for managing those same complexities. Nowhere is this more abundantly evident than in industry, commerce, and new service activities, where the marriage of computers with telecommunications is creating a fundamentally new basis for business transactions. Similarly complex, interlocking information and communications networks exist in government administrations and quasi-government organizations. Medicine and national defense systems are further examples of sophisticated applications of information technologies.

But as our capability to manage these complexities increases, so does our dependence on the technologies we use. Awareness of this vulnerability gives rise to concern for our safety — the safety of society as an organization and our safety as individuals. In the event of a technical or functional breakdown of these systems, or of politically or economically motivated abuse, the ensuing disruptions might cause grave harm to whole groups of society, business, and industries, or to the economy or whole society of a region or a nation.

As individuals, we are concerned for the security of information about our private lives. In the early stages of the computerization of society, the corporate sector — in particular banking, insurance, and private health — was believed to be the biggest threat to privacy. That threat is now associated more with the state. As a consequence of their wide-ranging activities in tax collection, health care, education, and social assistance, public authorities now collect, process, and store more personal data than anybody else. When thousands of terminals are connected to centralized data bases, the term *privacy* assumes a very different dimension. In a modern, computerized welfare society, there can be no such thing as absolute privacy or data security.

Nonetheless, experience gained in many Organization for Economic Cooperation and Development (OECD) countries has shown that privacy protection laws can be a valuable instrument for striking a balance between the information needs of bureaucracies and the rights of citizens to unsurveilled political and personal development. However, despite the important work done by the OECD and the Council of Europe, it is becoming increasingly clear that continuing technological developments and concomitant changes in both the sources of danger and the means of controlling them may necessitate new responses and strategies to safeguard individual liberties and to check the vulnerability of society.

This is not to say that data protection and freedom of information are necessarily conflicting notions; rather they are integral parts of a single comprehensive concept. Within reason, unhindered distribution of data and access to information gathered by industry and administrations is a constituent element of democratic society. Of course, equal opportunity to distribute and gain access to data is not constrained only by institutional and legal factors. Other barriers exist: availability of hardware and software; excessive information costs; uneven balance of power between and among individuals, organizations, and bureaucracies; and differences in computer literacy and skills in handling information technologies generally.

Apart from the problems of technical vulnerability, privacy, and access and distribution of data, the progressive diffusion of information technologies looks fairly certain to bring about far-reaching changes in individual and collective social behavior and in fundamental social and cultural value patterns. By its nature, this area is completely open to speculation, and the challenges to policy makers have still to emerge more clearly. Nevertheless, reflection is called for. Our societies must not be caught completely unawares when such profound changes begin to unfold.

The impact of information technologies on human contact is one such case. Will they facilitate interpersonal communications for people in remote areas or for the handicapped? Will they intensify social interaction generally? The optimistic view of this is that information technologies will lead to a sort of social revitalization — high-tech resulting in a higher rate of human contact. The more pessimistic among us may believe that the new technologies could transform many people's lifestyles into one of increasing social isolation and depersonalization of human communication.

Clearly, the extent to which either the revitalization or human isolation scenarios occurs also depends on the wider social context. Part of this wider context is man's relation to reality. Increasing use of information technologies can create an artificial environment in which the real world is replaced by one of a binary logic of yes/no and if/then. Such artificial realities can become a kind of "substitute knowledge" that unduly restricts living experience and leaves virtually no scope for the tolerance of ambiguity or acceptance of different points of view. Artificial worlds, though rational and self-contained as such, are devoid of meaning. They represent a threat to human creativity, limiting the ability to cope with problems encountered in work and other life situations and inhibiting our capacity to accommodate the unexpected, explore new avenues, and reason along new lines.

The likely impacts on society that have been touched upon here form but the tip of an iceberg. There are implications for language and other means of expression, for national and cultural identity, for possible shifts in morals and value patterns; the list is virtually infinite.

IMPLICATIONS OF INFORMATION TECHNOLOGY FOR THE ECONOMY

There is a noticeable tendency in many circles to persistently underestimate the contribution of information technologies — and for that matter, the contribution of technological change in general — to economic growth and welfare. At first glance this is surprising. Both theory and history should lead us to believe the contrary.

Theory tells us that, together with demand, technical progress is a major determinant of economic growth. Progress generally leads to increased demand for investment goods, and to the extent that it sharpens competition and raises profit margins, it enhances the economy's responsiveness to changing conditions through improved factor allocation. In areas where innovation is accompanied by positive income effects domestically and/or by improved competitiveness internationally, information technology (IT) creates further scope for economies of scale which may spill over into other activities. At the same time, demand for qualified labor rises, generating incentives for education and training.

History tells us that technological innovation has played a major role in the past in augmenting efficiency and welfare. Indeed, it would seem to be making an ever-increasing contribution to total factor productivity. According to studies done in the United States, technological innovation accounted for about half of total factor productivity growth in the United States between 1948 and 1966; for about 70 percent between 1966 and 1973; and for almost all the growth in total factor productivity between 1973 and the end of the decade. All major technical advances — and information and communications technologies fall into this category — tend to raise the productivity of labor: it is estimated that technological change has raised the productivity of the workforce at an average rate of about 2 percent a year over the past century. However, a particular feature of information technologies is that, at the same time, they also tend to raise the productivity of capital.

Failure to anticipate the contribution of technology to economic growth is due in part to the uneven incidence of the impacts of new technologies. This uneven incidence is due to at least two factors. First is the time scale. Many of the adverse economic and social effects of technological innovation typically occur in the short term. They are often concentrated on a few groups or areas and thus tend to be highly visible. The benefits of technological change, on the other hand, are of a more long-term nature and tend to be more diffuse. Second, there is the geographic factor. Not all countries benefit from new technologies to the same extent or with the same rapidity, so that some countries may be perceived as lagging in terms of technological development. But dynamic reorganization of the international division of labor leads to the gradual relocation of production activities toward the countries on the periphery of technological development, thus sustaining the momentum of global growth.

New technologies, and in particular information technologies, are proving to be a major driving force behind economic development and growth not only because the information technologies sector is in itself a highly dynamic and expanding field of activity that creates new markets and generates investment, income and new jobs, but because information technologies facilitate the adjustment of economic and industrial structures generally. This happens through a number of avenues: the impact of information technologies in established industries is in most cases a revitalizing one, assisting sectors to respond more rapidly and more efficiently to shifts in demand patterns and changes in international comparative advantage through more efficient production processes and new or improved products. Information technologies open up greater opportunities for the exploitation of economies of scale and scope; they make for more flexible production and use of labor and equipment and promote the internationalization of production and markets. Information technologies make for greater mobility and flexibility in capital and financial flows and services and are frequently the precondition for the creation of innovative financial instruments.

But it is becoming increasingly evident that the rapid changes taking place in financial markets and the growing internationalization of production and product markets are revealing supervisory structures to be inadequate and competitive and regulatory frameworks to be insufficiently dynamic and flexible. Technological advances in these fields, while enhancing adjustment, are also producing outcomes that tend to weaken government control over the course of the economy. For example, the increasing international mobility of financial capital flows due to faster communication reduces the effectiveness of monetary policy.

But the center stage in the debate surrounding the interaction between new technologies and structural adjustment is occupied by the employment question. Generally speaking, new technologies affect employment in two ways: they influence the level of employment, and they influence the composition of skills and jobs.

Public attention tends to focus on the negative implications of technological change on overall employment levels, and an unmistakably pessimistic note can be detected, particularly in Europe. Yet past events provide us with abundant grounds for optimism. Little convincing evidence has been provided to prove that high unemployment has been due chiefly to the spread of robotics, automatization, or other information technologies. In fact, the evidence could be interpreted as pointing in the opposite direction. A striking example is offered by the U.S. experience of the last fifteen years or so, a period marked strongly by both rapid technological progress and increasing job creation. European studies show that over the long term, employment gains tend to be concentrated in branches and companies that generate above-average increases in labor productivity. Conversely, job losses tend to be greatest in industries and companies that do not innovate.

The pessimistic bias in perceptions of longer-term employment prospects may have its roots in the fact that the employment-displacing effects of technological change are more readily visible and predictable than the job-creating effects. But what counts in the end is whether the overall balance is positive or negative.

Changes in the aggregate level of employment are, of course, the outcome of developments taking place at the industry, company, and workplace levels. The introduction of information technologies is already bringing about far-reaching modifications in the content and organization of work. Job scope and skill are shifting toward diagnosis and problem-solving, which emphasize the capacity for logical, analytical, and abstract thought. There is increasing emphasis in many industries on multiplicity of skills, involving the integration in one worker of tasks previously assigned to a number of operatives.

Traditional boundaries between scientists, engineers, technologists, technicians, craftsmen, and managers are becoming increasingly blurred. And an increasing interdependence can be observed between jobs, functions, departments, and plants.

What these developments in job requirements in fact reflect is a fundamental feature of new technologies: although they may eliminate jobs in one place, they create them in another. Many existing skills are set to become virtually obsolete (e.g., telephone operators, newspaper compositors), whereas others are already expanding dramatically (e.g., electronics engineers, business systems consultants). New skills will emerge (e.g., videotex page creators, data base designers and managers), whereas others "emigrate"; e.g., through the transfer of assembly operations to newly industrialized countries.

Many of the skill-requirement effects of new technologies can be adequately met by existing policies and programs, but the speed and pervasiveness of innovation and the sudden obsolescence of skills and entire occupations inevitably give rise to structural imbalances that are not easy to handle. Labor markets and social security systems are coming under considerable pressure, and the efficiency of education and training systems is already being severely tested.

IMPACT OF INFORMATION TECHNOLOGIES ON INTERNATIONAL RELATIONS

As new information technologies expand their uses and coverage, the world shrinks. Travel times become shorter, information flows faster and in more detail, and both personal and business contacts proliferate. The result is an unprecedented growth in interdependence, which, for all its virtues, impinges dramatically on every country's economic, political, and cultural autonomy. Not only have national economies become more susceptible to the effects of policy decisions taken at the international level, but hardly a policy area remains in which governments can implement measures at the domestic level without having some impact on the domestic policy of some other country. The pace of technological change, particularly in the field of information and communications, will likely accelerate the process. The chances are that its effect on international relations will prove to be double edged. It will put unwelcome strain on countries' economic and political relations with other states, but as governments find themselves faced with an expanding range of constraints, the pressure to cooperate may well increase.

Much, of course, will depend on the general economic environment in which the process of accelerating interdependence evolves.

The strains on international relations will, for example, probably lessen as world trade expands. But will the spread of information technologies promote or hinder the growth of world trade? Clearly, forces are working in both directions. The advance of telecommunications and computerization enlarges the scope for subjecting widely dispersed plants to direct managerial control from a single location; and computer-aided design and production and flexible manufacturing systems may well reduce the optimum scale of production facilities and make far more flexible batch production. The combination of these developments allows for decentralized production in market proximity with centralized financial control. This would seem to operate in favor of international investment, but against international trade. On the other hand, the internationalization of production and assembly will itself augment trade flows, cheap telecommunications permit long distance merchandising and direct order from distant sources of supply, lower transport costs promote trade in merchandise, and improved communications make for further expansion in the international exchange of services, such as banking and insurance. Perhaps more important than the impact of information technologies on the level of world trade, however, is that they will reorder the competitive standing of individual countries, change their comparative advantage, and create new trading patterns. As for the nations at the center of innovation, development and application of new technologies will pursue their transition to the high-tech and service-based economy, leaving much of the production and assembly of the more mature product groups to the industrializing countries at the periphery. The result could be a fundamental shift in the geographic flows not only of finished and semifinished goods but also of raw materials.

Reorganization of the international division of labor and production along these lines should prove generally beneficial for world growth and economic welfare in general. Major problems arise, however, for those industrialized countries caught in the middle: they would be confronted by a widening technological gap with the more advanced economies and a shortening industrial gap with the labor-abundant, price-competitive countries on the newly industrializing periphery. A realistic risk exists in the face of this dilemma: that these countries might perceive defensive measures (such as trade restrictions and subsidies to protect uncompetitive industries) as the only feasible course of action available to them, thus reducing the openness of their economies.

Scenarios such as these remind us of the vast degree to which countries differ in their technological capabilities. Increasingly, governments perceive themselves as playing an important role in narrowing the technology gap between them and their rivals. The dangers to international relations inherent in this strategy are broadly familiar: the tendency in some cases to competitive subsidization and to the build-up of surplus capacities and the risk of exporting the resultant adjustment problems to other countries. But the scope for constructive action within such a strategy must also be recognized. The opportunities for international collaboration to compensate for national deficiencies in technological capability are undoubtedly real.

In numerous other ways the international political landscape will change with the spread and increasing sophistication of information and communications technologies. In the not-too-distant future, political leaders or groups may be able to appeal directly to the public of another country. This would pave the way for the creation of transnational constituencies on a much greater scale than has ever occurred before. To the extent that direct address entails the circumvention of official channels in the target country or countries, it could lead to complex repercussions on international relations. But even small political groups and minority factions would be well placed to reach a much wider national and international audience in pleading their cause.

It is in this context that many countries view with concern the difficulty in maintaining cultural values and a degree of cultural identity in the face of advanced communications technologies. Not only do these tend to promote world markets and the consumption of similar goods, but they can also foster a common lifestyle across national borders. Not surprisingly, governments have already begun to develop a variety of defensive responses in the form of restrictions on access to or the movement of data and television programming across national frontiers. And at regional and local levels, in some countries, the advance of new information technologies has met with a vigorous opposition from groups seeking to preserve their cultural identities, traditions, and languages.

This is not to say that no progress at all has been made toward fostering an unhampered flow of information between countries. In their recent Declaration on Transborder Data Flows, OECD governments stated their intentions: to promote access to data and information and related services and to avoid the creation of unjustified barriers to the international exchange of data and information; to seek transparency in regulations and policies relating to information, computer, and communications services affecting transborder data flows; and to develop common approaches for dealing with issues related to transborder data flows and, when appropriate, develop harmonized solutions.

CONCLUSION

The diversity of the issues that emerge from this general overview of the effects of information and communications technologies on society, the economy, and international relations is matched only by the diversity in social and economic policy concerns and priorities pursued by the advanced industrialized nations. The main thrust of U.S. policy at the domestic level is on deregulation and, at the international level, on obstacles to trade and investment. Europe is preoccupied with the impact on domestic employment and, internationally, with problems of industrial and technological competitiveness. The focus of domestic interest in Japan is on the emerging information society, whereas at the international level it is acutely aware of the implications of information technologies for increasing global interdependence.

Given this wide range of policy issues on the one hand and the diversity of policy approach on the other, policy responses are urgently required at the national and international level. If these responses are to be successful in maximizing the opportunities offered by the advance of information and communications technology and in minimizing the attendant risks, three principles have to be observed. First, the diversity of the policy concerns and priorities that have been noted above need to be taken into account in a balanced way in the international dialogue. Second, in the light of increased world interdependence, domestic policies must be formulated that take account of their possible international implications. And third, awareness of the benefits of international cooperation should be heightened, in particular by demonstrating that global welfare can be significantly enhanced if domestic policies are oriented to an agreed-upon concept of internationally coherent action.

II

INTERDEPENDENCE
POLICY AND
PRACTICE

3

Deregulatory Trends in OECD Countries

MARCELLUS SNOW AND MEHEROO JUSSAWALLA

Telecommunications technologies are rapidly converging to open up a vast array of new opportunities for users and suppliers of networks. The economic impact of this revolution is beginning to emerge in a significant manner. After a century of stable development, the industry is facing massive upheavals that are challenging established institutional and industrial structures. At the heart of this process is the convergence of computing and communication technologies that affect industries other than telecommunications.

Electronic information highways have removed the distinctions between hitherto separate industries, lowering the barriers to entry by new competitors. This trend led Reuters to develop as a financial trading network provider. The full consequences of this transformation in economic and policy terms is an emerging critical issue for the Organization for Economic Cooperation and Development (OECD) countries.

TECHNOLOGY AND DEREGULATION

Conceptualizing Technology and Technological Progress

Where the engineer sees a vast landscape of novel and qualitatively diverse processes and components in information technology, the economist builds a conceptual black box and simply asks about the relationship between inputs and outputs (the production function) or between outputs and cost (the cost function). Either the cost or the production function, when correctly specified and estimated, constitutes all that is of interest in the technology from a purely economic point of view. In addition, these functions can be used to identify various kinds of economies inherent in the technology, as well as the pace and nature of technological progress. Such progress can be said to occur when more output can be derived from a given amount of input, or, equivalently, when a given output requires less input.

The Multiproduct Property of Information Technology

From an economic view, it is proper to identify outputs of the production process by patterns of consumer demand. Thus, what might be considered an output that can be considered an equivalent of bandwidth, from a purely technical standpoint, becomes a qualitatively diverse range of outputs or services when differing consumer demand and preferences are taken into account. For example, a given amount of bandwidth or capacity might be used for voice, data, or video. It might be a link from one sender to one receiver, from one sender to many receivers, or, as in the case of a conference call, among many senders and receivers. The transmission can occur at different times of day, on different days of the week, and under different technical and operational specifications, including quality of transmission, priority of service, and so forth. All of these characteristics make it clear that telecommunications and information technologies in general are inherently multiproduct in character.

Multiple outputs from a single production process have until recently escaped serious analysis by economic science. Since the mid-1970s, however, fundamental breakthroughs in microeconomic theory — specifically, in the economic subdiscipline of industrial organization — have greatly facilitated the scientific analysis of developments in information technology and their effects on domestic industrial structure. These developments will now be briefly outlined.

Central to the intellectual underpinning of any form of economic regulation is the concept of natural or de facto monopoly — a monopoly that inheres in cost relations and technological reality — in contrast to a de jure monopoly, which is imposed by regulatory, administrative, or legislative fiat. Seminal works by Baumol (1982), Baumol, Panzar, and Willig (1982), Zajac (1978), and others have yielded a simple, convincing, extremely robust, and versatile definition of *natural monopoly* as a property of the cost function. In essence, a natural monopoly exists if one firm is able to produce a given output of products more cheaply than can a combination of two or more firms.

Other concepts hinge on the notion of natural monopoly. If a firm produces only one output, then one property of natural monopoly turns out to be equivalent to the familiar attribute of economies of scale — average cost decreases as the level of output increases. If more than one output is allowed for, however, more and more novel results emerge. In the multiproduct framework, for example, economies of scope are said to obtain if a natural monopoly allows synergies of joint production to make it cheaper for a single firm to manufacture a given combination of outputs than for a number of firms to specialize in manufacturing those outputs individually.

The question of whether or not a natural monopoly should be protected by regulators in the public interest is of obvious policy concern. The traditional rationale for public control of natural monopolies in such sectors as telecommunications, energy, and transportation was to protect the public from potential abuses of the monopolists while preserving the monopolies themselves in the interest of economic efficiency. The nature and extent of desirable regulatory protection, however, depend on the extent to which cost and technological factors encourage competition by rivals with a firm endowed with natural monopoly attributes. For example, a natural monopoly is said to be *sustainable* if it can frustrate any attempt at entry into its product markets by smaller, more specializing rivals — in other words, if no financial incentives for such entry exist. A natural monopoly unable to withstand such entry is *unsustainable,* and an obvious argument exists for regulatory proscription of entry by competitors in the interest of economic efficiency. This is based on the fact that competition would prevent the least-cost output from being made available to consumers. Sustainability is an example of a concept uniquely meaningful in a multiproduct setting, because all single-product natural monopolies are (trivially) sustainable by virtue of economies of scale.

Another important recent idea in the economic analysis of information technology is that of *contestability* of market structure. The strong natural monopoly and multiproduct properties of many information technologies make the conventional economic abstraction of perfect competition — involving a large number of small, single-output firms, each of which has no influence over price — quite unrealistic. Contestability theory is an attempt to show that some of the values of the competitive process can be preserved in a market with a small number of large firms — in particular, a monopolist with several smaller potential rivals.

Two contestability concepts are particularly useful when applied to the deregulation of telecommunications and other information technologies. First, potential as well as actual competition can exert a galvanizing influence on the monopolist firm, inducing it, for example, to reduce prices, increase output, and become more responsive to user needs. Second, it must be relatively inexpensive for rival firms to enter and, if necessary, to leave markets they wish to "contest." Heavy barriers to entry in the form of extensive capital, legal, and lobbying costs that cannot be converted to other uses — known as *sunk costs* — make it more difficult for rivals to contemplate actual competition and thus for the established monopoly firm to accept competition as a credible threat.

A final example of advances in the area of multiproduct theory relevant for information technology involves the discovery of cost and production functions able to accommodate multiple outputs. The most common of these, which have been available since the early 1970s, are *translog* (transcendental logarithmic) functions, which among other uses have been applied to test for the presence of natural monopoly in the predivestiture American Telephone & Telegraph Company (AT&T) and INTELSAT.

The successive shifts and reverses in Federal Communications Commission (FCC) policy over the last three years show that decision makers cannot easily strike a balance between permitting smaller competitors to flourish and not imposing too many constraints on the dominant suppliers that would hinder their capacity to compete. The industrial structure on the supply side has to adjust to the loss of captive markets due to deregulations, increasing costs of R&D for new products, and the rapidly increasing cycle of innovation. These factors are driving suppliers to seek new global markets, and competition is whittling away profit margins on many products. Europe is even more vulnerable to these upheavals than the United States or Japan. Its home markets have failed to provide the kind of scale economies needed to absorb development costs.

On a per capita basis, Europe's investment in telecommunications equipment is a third of the U.S. level; European suppliers are trying to link up with international partners.

Schools of Regulatory Theory

Regulatory economics comprises a number of distinct traditions regarding both positive and normative aspects of the regulatory process. Those most relevant to information technologies will be briefly summarized here. They are the conventional or public interest theory, the capture school, the cooperative approach, and the political economy of deregulation.

Public interest regulation proceeds from the assumption of a monopolist producing a single output under economies of scale. Straightforward microeconomic theory suggests that this firm has an incentive to produce a smaller output at a higher price than it would under competition. The regulatory authorities preserve the monopoly as a legal entity to prevent "needless duplication of facilities" but require the firm to reduce prices and increase output according to certain criteria (such as recovering a "fair" or market-oriented rate of return on its invested capital).

The capture theory, identified with the University of Chicago but sharing some insights with more radical viewpoints, suggests that various flaws in the regulatory mechanism — such as delays and asymmetries of information and staff size between the regulated firms and the regulatory body — conspire to make regulators work in the interest of the regulated firms. They are in essence "captured" by the industries they are supposedly regulating in the public interest.

Cooperative approaches to regulation, tracing a line of intellectual ancestry to the English cooperative movement of the nineteenth century, are seldom found in practice. INTELSAT, the global intergovernmental commercial satellite consortium, is organized financially as a cooperative of owners and users. The French telecommunications authorities stress cooperation as an alternative to competition in obtaining goals of social welfare and economic efficiency. A German variant of cooperative theory, known as *Gemeinwirtschaft* (social economy), has been influential for decades in informing socialist arguments in that country for continued public ownership and operation of telecommunications and other public utilities.

The political economy of deregulation school, because of its recent origin, has been applied extensively to the regulation of information technology in industrialized countries. It stresses the role of the state, of interest groups, and of the institutional environment generally in affecting the outcome of policy debates. In particular, it addresses the following question: Why can the implementation of regulatory arrangements that are demonstrably superior to the status quo from purely "technical" perspectives (those of economics, law, and engineering, for example) be frustrated by interest group coalitions in the political process?

Telecompetition in OECD Countries

Britain and the United States have shown that even imperfect deregulation is better than none. Britain now has more than 600 value-added networks compared with one or two in France and Germany. The result is that the productivity of British business and industry is rapidly rising and attracting European telecom-munications business. The telecommunications industry in Western Europe, on the other hand, has been under stress. A study done by Arthur D. Little for the European Economic Community (EEC) Commission reports that EEC businesses use half as many telephones as their counterparts in the United States and that EEC homes have two-thirds as many telephones as U.S. homes. Prior to the merger of Satellite Business Systems with MCI, SBS's annual marketing budget was bigger than the total EEC expenditure on satellite communications each year. EEC's telecommunications investment per head has been 80 percent of the Japanese level and 40 percent of the U.S. level.

There are two major reasons for the weaker telecommunications sector in Europe. First of all, the European post, telegraph, and telecommunications authorities (PTTs) are removed from the market. Basic services are priced without reference to costs to meet the objective of universal service. Telecommunications revenues are used to subsidize losses from the postal service. The West German Bundespost has the highest-quality old-technology network in the world and in general discourages service alternatives like value-added networks (VANs) and leased lines. The second reason for Europe's comparatively weak telecommunications sector is the fragmentation of the European markets. Before the microchip revolution, a central office switch had a life span of twenty to thirty years. A modern switch requires an investment of $50 million to $1 billion, which must be recovered within ten years for fear of the technology's obsolescence. Furthermore, European countries do not collaborate on standards, and this results in a less than optimal allocation of scarce resources. The chances of liberalization are slimmer in Europe than are the chances of privatization. Privatization helps the government to get cash, the shareholders to get a profitable company, and the telecommunication managers to get rid of government intervention. Liberalization introduces competition, which may be disturbing to Western European PTTs.

In the mid-1960s, microchips and computers hastened the demise of the natural monopoly. In the United States there was no question that monopolies would have to go because technology has changed market demand and monopolies stand in the way of the market trends. The industry structure itself is changing in such a way that the combination of wire and nonwire services and the competition between them may destroy the last remnants of monopoly during the 1990s.

Apart from the political and social problems related to reforming monopolies, a major issue stems from deregulation. The newly deregulated monopoly enters the competitive market armed with huge sums of rate-payer investment, the confidence of former customers, and a knowledge of the existing network. The new competitors have none of these advantages. Policy makers find this "competitive" environment confusing. Technology is forcing computer and telecommunications providers to compete in a framework of systems integration that undermines the regulatory structure. The social and economic transformation caused by this process will raise issues for decision makers for some years in the future. The economic pressures creating the integration of systems will be first felt in offices and factories before they reach the homes of users.

SUMMARY OF DEREGULATORY TRENDS IN SOME OECD COUNTRIES

Canada

Industrial structure and deregulatory timetables in information industries are remarkably similar in Canada and the United States. Technological developments have been essentially simultaneous, due in part to extensive patent and licensing agreements. A lag of several years between initial deregulatory developments in the United States and analogous events in Canada has been noted by researchers.

Despite this similarity, Canadian policy toward regulating information technologies has been more systematically considered and implemented and lacks the ideological flavor of U.S.-style deregulation. There is as yet, for example, no real conviction among Canadian policymakers that natural monopoly has disappeared in information equipment or service markets. Nonetheless, in 1982, the same suit as against AT&T was approved; shareholders of Bell Canada voted for a sweeping corporate reorganization that paralleled developments in the United States.

The major structural adjustments of information and telecommunications industries in Canada have to do with restrictions by regulatory authorities on the permissible scope of Bell Canada's activities. By any account, information industries in Canada, particularly telecommunications, have been radically restructured in recent years. The implications of this massive transformation are yet to be realized fully. In addition, the concrete effects of deregulatory proceedings by Canadian authorities have not yet become clear. These proceedings involve policies in such areas as enhanced services, resale, and complete system interconnection. Which consumer groups will be hurt and which benefited is uncertain. New market niches, however, will probably be created for bold entrants willing to offer new services to users.

The consensus in Canada is that although industrial restructuring and deregulation of information technologies have introduced uncertainty and some distributional inequities into the economy, the costs of standing still would have been even greater.

France

France is unique among major industrialized countries in its defense of ministerial monopoly in furnishing telecommunications services and in the role of the state generally in providing industrial structures and economic incentives promoting advances in information technology. Its PTT administration prefers cooperation to competition and is pursuing decentralization of telecommunications and broadcasting as an alternative to deregulation.

In its activist role, the French PTT has numerous subsidiaries, including several abroad, that function along commercial lines. In addition, three large telecommunications manufacturers were nationalized in 1981. France sees its PTT monopoly as being exercised in a liberal and enlightened manner; for example, competition has been allowed in the terminal equipment market since 1920. The countervailing advantages of monopoly in telecommunications service provision are seen in France as universality of service; reliable and secure networks; uniform tariffs with no incentives for cream skimming; and common technical standards. As for the alleged lack of initiative and dynamism in ministerial monopoly, France points to its early development of digital telephone switching; telematics and data communications, including the Transpac packet-switched public data network; and the recent "recabling of France" authorization to implement interactive cable television and videocommunication networks using optical fibers and other advanced concepts.

As for future policies in information technology, the French government anticipates continued expansion of public data networks; implementation of a new tariff policy approximating user charges to actual costs; measures favorable to the development of value-added services using public networks; and continued liberalism regarding competition in the terminal equipment sector.

Deregulation of a kind, certainly decentralization, can be said to have resulted from the Audiovisual Communication Law of July 1982, which eliminated the state's monopoly for both programming and broadcasting and allowed for substantial local initiative in both. In contrast, the state retains an activist role in computers and information processing, particularly in legal safeguards for privacy of data files and restrictions on their transmission outside France.

West Germany

Recent declines in its export shares in high-technology products have induced the West German government to take a stronger role in formulating an industrial strategy to promote the development of microelectronics, information, and communications technology. It sees this action as paralleling massive government expenditures in the United States for defense and space and strategic interaction in Japan between government and industry. Among the thirty-two different projects and DM 3 billion committed to this industrial promotion program by the West German government is an integrated services digital network (ISDN) to begin operation in 1989 on an experimental basis.

It is safe to say that deregulation of the telecommunications sector in West Germany has been very carefully studied by many interested parties but not yet implemented to an appreciable degree. Such analyses include an influential assessment by three industrial organization economists hired by the West German Monopolies Commission. Although their report recommended a number of deregulatory reforms, it stopped short of suggesting that the Deutsche Bundespost (DBP) be prohibited from competing in terminal equipment markets, on the ground that it might enjoy economies of scope in doing so. Later but less straightforward parliamentary reports and evaluations followed. The DBP now has its own Research Institute for Communications Services that actively investigates economic and policy issues impinging on areas falling under the DBP's statutory "telecommunications sovereignty."

Regulatory changes to date include administrative separation of the DBP's licensing and inspection functions; judicial and administrative decisions promotive of private, commercial radio and television broadcasting; and some concessions to more transparent DBP procurement procedures. Nonetheless, as Western Europe's largest enterprise and employer, the DBP is frank about its "social" objectives — such as universal service, cross-service subsidies of various sorts, and uniform engineering standards — that have achieved a certain political consensus at the cost of economic efficiency narrowly construed.

Finally, there is a complex, constitutionally mandated interplay of state and federal competence relating to West Germany's radio and television broadcasting, which, while facilitating diversity and pluralism, has led to practical difficulties in arriving at an overall policy.

Japan

Two laws of "Copernican" import became effective in Japan in 1985. The first abolished the monopoly of Nippon Telegraph and Telephone (NTT), the domestic telecommunications carrier, by allowing other firms, including foreign ones, to compete. The second converted NTT from a state-owned enterprise to a private, joint-stock company. By this stroke of legislation, Japan vaulted decades forward into the kind of deregulation that has accumulated slowly and somewhat unpredictably in the United States.

Japanese policy can be seen as having emerged from two different conceptions of the role of telecommunications and information technology generally. The one, espoused by the Ministry of International Trade and Industry (MITI), sees telecommunications as part of a microeconomic "industry" policy. The other, favored by the Ministry of Posts and Telecommunications (MPT), takes a broader social view, urging the application of new telecommunications technologies in various experiments encouraging social interaction and information exchange. In addition, the ministries had differing perceptions of the emerging interface of communications and information in Japan: MPT regarded it as part of the telecommunications industry, whereas for MITI it was an information processing industry.

Less deregulatory pressure has been brought to bear on Japanese broadcasting, because it has already achieved a broad social consensus. A creative tension exists between commercial broadcasting, which helps prevent the government-operated system from becoming inefficient and unresponsive, and the state-run Nippon Broadcast Corporation (NHK) networks, which have maintained a certain level of quality in Japanese radio and television programming.

Thus, deregulation of the telecommunications sector can be seen in a pragmatic rather than in an ideological light. It is an aspect of Japan's well-known "industrial policy," according to which promising growth industries are encouraged by various public incentives and interactions with the private sector. This contrasts with analogous policies in a number of other industrialized countries, where interest-group politics lays greater stress on subsidies, loans, and fiscal incentives to save declining industries.

The United Kingdom

Much like Japan did, the United Kingdom recently enacted sweeping legislation with two major effects. First, British Telecom (BT), the government communications carrier, was privatized by the sale of its shares to the public. Second, limited competition with BT was allowed by the licensing of the Mercury consortium as a second network carrier.

These major readjustments of British industrial structure were significantly influenced by input from the academic community and can be said to reflect long-standing political views of the British government favoring both the encouragement of competition and the dismantling of various forms of state entrepreneurship.

Particular steps toward liberalization of information-related activities also include easier entry into terminal equipment markets; encouragement of value-added network services (VANS); and the establishment of a separate, nonprofit standards board to test equipment and ensure its compatibility with BT's network.

The 1984 telecommunications legislation granted British Telecom a twenty-five-year operating license. BT's price increases for the first five years will be limited to 3 percent less than the annual increases in the retail price index. The license also obliges BT to provide rural and ship-to-shore services, public call boxes, services for the disabled, and emergency services. In addition, BT is required to continue providing maintenance and installation services throughout the country according to a uniform charging scale. BT must also provide universal service unless a computer does so.

Deregulation of emerging cable television and satellite broadcasting services has been more gradual and is still under way. A 1980 government statement favoring competition in cable television led to the granting of a number of experimental pay-TV licenses. Since then, government policy and commissioned studies have dealt with difficult choices involving network architecture, program content, and the nature and extent of interactive video services. Progress toward direct broadcasting satellites for Great Britain has been fueled both by the desire to provide a wider range of programming and the goal of promoting British information and aerospace technologies.

The United States

Deregulation has a long but uneven history in the United States. There are both positive and negative lessons for other countries wishing to learn from the U.S. experience.

Information industry policy dates from at least 1956, when AT&T and the U.S. government entered into a consent decree enjoining AT&T and Western Electric, its subsidiary, from engaging in business activities other than common carriage of communications service. Since then the Federal Communications Commission (FCC) has gradually introduced more competitive influence into three main areas: terminal equipment, long distance, and international telecommunications.

The most striking recent development is of course the agreement in 1982 between AT&T and the U.S. Department of Justice providing for the divestiture of AT&T as of January 1, 1984. As a result, AT&T lost its local operating companies, which are now grouped into seven new regional groupings. AT&T has retained its nationwide intercity network composed of its Long Lines Department; the intercity facilities of the Bell operating companies; Bell Laboratories; and Western Electric. In return, AT&T is now allowed to enter computer, computer-related, and information-services markets. It is vigorously competing in these activities with the new regional Bell firms, established computer companies, and other long-distance companies.

The decision to divest AT&T of its local operating companies in the name of economic efficiency was not universally popular in the United States, despite the broad political and economic consensus that made it possible. One result of the change has been for competition to align prices more exactly with costs of individual services, thereby doing away with time-honored patterns of cross-subsidization. Something of a political reaction accumulated in the U.S. Congress, which opposed the addition of network access charges to residential telephone bills unless the FCC agreed to introduce them gradually. Congress, for its part, has been unable, despite at least two concerted attempts, to provide comprehensive legislation to replace the Communications Act of 1934.

Finally, current U.S. government policy regarding international deregulation, while consonant with the views of business and other user groups, has met opposition abroad, particularly from European PTT administrations. In addition, INTELSAT opposes the U.S. government's approval of limited competition by private commercial satellite systems on the North Atlantic and other routes.

COMPETITION AND GLOBAL MARKETS

Competitiveness of Domestic Information Technology Industries in Overseas Markets

As noted above, West Germany is taking steps to restructure its information industries to make them more competitive abroad, particularly in developing countries with no domestic markets of their own to protect. A number of OECD countries face the difficult choice of maintaining comfortable but restrictive procurement procedures between the PTT and a few large firms or of loosening the procurement process in favor of more competitors and greater diversity of supply. The latter policy, although often entailing painful readjustments in the domestic industry, allows the forces of competition to make industry more viable in competing for telecommunications, aerospace, and other information-related contracts abroad.

Deregulation in countries like the United States and Japan has opened domestic telecommunications markets and information markets generally to foreign entrants. For example, certain commercial subsidiaries of the French PTT are active in the United States, and the United States lobbied vigorously and successfully to have the recent Japanese telecommunications bills allow liberal entry by foreign competitors. Thus, telecommunications administrations and industries in countries that may not allow particularly liberal access to their own domestic service and equipment markets are finding themselves the beneficiaries of liberalized access to similar markets in other countries. Inevitably, the question of reciprocity must arise. Depending on how it is answered, ease of access to overseas information markets will either increase or be reversed by protectionist pressures.

Service versus Facilities Competition

Whether or not existing network or other capital-equipment facilities are duplicated as the result of liberalized competition has obvious implications for the structure of domestic information industries. Duplication of existing networks is an extreme example of competition; the economic viability of this approach depends on the presence or absence of a natural monopoly in the cost function of the technology in question. Competition can also develop at the fringes of the network, in terms of terminal equipment and services offered by various enterprises, including the PTT itself. Such service competition occurs when a vertically integrated firm — providing, for example, both a network and communications services — is obliged to allow a competitor access to its own facilities in order to compete with those services. One can think of facilities competition as horizontal in nature: AT&T versus MCI in the United States or British Telecom versus Mercury in the United Kingdom. Service competition, as noted, is vertical, involving asymmetries in the extent to which competitors are vertically integrated. Telematically, this might be reflected in competition between AT&T and IBM in the United States, or between British Telecom and IBM in the United States, or between British Telecom and IBM in the United Kingdom. Value-added or enhanced services are, of course, examples of service competition. In international terms, INTELSAT has declared itself amenable under certain circumstances to service competition on its own facilities, while vigorously opposing the establishment of facilities competition in the form of physically separate satellite systems.

Premature deregulation of special services could thwart competition in the telecommunications industry. Special services involve stable, long-term, custom-made offerings. Carriers and users dispute the principle that special activities are not in fact common carrier services. The questions then arise of whether or not market forces are sufficient to assure universal availability of special services and of whether or not private spectrum should be used for such services. Private spectrum use may aggravate existing private radio frequency congestion in the face of dwindling spectrum availability. In the United States, carriers and users have been aware that the Federal Communications Commission has regulated additional or special services to keep them relatively free of abuse. There is apprehension that market forces are not yet sufficient to protect users more effectively than existing tariff processes. Special services offered by dominant carriers are unregulated, and it becomes possible for them to be cross-subsidized if competition develops. The whole issue becomes a Catch-22. On the one hand, frequency shortage prevents users from building a private system and on the other they have to turn to the dominant carrier to meet their needs, and they must pay whatever the carrier demands in an unregulated, noncompetitive environment.

Telecommunications Deregulation and the Information Economy

We conclude by examining what is arguably the most profound of all domestic structural adjustments in industrializing countries: the replacement of manufacturing by information activities as the primary output of the late-twentieth-century global economy. It is clear that deregulation of the telecommunications sector of the OECD and other industrialized countries has been instrumental in this historic transformation. Indeed, it is comparable in extent and import to the Industrial Revolution, which replaced agriculture with manufacturing as the major economic activity of the nineteenth century.

Virtually all observers agree that deregulation has introduced greater diversity and user responsiveness into telecommunications markets. We have noted previously that telecommunications is a vital common element in many information services. Thus, in ways still difficult to characterize with any precision, it can be seen that cheaper, more diverse, and more user-responsive telecommunications facilities have played a crucial role in ushering in the information economy. Can the information society be far behind?

BIBLIOGRAPHY

Akutsu, Yoshiro. 1978. "The Japanese Path Toward an Information Society." In *Information Societies: Comparing the Japanese and American Experiences*, edited by Alex S. Edelstein, John E. Bowes, and Sheldon M. Harsel, 191–94. Seattle: U. of Washington Press.

Baer, Walter. 1978. "Telecommunications Technology in the 1980s." In *Communications for Tomorrow: Policy Perspectives for the 1980s*, edited by Glen O. Robinson, 61–123. New York: Praeger.

Bailey, Elizabeth E., and William J. Baumol. 1984. "Deregulation and the Theory of Contestable Markets." *Yale J. on Reg.* (2):111–38.

Bailey, Elizabeth E., and Ann Friedlaender. 1982. "Market Structure and Multiproduct Industries." *J. Econ. Lit.* 20(3): 1024–48.

Baughcum, Alan. 1986. "Deregulation, Divestiture, and Competition in U.S. Telecommunications: Lessons for Other Countries." In *Marketplace for Telecommunications: Regulation and Deregulation in Industrialized Democracies*, edited by Marcellus S. Snow, 69–105. New York: Longmans.

Baumol, William J. 1982. "Contestable Markets: An Uprising in the Theory of Industry Structure." *Amer. Econ. Rev.* 72(1):1–15.

Baumol, William J., John C. Panzar, and Robert D. Willig. 1982. *Contestable Markets and the Theory of Industry Structure*. New York: Harcourt Brace Jovanovich.

Beesley, Michael E. 1981. "Liberalization of the Use of British Telecommunications Network." Report to the Secretary of State. London: Her Majesty's Stationery Office.

____. 1985. "Progress in U.K. Telecoms Regulation and Competition." In *The Washington Round: World Telecommunication Forum, Washington, D.C., 18–19 April 1985*, 241–51. Geneva: ITU.

Beesley, Michael E., and Steven Littlechild. 1983. "Privatization: Principles, Problems and Priorities." *Lloyd's Bank Rev.* 149:1–20.

Bowes, John E. 1981. "Japan's Approach to an Information Society: A Critical Perspective." *Keio Communication Rev.* 2:39–49.

Christensen, Laurits R., D. Cummings, and Philip E. Schoech. 1983. "Econometric Estimation of Scale Economies in Telecommunications." In *Economic Analysis of Telecommunications: Theory and Applications*, edited by Leon Courville, Alain de Fontenay, and Rodney Dobell, 27–53. New York: North-Holland.

Coursey, Don, R. Mark Isaac, and Vernon L. Smith. 1984. "Natural Monopoly and Contested Markets: Some Experimental Results." *J. Law Econ.* 27(1):91–114.

Evans, David S., and James J. Heckman. 1983. "Multiproduct Cost Function Estimates and Natural Monopoly Tests for the Bell System." In *Breaking up Bell: Essays on Industrial Organization and Regulation*, edited by David S. Evans, 253–82. New York: North-Holland.

____. 1984. "A Test for Subadditivity of the Cost Function with an Application to the Bell System." *Amer. Econ. Rev.* 74(4):615–23.

Forester, Tom, ed. 1985. *The Information Technology Revolution*. Cambridge, Mass.: MIT Press.

Fujitake, Akira. 1978. "The Development of an Information Society in Japan." In *Information Societies: Comparing the American and Japanese Experiences*, edited by Alex S. Edelstein, John E. Bowes, and Sheldon M. Harsel, 125–34. Seattle: U. of Washington Press.

Germany, Federal Republic. Monopolkomission. 1981. *Die Rolle der Deutschen Bundespost im Fernmeldewesen.* Bonn: Bundespost.

Hudson, Heather E., E. Parker, A. Hardy, and D. Goldschmidth. 1979. *The Role of Telecommunications in Socio-Economic Development: A Review of the Literature with Guidelines for Further Investigations.* Washington, D.C.: Keewatin Communications.

Ito, Youichi. 1981. "The 'Johaka Shakai' Approach to the Study of Communication in Japan." In *Mass Communication Review Yearbook, Volume 2,* edited by G. Cleveland Wilhoit and Harold de Bock. Beverly Hills: Sage.

_____. 1985. "Implications of the Telecommunications Policy Reform in Japan." *Keio Communication Rev.* 6:7–18.

_____. 1986. "Telecommunications and Industrial Policies in Japan: Recent Developments." In *Marketplace for Telecommunications: Regulation and Deregulation in Industrialized Democracies,* edited by Marcellus S. Snow, 210–30. New York: Longmans.

Ito, Youichi, and Morikazu Takahashi. 1985. "Implications of the Japanese Telecommunications Policy Reform for International." In *The Washington Round: World Telecommunication Forum, Washington, D.C., 18–19 April 1985,* 91–101. Geneva: ITU.

Jonscher, Charles. 1986. "Telecommunications and Industrial Policies in Japan: Recent Developments." In *Marketplace for Telecommunications: Regulation and Deregulation in Industrialized Democracies,* edited by Marcellus S. Snow, 210–30. New York: Longmans.

Joskow, Paul L., and Roger G. Noll. 1981. "Regulation in Theory and Practice: An Overview." In *Studies in Public Regulation,* edited by Gary Fromm, 1–65. Cambridge, Mass.: MIT Press.

Jussawalla, Meheroo. 1986. "The Policy Relevance of an Information Economy." In *Telecommunications and Development,* edited by Walter Richter. Geneva: ITU.

_____. 1984. "The Future of the Information Economy." *Journal of Communication* (Keio University).

Jussawalla, Meheroo, and Don M. Lamberton, eds. 1982. *Communication Economics and Development.* New York: Pergamon.

Jussawalla, Meheroo, Don M. Lamberton, and Neil Karunaratne, eds. 1988. *The Cost of Thinking: Information Economies of Ten Pacific Region Countries,* 15–41. Norwood, N.J.: Ablex.

Kaiser, Gordon E. 1986. "Developments in Canadian Telecommunication Regulation." In *Marketplace for Telecommunications: Regulation and Deregulation in Industrialized Democracies,* edited by Marcellus S. Snow, 173–200. New York: Longmans.

Kaufer, Erich, and Charles Beat Blankart. 1983. "Regulation in Western Germany: The State of the Debate." *Zeitschrift fur die gesamte Staatswissenschaft* 139(3):435–51.

Keeler, Theodore E. 1984. "Theories of Regulation and the Deregulation Movement." *Public Choice* 44(1):103–45.

Knieps, Guenter, Juergen Mueller, and Carl Christian Von Weizsacker. 1981. *Die Rolle des Wettbewerbs im Fernmeldebereich.* Baden-Baden: Nomos.

____. 1982. "Telecommunications Policy in West Germany and Challenges from Technical and Market Development." *Zeitschrift fur Nationalokomomie,* Supplement 2:205–22.

Lamberton, Don M. 1986. "Australian Regulatory Policy." In *Marketplace for Telecommunications: Regulation and Deregulation in Industrialized Democracies,* edited by Marcellus S. Snow, 231–52. New York: Longmans.

Leff, Nathaniel H. 1984a. "Externalities, Information Costs, and Social Benefit-Cost Analysis for Economic Development: An Example from Telecommunications." *Econ. Dvlpt. Cultural Change* 34(2):255–76.

____. 1984b. "Social Benefit-Cost Analysis and Telecommunications in Developing Countries." *Information Econ. Policy* 1(3):217–27.

Littlechild, Stephen C. 1980. *The Fallacy of the Mixed Economy: An Austrian Critique of Conventional Mainstream Economics and of British Economic Policy.* London: Institute of Economic Affairs.

____. 1983. *Regulation of British Telecommunications Profitability: Report to the Secretary of State.* London: Her Majesty's Stationery Office.

Maitland, Donald (Sir). 1984. *The Missing Link.* Report of the Independent Commission for World Wide Telecommunications Development. Geneva: ITU.

Neumann, Karl-Heinz. 1986. "Economic Policy Toward Telecommunications, Information and the Media in West Germany." In *Marketplace for Telecommunications: Regulation and Deregulation in Industrialized Democracies,* edited by Marcellus S. Snow, 131–52. New York: Longmans.

Neumann, Karl-Heinz, Urs Schweizer, and Carl Christian Von Weizsacker. 1983. "Welfare Analysis of Telecommunications Tariffs in Germany." In *Public Sector Economics,* edited by JRG Finsinger, 65–85. New York: St. Martin's Press.

Neumann, Karl-Heinz, and Thomas Schnoering. 1985. "Das ISDN — Ein Problemfeld aus volkswirtschaftlicher und gesellschaftspolisher Sicht." Diskussionsbeitrage zur Telekommunikationsforschung. Bad Honnef, West Germany: Deutsche Bundespost, Wissenschaftliches Institut fur Kommunikationsdienste.

Neumann, Karl-Heinz, and Berhnard Wieland. 1985. "Competition and Social Objectives: The Case of West German Telecommunications." Bad Honnef, West Germany: Deutsche Bundespost, Wissenschaftliches Institut fur Kommunikationsdienste.

Noam, Eli M. 1986. "Telecommunications Policy on the Two Sides of the Atlantic: Divergence and Outlook." In *Marketplace for Telecommunications: Regulation and Deregulation in Industrialized Democracies,* edited by Marcellus S. Snow, 255–74. New York: Longmans.

Noll, Roger G. 1983a. "The Future of Telecommunications Regulation." In *Telecommunications Regulation Today and Tomorrow,* edited by Eli M. Noam, 41–71. New York: Harcourt Brace Jovanovich.

____. 1983b. "The Political and Institutional Context of Communications Policy." *Zeitschrift fur die gesamte Staatswissenschaft* 139(3):377–404.

____. 1986. "The Political and Institutional Context of Communications Policy." In *Marketplace for Telecommunications: Regulation and Deregulation in Industrialized Democracies,* edited by Marcellus S. Snow, 42–65. New York: Longmans.

Nora, Simon, and Alain Minc. 1980. *The Computerization of Society.* Cambridge, Mass.: MIT Press.

Olson, Mancur. 1982. *The Rise and Decline of Nations: Economic Growth, Stagflation, and Social Rigidities.* New Haven: Yale U. Press.

Pavlic, Breda, and Cees J. Hamelink. 1985. *The New International Economic Order: Links between Economics and Communications.* Paris: UNESCO.

Peltzman, Sam. 1976. "Toward a More General Theory of Regulation." *J. Law Econ.* 19(2):211–40.

____. 1981. "Current Developments in the Economics of Regulations." In *Studies in Public Regulation,* edited by Gary Fromm, 371–84. Cambridge, Mass.: MIT Press.

Pierce, William, and Nicholas Jequier. 1983. *Telecommunications for Development.* Geneva: ITU.

Porat, Marc U. 1977. *The Information Economy.* Washington, D.C.: U.S. Department of Commerce, Office of Telecommunications.

____. 1978. "Global Implications of the Information Society." *J. Communication* 23(1):70–80.

Saunders, Robert J., Jeremy J. Warford, and Bjorn Wellenius. 1983. *Telecommunications and Economic Development.* Baltimore: Johns Hopkins U. Press.

Sharkey, William W. 1982. *The Theory of Natural Monopoly.* New York: Cambridge U. Press.

Shepherd, William G. 1984. "Contestability vs. Competition." *Amer. Econ. Rev.* 74(4):572–87.

Snow, Marcellus S. 1975. "Investment Cost Minimization for Communications Satellite Capacity: Refinement and Application of the Chenery-Manne-Srinivasan Model." *Bell J. Econ.* 6(2):621–43.

____. 1976. *International Commercial Satellite Communications: Economic and Political Issues of the First Decade of INTELSAT.* New York: Praeger.

____. 1982. "Telecommunications and Media Policy in West Germany: Recent Developments." *J. Communication* 32(3):10–32.

____. 1983. "Telecommunications Deregulation in the Federal Republic of Germany." *Columbia J. World Business* 18(1):52–61.

____. 1984. "The State as Stopgap: Social Economy and Sustainability of Monopoly in the Telecommunications Sector." Mimeo.

____. 1985a. "Arguments For and Against Competition in International Satellite Facilities and Services: A U.S. Perspective." *J. Communication* 35(3):51–79.

____. 1985b. "Policy Questions in Economic Regulation of Information Societies: Evidence from Japan, the United States, and Other Industrialized Countries." *Keio Communication Rev.* 6:19–38.

____. 1985c. "Regulation to Deregulation: The Telecommunications Sector and Industrialization, with Examples from the Pacific Rim and Basin." *Telec. Policy* 9(4):281–90.

____. 1986a. "Communications Policy in Seven Developed Countries: Introduction, Background, and Conclusions." In *Marketplace for Telecommunications: Regulation and Deregulation in Industrialized Democracies,* edited by Marcellus S. Snow, 3–19. New York: Longmans.

____, ed. 1986b. *Marketplace for Telecommunications: Regulation and Deregulation in Industrialized Democracies.* New York: Longmans.

____. 1986c. "Regulating Telecommunications, Information and the Media: An Agenda for Future Comparative Research." In *Marketplace for Telecommunications: Regulation and Deregulation in Industrialized Democracies,* edited by Marcellus S. Snow, 275–94. New York: Longmans.

____. 1986d. "Statistical Tests for Natural Monopoly Properties in International Satellite Communications." Presented at Symposium on Explorations in Space Policy: Emerging Economic and Technical Issues, Washington, D.C., June. Mimeo.

Spence, A. Michael. 1983. *"Contestable Markets and the Theory of Industry Structure*: A Review Article." *J. Econ. Lit.* 21(3):981–90.

Stigler, George J. 1971. "The Theory of Economic Regulation." *Bell J. Econ. Manage. Sci.* 2(1):3–21.

Telecommunications: Pressures and Policies for Change. 1983. Paris: OECD.

Thiemeyer, Theo. 1983. "Deregulation in the Perspective of the German *Gemeinwirtschaftslehre.*" *Zeitschrift fur die gesamte Staatwissenschaft* 139(3):405–18.

Tomita, Tetsuro. 1984. "Japan's Policy on Monopoly and Competition in Telecommunications." *Telec. Policy* 8(1):44–50.

Voge, Jean P. 1986. "Survey of French Regulatory Policy." In *Marketplace for Telecommunications: Regulation and Deregulation in Industrialized Democracies,* edited by Marcellus S. Snow, 106–30. New York: Longmans.

Von Weizsacker, Carl Christian. 1984. "Free Entry into Telecommunications?" *Information Econ. Policy* 1:197–216. (Reprinted in *Marketplace for Telecommunications: Regulation and Deregulation in Industrialized Democracies,* edited by Marcellus S. Snow, 20–41. New York: Longmans, 1986).

Wiley, Richard E. 1980. "Competition and Deregulation in Telecommunications: The American Experience." In *Kommunikation ohne Monopole: Über Legitimation und Grenzen des Fernmeldemonopols,* edited by Ernst-Joachim Mestmacker, 31–50. Baden-Baden: Nomos.

Zajac, Edward E. 1978. *Fairness or Efficiency: An Introduction to Public Utility Pricing.* Cambridge, Mass.: Ballinger.

4

Information Technology and the Relationships among OECD Countries

Peter Robinson

There have been reports on the impacts of information technology (IT) on individuals (in terms of threats to privacy and changes in skill requirements, for example), reports on impacts on corporations in terms of maintaining competitiveness or improving productivity, and reports on changes in the ways that industry is operating and in the growing range of innovative services now possible. But little has been reported on the impacts of developments in information technology on international relationships among countries, although it is at this level that we must now begin to understand and deal with many of the issues if progress is to be made in resolving them.

No government can claim to understand the broad range of implications of IT nor of actions taken to deal with it; no government can claim to know unequivocally the answers even for itself, let alone for others. All are dealing with a phenomenon that they do not fully understand, and they are using their own experience, objectives, and ideologies to determine their responses.

In this chapter I will describe four sets of issues raised by developments in information technology, with suggestions of possible implications for relationships among nations, with particular emphasis on growing interdependence. In addition, a growing need for developing greater understanding — of trends, issues, attitudes, and concerns — is identified. The means for achieving this understanding are discussed.

TELECOMMUNICATIONS

Telecommunications is so central to much of the change that is now taking place in international relationships that it is difficult to ignore. This means that telecommunications policies must be considered in their broader international context in the same way that financial and industrial policies are. No longer can telecommunications be considered solely in terms of domestic requirements, with international considerations consisting mostly of technological means of ensuring "plug-in" compatibility with neighboring communications systems. No longer is it possible to assume that telecommunications services for international requirements will continue to be offered in a cooperative manner, as in the past. Competition is creeping into the international arena, at least in terms of global or regional (and perhaps private) satellite systems, between satellite and terrestrial systems, and among countries for transit services.

The development of integrated services digital network (ISDN) and open systems interconnection (OSI) will result in a wide range of new opportunities for innovative services. The extent to which intelligence should be incorporated into the network or into the attached equipment is a contentious issue, and decisions made now will have long-term implications for international relationships. Regulatory decisions — regarding attachment of equipment to the network, for example — will affect international relations, at least in terms of trade and comparative advantage of domestic versus foreign industry.

Monopoly provision of telecommunications services will certainly continue in many countries for some time, and there is need to develop an amicable modus operandi at the international level to accommodate both monopoly provision and competitive provision of many such services. What changes will be necessary to achieve this?

Much of the current debate reflects differences in ideology. Is it possible to get beneath this level of debate to what some might regard as the "real" issues? What recommendations might be made to deal with the major issues that are identified, so as to develop greater international cooperation in dealing with them?

TRADE IN DATA-RELATED SERVICES

Trade in services is another area of international sensitivity. Discussions on the topic are already having important impacts on international relations. As discussions proceed in the face of growing pressures for protectionism, and as agreements are eventually reached, further changes in relationships will take place.

An interesting question that might be considered here is the extent to which data-related services might be regarded as a vertical set of services, in much the same way that financial services or tourism services are regarded, or whether, because of their broad pervasiveness and the support they provide for many other service sectors, they might be considered more of a horizontal approach. What are the implications of the answer to this question? Could data-related services perhaps be considered in terms of a "core agreement" on services? Or is this impracticable, particularly if progress is to be made in considering the broader range of services and related requirements? What changes in international relationships will emerge as discussions continue and trade in services increases? Are the changes brought about by data-related services likely to differ in kind or degree from changes brought about by trade in other services?

A possible new requirement for trade in data-related services, different from the concepts developed for trade in goods, are "rules of the road" for access to data and information and related services. Work on this, for example, has already been carried out in the Organization for Economic Cooperation and Development (OECD) and elsewhere in regard to the protection of personal data and in regard to determining what types of access to data should be considered reprehensible and might be included in the criminal code. But other access issues have arisen. Confusion regarding inaccessible data and information will have negative impacts on trade and lead to increasing requirements for domestic storage and processing.

These and other issues, including the degree of applicability of concepts developed for trade in goods, could profitably be discussed. For example, a basic question might be, To what extent does trade in data-related services differ from trade in other services in terms of, for example, necessary concepts?

CHANGES IN INDUSTRY

Over the past two decades, technological change has eroded the clear distinctions that existed in the market place. A computing service was clearly distinct from a telecommunications service, which was quite different from a postal service. Today those distinctions no longer hold. Nor is it so easy to determine what is a banking service and what is not. Hotel chains are getting into the business of teleconferencing; department stores are offering financial services; banks are getting into electronic publishing. Manufacturers are diversifying into services, often by takeovers or joint ventures.

These changes in *what* corporations are doing, as well as changes in *ways* of doing things, are posing significant policy challenges. Far-reaching questions about regulation arise. For example, is it possible to define *banking services* sufficiently clearly to ensure that only banks engage in such services or to ensure that they do not branch out beyond the boundaries of those services? Even if such a definition were possible, is it desirable to curtail the activities of corporations that are able to compete in world markets? Or would allowing expansion into other services result in serious problems for other smaller corporations? Similar questions arise in regard to other regulated industries.

Technological change, in addition to affecting markets and products, has had profound impacts on the internal operations of business. Functions have become easily transferable from one location to another, and labor has been replaced by information technology equipment. In addition, some services that were provided in house are now being sold in the market; and some services that were purchased are now being provided in house. Further, there has been a greater integration and coordination of functions to improve productivity, through, for example, better planning, lower inventory and improved distribution.

These changes raise further issues that challenge governments. If functions are transferred out of the country, for example, concerns about too high a dependence on foreign sources of services and about dangers of denial of access arise. There are also concerns about impacts on domestic employment. It has been suggested, for example, that governments need contingency plans for "jobless growth," because wealth creation can no longer be equated to job creation. Yet, at the same time, governments recognize that placing constraints on business with regard to where functions can be performed can be counterproductive.

In effect, these changes, together with those for improved planning and coordination, are resulting in a greater "sharing" of responsibility and workload among the different locations of a transnational corporation — perhaps a growing interdependence among the various branches and subsidiaries. Will this inevitably lead, of itself, to growing interdependence among nations, or are these changes merely part of a much broader trend toward growing interdependence? What will changes in these types of business relationships mean in terms of changes in the relationships among countries?

SOCIOLEGAL ISSUES

Many transborder data flow (TBDF) issues arise because a user of TBDF is involved in activities occurring virtually simultaneously under two (or more) different political and legal jurisdictions. Such a user is in danger of being in breach of one or another national law or of acting in contravention of the laws of other jurisdictions. Innocent third parties can also be caught between conflicting legal requirements. As the volume of TBDF increases, as it undoubtedly will, pressures will increase for greater compatibility among countries in the ways in which issues are resolved.

Probably the most visible sociolegal issue that has arisen from developments in information technology is the protection of personal privacy. Concerns in this regard have led to the development of the OECD Guidelines on the Protection of Privacy and the Transborder Flows of Personal Data, and to the Council of Europe Convention for the Protection of Individuals with Regard to Automatic Processing of Personal Data. Although certain issues remain, major concerns appear to have been overcome. Is there need to do more at this stage than monitor developments in regard to personal privacy protection?

Another particular concern of some governments has been a fear of increasing foreign cultural domination, assisted by technological developments that allow easy transfer of cultural products from one country to another, through, for example, videocassettes and TV broadcasting. Low-cost "cultural" imports can squeeze out domestic products and affect values and attitudes. What are the implications for international relationships? Is there likely to be a greater homogenization of cultures, or will sensitivities escalate and create additional difficulties?

Advertising products may also alter values and attitudes, and, already, governments of some developing countries have expressed concern about this happening to their citizens. Is it likely to happen in OECD countries? Advertisements that are legal in one country may be illegal in another because of certain types of legislation such as that for consumer protection: what impacts is this likely to have on international relations?

What are the most pressing sociolegal issues today? Are others emerging that could be more important? How should governments deal with these requirements? Which international forums are likely to deal with them? Will growing interdependency among nations help reduce or increase differences and difficulties in dealing with sociolegal issues?

Is there a real danger that some legal systems and constitutional requirements are too inflexible to be easily changed to harmonize with an international consensus that has developed in the rest of the world?

BUILDING UNDERSTANDING

Information technology, particularly developments in telecommunications, has had significant impacts on the speed, frequency, type, and degree of international contacts made between people and institutions. Today, an action taken in one country can have repercussions in other parts of the world in a matter of seconds. In many cases, these may be minor impacts, such as debitting a charge account; in others the implications may be much more pervasive. For example, changes in regulation in the United States have led to changes in many other countries; concern over privacy protection in Europe has led to changes in legislation in many countries.

This internationalization of events and their implications has led to a growing interdependence among countries. What does growing interdependence mean in practical terms, and what issues does it raise? These questions are at the core of changing international relationships. Some people appear to be trying to deny that growing interdependence is really happening and trying to hold fast to old opinions and old ways of doing things. More specifically, and more difficult to deal with, some actually fear this trend and see a reversion to colonial status of full dependency, because of the obvious asymmetry in many present-day relationships.

It has often been said that we do not understand an activity unless it can be expressed in numbers. One requirement might then be, for example, greater and more meaningful and consistent attention to building up a statistical data base. Is lack of success in this area due to lack of political will, lack of recognition of the need at senior bureaucratic levels, lack of adequate concepts, lack of appropriate theoretical approaches and practical tools, or a combination of these?

Another requirement might be the establishment of an appropriate forum in which mutual understanding and consensus building can take place. Such a forum has in large part existed for OECD member countries in the Committee for Information, Computer, and Communications Policy (ICCP) and its Working Party on Transborder Data Flow. But a forum with adequate interdisciplinary expertise does not exist, one where industrialized and developing countries can get together on a regular basis. Is such a forum necessary? What other measures might be taken to improve understanding, with a view to improving interrelationships among countries?

CONCLUSION

In assessing impacts of information technology on international relationships, particularly growing interdependencies, changing perceptions are at least as important as changing technology. It is for this reason that this chapter puts emphasis on building understanding, so that there is a firmer foundation for policy development, and so that there is a greater chance of avoiding misconceptions.

International interrelationships, and whether these are in large part good or suffering from an inability to keep pace with technological change, are particularly important in resolving current and emerging issues.

5

Some Public Policy Implications of the Information Revolution

ROGER BENJAMIN

DEFINITION OF CONTEXT

The dramatic growth of information trade accelerates the development of postindustrial societies. The Organization for Economic Cooperation and Development (OECD) countries are no longer primarily industrial societies; the emphasis on economic activity has shifted from the production of goods to the production of services that are information intensive. There are many consequences of this transformation, but I will touch on only the most salient points. First, the OECD countries, especially the United States and Japan, have been the engines of global economic development. What are the international consequences when the industrial sectors of these countries decline? Second, the measurement of economic activity remains biased toward the production of goods. Much of the service economy, especially the public sector, is not easily captured by standard neoclassical economics. In fact, productivity, as measured by standard economic models, declines in service- and public sector-dominated economies. It may be that relationships between OECD economies and industrial and developing states will become much different in the future than in the past.

We are moving into a phase of change in which *international interdependence* and the *globalization of domestic economies* are no longer mere catch words. Consider a few examples. Both in the real world of politics and economics and in the minds of the scholars who think about these subjects, one distinguishes between domestic and foreign public policy systems. We still speak about domestic economic policy initiatives as if inflation, low or high interest rates, and strong or weak currencies were not heavily influenced by the international economic policy system. U.S. farmers complain about agricultural policy in Washington when prices for their crops are increasingly determined by what happens to crops in other countries. Even though sensitive observers of the problem faced by U.S. and European heavy industries know better, the primary focus of attention is on reindustrialization of steel and auto industries without a substantial examination of the development of these same industries in the Pacific Basin countries. The United States and its Western European counterparts worry a good deal about immigration (legal and illegal) in the 1980s. Yet, immigration, labor, and capital investment policies between the donor and recipient nations are clearly inextricably linked. Tariff barriers preventing capital investment in a nation poor in capital funds may lead to increased immigration. Finally, we still speak of national security at least in the two superpowers, the Soviet Union and the United States, at a time when national security cannot be guaranteed for any nation.

In part, the breakdown between the domestic and international systems is due to the reunion between politics and economics. Perhaps only in the United States did political scientists clearly distinguish the polity from the economy. The pluralist vision considers the economy operating separately from the state, which acts as a neutral arbiter by keeping the various interest groups playing by the rules of the game. Now, however, such a vision is really only of historical interest (assuming, that is, it once had merit). In a world of slow economic growth and increasing interdependence, economic choices are political choices, as well. Where, for instance, does the state begin and the economy end? Observers disagree as to how to answer this question, but they do agree that it is important. So, too, the question of the relative autonomy of the state from the economy becomes an issue. And whether the state is or is not thought autonomous directly relates to how one conceptualizes the foreign policy process.

The "threshold" change I speak of also involves the apparently new set of relationships between modernizing and industrializing countries and postindustrial societies. Postindustrial societies, with their emphasis on the Information Revolution — its production, sharing, storing, and retrieving on the one hand and declining industrial bases on the other — present a new set of opportunities and constraints in both international and domestic policy arenas.

Why, however, is this transformation from industry to a service and public sector emphasis underway? Within postindustrial societies an evolutionary process has been underway for some time. Although I do not believe we have an explanation, it is possible to develop efficient descriptions of this process of change. Once an industrial infrastructure of a society is built — railroads, airlines and roads, communication networks, and the light and heavy industrial base itself — economic attention may turn, *relatively*, to the production and consumption of nondurable goods. This may to some extent be the case because once housing stocks are in place, once citizens have adequate amounts of the things of industrial civilization, a relative point of saturation may be reached and attention shifts to goods (wants) of a social, nonmaterial nature.

The impact of these changes is to redefine the limits of politics. One may, for example, speak of the decline of government and the rise of politics at the same time. While governmental stability and perhaps political parties decline, litigation, strikes, and confrontations of various sorts between groups increase. All of the above leads to increased demands on government, an already overburdened government beset by declining tax revenues.

On the production side, the major question concerns how institutional arrangements affect the performance level or efficiency of the institution. If a good being produced is capital intensive, then a large initial investment is spread over the quantity of output. It is in the production of such goods that familiar economies of scale accrue; that is, the greater the size of the organization, the greater the level of efficiency. There are, however, a great many goods for which one encounters significant information distortion or bias and loss of control in larger compared to smaller production units, goods that are information sensitive (requiring many sender-receiver interactions). Economic theorists of organizations are thus led to assume that the greater the number of vertical channels information must pass through, the greater the possibility for information distortion. For many goods, diseconomies rather than economies of scale result from the centralization of tasks.

These bewildering information-centered changes have very different consequences in newly industrializing states compared to advanced or postindustrial societies. The purpose of the next section is to sketch the basic elements of a model that differentiates types of states in capitalist societies. We will then be in a position to end this chapter with more useful projections about public policy relevant trends.

As Table 5.1 indicates, the fundamental nature of postindustrial states differs from newly industrializing states. In newly industrializing states, the administrative order is fairly distinct from the rest of society and oriented toward the production of "pure" public goods. The administrative apparatus of the state drives the effort to industrialize and, in that context, reshape the written and/or unwritten traditional legal order that may be outmoded. By comparison, in the postindustrial, information-dominant society the state as legal order is where the action is. The fundamental socioeconomic and cultural changes extant in postindustrial society require changes in the legal order and will lead to a redesigned administrative apparatus. In other words, the fundamental public policy agenda differs in *kind* in our postindustrial societies. The primary public policy agenda for postindustrial societies will be the redesign of the institutional arrangements in the

TABLE 5.1

Fundamental Differences in Postindustrial and Newly Industrializing Capitalist States

Distinguishing Dimension	Postindustrial State*	Newly Industrializing State*
INSTITUTIONAL-LEGAL ORDER		
Notion of rights	Property rights as infringed upon by extensive "quality of life" rights	Property rights are paramount
Public and private domains	Distinction between public and private is blurred as collective externalities are widely recognized	Public domain is limited and clearly demarcated from private domain
Tensions among freedom, equality, order, and justice	Commitment to economic freedom and social order is challenged by commitment to social equality and distributive justice, with resultant ambiguity	Commitment to economic (entrepreneurial) freedom and social order is dominant
ADMINISTRATIVE APPARATUS AS ORGANIZED WHOLE		
Functional scope and orientation	Virtually unlimited, with extensive intervention on the consumption side; welfare state	Limited to provision of "pure" public goods and intervention on production side; state capitalism
Social composition	Socially indistinct from extensive, heterogeneous "middle stream" of private sector	Socially distinct as technobureaucratic elite with Western orientation
Structural relations with government and legal order	Constrained by legal order; constrains government	Constrained by government; constrains legal order

*Postindustrial state, for example, Japan, United States, Great Britain; Newly Industrializing State, for example, South Korea, Brazil, Turkey.

Source: Compiled by the author.

administrative order to make them more responsive to the information-sensitive collective goods dominant in these societies. This redesign is, in fact, well underway and is a centered system itself.

FURTHER PUBLIC POLICY IMPLICATIONS

One may visualize goods, meaning anything humans desire, along a continuum from public to private. Manufacturing and agricultural goods are divisible. Goods that are information sensitive are much more difficult to divide. They are to varying degrees collective goods. Collective goods are messy because of the uncertainty concerning who receives what proportion of the benefits (of the consumption) of the good and who pays what proportion of the costs of the production of the good. Moreover, the greater the degree the good is information centered, the greater the level of externalities (spillover effects) attached to the good. No one minds consuming positive externalities, but if the externalities are negative, the matter is different.

The point is, if construction and change of largely centralized socioeconomic and political institutions are the hallmark of the industrial era, then efforts to cope with the effects of these changes, human services, and the redesign of these institutions describe the present and future in postindustrial societies. Redesign rather than decentralization is called for, because the debate over centralization of governmental institutions is miscast. It is a matter of matching the size of the government unit with the good to be delivered, public or collective, and linking these to the catchment area (community) appropriate for consumption of the good. Because publics are more diverse and better educated than ever before, their wants are also more diverse. This suggests that equal diversity in the design of political institutions is required. In addition, there are a number of other implications of the argument relevant to political and public policy.

EXAMPLES

Property Rights

Is there to be no space commons so that all countries can have access to satellite slots for their own direct broadcast satellite (DBS) purposes? How can we, if we should, ensure intellectual property rights? Computer software — e.g., intelligent systems programs — require enormous application of human capital, but can be copied, hence "stolen," as soon as they are produced. Similar problems abound in field after field of scientific application (e.g., molecular genetics, computer engineering, polymers). Should we even try to protect intellectual property the way we patent products?

Disjunctures across national boundaries abound. Here are two of the most important cases. Preservation of cultural identity becomes a serious issue for developing societies overwhelmed by the global information system emanating from postindustrial societies. I have been participating in a survey research project in South Korea since 1978 that seeks to examine individual reaction to the modernization process, which, among many other things, presents "modern" cultural symbol systems that present radical disjunctures from the existing value systems. The cultural identity problem is not trivial and is particularly acute in the newly industrializing states undergoing the most rapid socioeconomic change. While Koreans and Malaysians worry about the impact of the new information world that spawns collective goods on them, the Rust Belt sections of Western Europe and North America reel from assaults of imports of material goods from newly industrializing countries. There are intermittent calls for reindustrialization in the Rust Belt areas and calls to limit imports.

The real impact of this accelerated change is confusion and incoherence in and among public policies, outmoded institutional arrangements, and needed fundamental concepts such as national sovereignty. Here are just a few examples. We lack a stable international monetary system. Although decisions in board rooms in Tokyo often more directly affect Pittsburgh steel workers than do actions in New York or Washington, D.C., we lack public policy forums that address this. In fact, sovereignty itself is likely to undergo redefinition. The production and consumption of collective goods (bads) spills across all national boundaries, and even the Soviet Union finds limits to acceptable national behavior when nuclear power plant accidents produce radiation (a collective bad), a prime example of a negative externality that other states are forced to consume.

Table 5.1 suggests another point. The basic thrust and direction of postindustrial states differs in kind, not degree, from industrial or newly industrializing states. Thus, the first-order sets of public policy concerns in each country listed are different from those of other countries. The focus is on the administrative state's attempt to provide sufficient infrastructure to promote industrial development in newly industrializing countries. In these states, the administrative elite attempts to transform the legal order, which may be incongruent with the needs of the industrial age, into one reflecting the state's focus on manufacturing goods. By comparison, in postindustrial states, the changing emphasis from manufacturing to collective goods because of the information revolution itself creates a need for redesign of the administrative order. The growth and expansion of collective goods is the reason one can speak of the simultaneous decline of government and rise of politics. Litigation becomes a prime public policy instrument, as individuals and collective action groups struggle with the externality problems associated with the collective good in postindustrial societies. If the foregoing is correct, then very different public policy concerns and emphases will be found in debates and interactions between the elites of postindustrial states compared to leaders of newly industrializing states. So it should not be surprising that political leaders in South Korea are more interested in material-goods production and growth than in the elimination of negative externalities flowing from the production of those goods, e.g., pollution.

6

International Communications Policy of Japan

MASAKATSU YONEZAWA

LEADING ROLE OF TELECOMMUNICATIONS IN THE TWENTY-FIRST CENTURY

With the development of industrial society, people have come to enjoy material satisfaction and to pay more attention to mental satisfaction. It is now said to be a transitional stage from the industrial society to the advanced information society, in which people place more importance on information.

Telecommunications that handle information are expected to play a leading role in the advanced information society in the twenty-first century.

JAPAN'S INTERNATIONAL COMMUNICATIONS POLICY

With changes in circumstances surrounding telecommunications it became necessary for Japan to formulate a new telecommunications policy, which aimed at achieving an advanced information society.

I would like to introduce some items concerning international telecommunications in the newly established telecommunications policy of Japan.

The Formation of a Dynamic Telecommunications Market

The first item is the formation of a dynamic telecommunications market. Various measures for that purpose were taken, such as introduction of competition into all areas of telecommunications.

We introduced competition into all areas of telecommunications on April 1, 1985. The telecommunications services that were provided only by Nippon Telegraph and Telephone (NTT) domestically and by Kokushei Denshin Denwa (KDD) internationally are now open to the private sector.

As of May 7, 1985, five Type I telecommunications carriers obtained permission from the Ministry of Posts and Telecommunications, and 222 Type II telecommunications carriers are registered with or submitted notification to the Ministry of Posts and Telecommunications.

In addition, various restrictions on terminal equipment were removed. Today users can choose freely from the great variety of Japanese- and foreign-made terminals, as long as these terminals conform to the minimum technical requirements of "no harm to the network."

Telecommunications systems have a great influence on daily business activities and social activities. In order to establish a telecommunications network that people can depend on, measures are necessary to fully guarantee security and reliability of the system. Therefore, the Telecommunications Business Law requires the telecommunications carriers to observe technical standards for telecommunications facilities. Various measures such as "Data Communication Network Security and Reliability Standards" and "Data Communication Network Registration System" are recommended.

Comprehensive guidelines of security and reliability for telecommunications systems are studied further at the Telecommunications Technology Council and a report of the council was submitted in June 1986. Loans are available to fund measures taken for security and reliability of data communications systems. Guidelines concerning relief measures after trouble is detected in the network will be drawn up and made public.

Promotion of International Coordination and Cooperation

As society and economy become more involved internationally, problems such as trade friction are increasing. At the same time, networks are being constructed rapidly at the international level. The following policies aim at encouraging international coordination and contributing to the smooth development of an international network.

Promotion of Imports

The trade imbalance of telecommunications equipment is one of the causes of trade friction. For Japan, which is highly dependent on international trade, maintaining the free-trade system is extremely important, and the supply of low-priced equipment and services of good quality, whether they be of Japanese or foreign origin, is consistent with the benefits to society. It is, therefore, necessary to maintain a free market for Japan's telecommunications and also to encourage purchase and use of telecommunications equipment of foreign manufacture, including communications satellites. Tax measures and financial loans are part of this policy.

Contribution to International Standardization Studies

International standardization not only promotes greater distribution of equipment and services and increases the convenience of users, but also contributes in many ways to expanding trade. For this reason, it is important that Japan give positive support to international standardization studies, including those of the International Telecommunication Union (ITU). Under the Telecommunications Business Law, the standard and certification of terminal equipment became simple, clear, and unbiased in regard to country of manufacture. The Organization for Economic Cooperation and Development (OECD) is also studying this question of standard and certification insofar as it affects trade. Active study will be continued in order to secure international conformity to Japanese standards for telecommunications equipment.

Study on Transborder Data-Flow Problems

As world society and economy become more interdependent a problem which has been receiving international attention is that of transborder data flow (TDF), or in other words how to maintain a free data flow between countries while giving full consideration to the protection of privacy. This problem is at present a lively topic of discussion at OECD. Since it is closely related to the process of international network construction, the growth of data communications industries and the promotion of high technology, it is necessary to study it positively by reinforcing synthetic research and study, exchanging information with other countries, and participating in OECD activities.

There is much concern that the rapid advance of informatization in the developed countries is widening the gap in telecommunications infrastructure between those countries and developing countries, and is aggravating the problems between north and south. The following policies are therefore employed to improve the quality of telecommunications as a whole in the developing countries.

Cooperation in Training Telecommunications Personnel in Developing Countries

Training of telecommunications engineers for developing countries should be promoted, especially in neighboring Asia and the Pacific countries, and assistance should be increased through the Japan International Cooperation Agency. An international exchange center for telecommunications should be established and extended to undertake technical cooperation with the private sector in various ways. This center will, for example, cooperate with the Center for Telecommunications Development to establish a site in Geneva, accept trainees, train experts and instructors, and develop teaching materials.

Cooperation in Formulating ISDN Plans in Developing Countries

The transition to the advanced information society is a worldwide phenomenon and recently, opportunities for constructing integrated services digital network (ISDN) have been increasing not only in the developed countries but in the developing countries, which are seeking to improve the performance of telecommunications networks. In this situation, Japan, as one of the nations advanced in ISDN research, should contribute to the construction of ISDN in the developing countries.

Promotion of Mutual International Understanding

This activity is proposed with the presupposition that Japan gives accurate information about national markets, legislation, and policy to other countries, so as to enrich their knowledge and understanding of Japan. At the same time, Japan must comprehend the situations in other countries and promote common international understanding. In this connection, international broadcasting — which is an extremely effective medium for conveying Japan's opinion and position to the rest of the world and for deepening international understanding of Japan — is becoming increasingly important. Measures will therefore be taken to improve international broadcasting and to encourage the international exchange of programs and video material. Regular bilateral conferences and forums should also be promoted, and comprehensive measures for the furtherance of international understanding should be developed.

The Report of the Study Group on Japan's International Telecommunications Role

The study group on Japan's role in the world in telecommunications was set up in October 1984. This study group, chaired by Ichiro Kato, emeritus professor of Tokyo University, submitted a report to the minister of posts and telecommunications in March 1986 after eighteen months' study on Japan's internal telecommunications policy. Because this report is voluminous, I would like to explain the outline of recommendations made. These recommendations are based on the following three considerations:

1. Promotion of mutual understanding among the countries of the world is necessary, for which effective communications are crucial. To do this, Japan should enhance bilateral and multilateral consultations among governments for information exchange and adjustment of telecommunications policies.
2. Further qualitative and quantitative improvements in international telecommunications services should be achieved. Telecommunications are necessary and indispensable for the international flow of information. Measures to promote the establishment of an advanced and stable international telecommunications network should be employed. Efforts should be made for early realization of international value-added network (VAN) services using international leased circuits in order to promote further development of VAN services. For this purpose, a positive contribution should be made so that the provider of VAN services may be regarded as an international telecommunications carrier under the international telecommunications law. At the same time, separate study of ways to make such services possible temporarily, taking into consideration the extremely strong demand in industries for international VAN services, is necessary.
3. Japan should fulfill its responsibilities to the global development of telecommunications with correct recognition of its position in international society. From a global viewpoint, Japan should pursue policies and measures contributing to peace and stability. With regard to the problem of the international satellite communications systems separate from INTELSAT, Japan should respect the role of INTELSAT in the international society and should continue to support INTELSAT. At the same time, considering the increase of demand for international telecommunications and the requirement for sophistication and diversification of international telecommunications services, Japan should recognize international satellite communications systems other than INTELSAT for further

development of international satellite communications services, as long as such systems do not cause significant economic harm to INTELSAT.

In international cooperation, priority should be given to training such personnel in developing countries as maintenance and operation personnel and senior engineers who are currently in extremely short supply.

7

Cooperative Communications Policies: Europe's Contribution to the International Information Economy

KLAUS W. GREWLICH

An increasingly close-knit network of communications systems is spanning the globe. A cloak of highly artificial structures lies over the earth and its inhabitants. Bombarded by the frequency waves of modern communications technology and telecommunications networks and circled by aircraft and satellites, we experience our planet's oneness "for better or for worse."

The conquest of space and time through advanced telematics and the ability to produce information as a trading commodity or as a "cultural property" and then transmit it transcontinentally (thus creating a state of simultaneity and omnipresence) may clear the way for mankind's step from speculative to effective planetarization.

But this planetary situation is ambivalent. The people are united and linked to each other, but they are also dependent and at each other's mercy. The newly conquered element, air, can become the conveyor of global death. Missiles with nuclear warheads, airborne warning and surveillance devices, modern combat planes, and military communications systems make the possibility of total destruction everpresent.

Civilian transnational communication of information and data also entails potential conflicts. The control of the flow of information and data in general and data bases in particular means power and economic advantages. Telecommunications and computer-based informatics, partly industry, partly services, have been identified as the basis of the "third industrial revolution." Where telecommunications were seen in the old days as a piece of useful infrastructure, telematics is seen as a make-or-break ticket to economic, cultural, and political development.

Thus, competition in the "international information economy" has ceased to be a game among merchant princes and has become a high-stakes race.

Domination of key technologies or systems knowledge is seen as a matter of "economic security." The stakes in the amazing high-tech race are not just markets as such, but are a perceived need of the major technological powers of the West, which believe they must capture a share of world production in growth sectors to offset the inevitable decline in others. Probably due to this perception, in many countries and regions government-industry relations oriented toward structural adjustment may become competition-oriented modernization policies, and telematics and traded information and information services may become increasingly central to that strategy.

So far, the leading Organization for Economic Cooperation and Development (OECD) nations have been able to keep the conflict potential inherent in the struggle for high-tech dominance under control. To ensure that this control is maintained in the future as well will be one of the decisive political and legal tasks in the years to come. The economic-technological race on which the technological powers of the West have embarked must lead to a strengthening of the West. On no account must it degenerate into ruinous cutthroat competition of self-defeating protectionism.

The ideal safeguard against such an adverse development would be: to establish an appropriate framework for global cooperation; i.e., improved "rules of the game"; and to achieve a mutually beneficial division of labor on the basis of converging industrial-technological performance.

The second point presupposes that the Europeans in particular will ensure their place among those in the technological vanguard. A European pillar is needed for the political and economic-technological partnership within the West and for the relationship with newly industrialized countries and the third world.

THE EUROPEAN CONTRIBUTION

Europeans ask themselves, "Where do we stand?" The answer given by others is often not very flattering. U.S. and Japanese respondents might shake their heads and say, "You Europeans are not any more in the race, the future lies in the Pacific." Indeed, if Europe actually fell behind in the high-tech race, the Atlantic Alliance would sound an alarm signal. For how can its cohesion be maintained in the long run, if the U.S. economy and society make the transition into a new age and Europe can't keep up?

In the past five years we have seen plenty of analyses of and opinions on the technological competitiveness of Europe as a whole — some lachrymose and dramatizing, others deliberately minimizing potential dangers. A more balanced view now appears to have crystallized:

The economic-technological capacity of the more advanced countries in Western Europe is now underestimated. Europe's growing role in space, for instance, or the export performance of some of the more advanced European countries, or recent events such as the 1986 Hannover Forum for World High-Tech (one of the biggest industrial fairs), may be taken as indications that the once creeping fear of being left helplessly behind the United States and Japan in the race for technological hegemony has become much less significant. Gaps remain, however, in such vital fields as microelectronics and major data processing and possibly also biotechnology. Their closing will require an all-out effort. Europe has the ability to close some of these gaps.

For a number of strategically important areas of high technology (notably in the fields of information and communication technology and critical new materials), the Europeans need transborder cooperation and, above all, the combining of Europe's own talent, as appropriate on the basis of "variable geometry" (i.e., varying partners, enterprises, and research institutes, from different European nations with comparable technological potential and similar interests would pragmatically cooperate and combine their technological and financial potential).

Cooperation within Europe and with the United States and Japan are not mutually exclusive. European cooperation — e.g., in the aerospace industry — shows that such cooperation may lead to a genuine partnership with other leading high-tech powers, because united the Europeans can offer more than each European nation can. The objective of a European telecommunications policy, for instance, is not to reverse existing alliances between European and U.S. firms, but quite the opposite: to strengthen reciprocal market access and technology exchange.

It can be said that if the European community were to be founded today, research, technology, and telematics would have to be focal points of a treaty, because no individual member state by itself stands a real chance of mastering all the critical high technologies and their applications to the extent needed to comprehensively secure its economic future.

What will matter in Western Europe in terms of a pragmatic approach "from the bottom up" will be to start by breaking up economic and social ossification (i.e., to liberate market forces, to create an entrepreneurial and innovative economy by facilitating positive adjustment policies), thereby creating functioning markets for risk capital and introducing fiscal policies that encourage innovations. Intensified efforts in the fields of information and education (including preparing every individual for life in an information society and establishing high-performance elites based on equal opportunity) should create conditions that provide maximum scope for economic and cultural creativity. This means, among other things, introducing new forms of cooperation between universities and industry; setting up models of equality-based cooperation among major corporations already established in the market, creative researchers, and young entrepreneurs; and making decentralized work possible and opening up the wide variety of new media to the shapers of cultural life.

The full use of the continental dimension of Europe's internal market, a market open to the world, is a necessary precondition for the full utilization and mobilization of productive forces and technological development capacities. No enterprise can risk a major investment geared to an all-European volume of demand without access to all individual European markets. And, even more important, seen from a world-market vantage point, and it is this market that matters considering costs and the specific competitive situation in technology-intensive sectors of the economy, the utilization of the base European community (EC) market, which (like the U.S. domestic market) permits the production and sale of units in large numbers and hence at favorable per unit prices, provides a springboard for trading success on a global scale.

These are some of the measures that are needed now: an even further simplification of border formalities; simplification and, where necessary, harmonization of technical standards and regulations; the opening up of public-sector procurement markets; creation of a legal framework for the integration of business functions; greater liberalization of the capital flows; appropriate adjustment of competition laws and policy; and a further adaptation of fiscal regulations, including the provisions governing affiliate enterprises.

Let us now address the issue of joint European technological-industrial and cultural programs pertaining to the information economy. This is not a defense for a concept of a European industrial policy that uses intervention instruments for "picking the winners" without framing this in an overall socioeconomic context, thus running the risk of being abused to "protect the losers." But it will become necessary in Europe whenever it is feasible and meaningful to combine high-tech research and industrial efforts to arrive at critical masses (as seen from the vantage point of international competition) and/or to pursue parallel projects and then exchange the results.

European research and technology cooperation has made some progress in the past years; for example, in thermonuclear fusion, space technology, and above all information and communication technology. As for the last, the ESPRIT program (European Strategic Programme for Research in Information Technologies) was jointly formulated by Europe's electronic industry, the EC commission, and representatives of the EC member nations.

The envisaged projects include a concept for common research for the broadband communications network of the future, starting with a reference model (RACE), a strategy for the digitalization (ISDN), mobile telephone, and a Europe-wide glass fiber network, including satellite links. Increasing liberalization of the terminals market and of services and the harmonization of the relevant norms on the basis of the Consultative Committee on International Telegraph and Telephone (CCITT) and the Committee on European Post and Telecommunications (CEPT) standards would go hand in hand with such major projects. Public sector procurement markets would continuously be opened up, a number of European telecommunication enterprises would strengthen technological cooperation with a view of establishing, as necessary, consortia able to achieve the economies of scale needed for a leading position in the world market. The European telecommunications administrations (together with British Telecom) would concert their introduction strategies.

All this could be boosted by the simultaneous intensification of efforts to create a homogeneous market for information services, notably specialized information (data banks, machine translation), and a bid to realize the common market for media products (such as TV and video). Indeed, in an unusual display of cooperation, several of Europe's largest manufacturers have agreed to establish and promote OSI (open system interconnection), a common data communication protocol, as the standard for European data communication. Moreover, to give another example, a number of major European telecommunications equipment manufacturers intend to develop jointly vital parts of the broadband switching stations designed to function in the future glass fiber network.

The Eureka process might generate a bottom-up approach (i.e., companies would have the initiative) and a number of ambitious projects. An important consideration is not to tackle the high-tech issue as an isolated element but in the broader context of socioeconomic policies, European internal market policy, cooperation within the North America–Europe–Pacific triangle.

Telecommunications is a technology-intensive growth sector of strategic importance, in which the more advanced countries of Western Europe remain competitive with the United States and Japan. The objective of a European telecommunications consolidation would be to strengthen this position. The parameters of a community tele-communications policy are set by at least four constraints: (1) developments in the world market and competitive positions in the international technoindustrial race; (2) the regulatory framework in the EC member states; (3) corporate strategies; and (4) the role of the EC commission and of community law.

It can certainly not be the objective of a European telecommunications policy to hamper or reverse cooperation with enterprises originating from the United States and Japan; quite the contrary. Major European telecommunication enterprises are determined to enter the U.S. market through direct investment and joint ventures. The EC market, on the other hand, must be an open one. But the European component in the emerging global telematic industry must present as high a profile as possible. A stronger European position could be boosted by joint R&D cooperation, joint ventures, and major telecommunication infrastructure projects. According to estimates by the EC commission, to compete with the average Japanese telecommunications company, the European firms would not only need larger markets but a number of them would have to cooperate to such an extent that instead of the eight larger and a few smaller European telecommunications firms, only four combines would remain. In order to cope with the U.S. competitors, notably AT&T and IBM, collaboration would have to go very far, because European industry and post, telegraph, and telecommunications authorities (PTTs) are beginning to understand that a world market needs international players and not privileged national champions. At the same time, extremely advanced communications software would have to be designed; glass fiber networks could be used as central networks to which local networks of differing designs could be hooked up. This would include supercomputers, large computers, computer groupings, and data banks.

The EC commission has initiated a number of complaints to encourage free and open competition in the telecommunications market. The commission's most notable involvement was its antitrust case against IBM; the action was settled in return for commitments by

IBM that it would release information about equipment standards, thus ensuring that private industry standards do not limit competitive opportunities for European manufacturers.

The EC commission has also filed a complaint against the German Bundespost alleging an "abuse of dominant position" under Article 86 of the Treaty of Rome. The commission's role in enforcing competition policy was recently given impetus by the March 1985 decision of the Court of Justice of the European Communities upholding a December 1982 commission decision in which the commission held that British Telecom had abused its dominant position by prohibiting private message forwarding activities to the United Kingdom. The court's decision in the British Telecom case may accord the EC commission rather broad discretion to challenge activities or practices by PTTs that it views as impediments to competition. Another field in which the EC commission may have to act is in state aid for the telecommunications sector, a thorny question, with a view to limit distortion of competition.

From a legal point of view, one may conclude that the community has an overriding duty to act in telecommunications and that it has the tools at its disposal to contribute substantially to the creation of the European telecommunications dimension.

IMPROVING THE RULES OF THE GAME

The political and legal control of potential conflicts in the international information economy and cultural interdependence is becoming an important subject on the international agenda. Asking for a revolutionary leap toward a "new legal regime," however, for the international information economy and the pertinent cultural exchanges is not realistic. As in other areas of international relations and public international economic law, a comparatively slow development is likely to take place. This, however, does not mean that no action is necessary; in fact, the enhancement of pragmatic approaches already in evolution should not be further delayed.

A major area for cooperation is the reduction of barriers to high-technology trade. The enormous start-up costs for innovation in high-technology industries mean that access to international markets is crucial. Bilateral discussions (e.g., between the United States and the European communities) and notably the new round of General Agreement on Tariffs and Trade (GATT) negotiations including the very important negotiations on trade in services, may contribute to reduce, in some cases to remove, the barriers that still exist in such areas as tariffs, standards, public or quasi-public procurement, rules of origin, and intellectual property. Consultations based on political arrangements — as, for instance, the OECD Declaration on Transborder Data Flows or the general understanding on positive adjustment policies (the "rules of the game for structural change") — could prove helpful, especially if they contribute to the international law-making process.

The OECD Working Party on Transborder Data Flows of the Committee on Computer, Information and Communications Policy is instrumental in this process. The mandate given to this working party was to concentrate its work primarily on the economic, legal and social policy issues raised by transborder data flows. In particular, it is required to examine the extent and impact of these flows, analyze the principle factors underlying their growth, identify the major government policies which have an impact on these flows, ascertain what legal or other measures might be required to deal with these issues and recommend areas for international cooperation.

The Council of Europe's privacy convention and the OECD guidelines call on the states to adopt the agreed-upon measures for the protection of the individual's privacy. At the same time, both documents recognize the fact that the free flow of personal data is essential for transborder economic activities and limit state interference with the free flow of commercial data in the name of privacy. The objective is to achieve an optimal balance of conflicting necessities in order to safeguard privacy while at the same time ensuring that the free flow of information remains an integral element of the economic process within the international system.

This declaration, though not legally binding, is of high political importance and may under the established conditions of public international law (notably *longa consuetudo* and *opinio juris*) contribute to some extent to the evolution of customary law. The declaration reflects a careful balance between access to data and information ("active export liberalization to avoid inter alia the problem of dependence") and the removal of unjustified barriers to the international exchange of data and information ("classical import liberalization").

The OECD declaration is a living document to be continuously enriched by future consultations on pertinent cases and by further work concentrating on issues emerging from the following types of transborder data flows: flows of data accompanying international trade; marketed computer services and computerized information services; and intracorporate data flows.

Notwithstanding the wide gap between the more industrially advanced OECD countries, the threshold nations, and other third world countries — a gap particularly pronounced in the international information economy — it is ethically, political, economically, and from the point of view of public international law out of the question for the OECD countries to settle the problems pertaining to the international information economy and the use of information resources by themselves. The third world has vested interests in this field, along with a certain problem-causing potential, which could be used to interrupt, for instance, the global data exchange. The OECD countries will therefore have to deal early with the problem of the international forums in which to discuss the issues pertaining to the global information economy. This could be the International Telecommunication Union (though the primary task of this organization is technical and functional), GATT (which will deal with the issues of high-technology trade and trade in services), the United Nations Center for Transnational Corporations, United Nations Conference on Trade and Development, and the Intergovernmental Bureau for Informatics (which has established the International Consultative Commission on Transborder Data Flow Policies). In any case, high priority should be given to practical measures for establishing suitable information and communication infrastructures, which are also needed to integrate the third world into the emerging information economy.

8

Telecommunications Policy in the United States

Suzanne R. Settle

It has become a truism that policy and law more often than not play a catching up role in the fast-paced advanced technology environment of today. Decisions are normally made in response to, rather than in anticipation of, technological developments. One reason for this, of course, is that policy making is rarely a scientific exercise. Instead, it reflects the balance struck between sometimes-competing social, economic, and political goals in the face of technology-induced pressures for change.

Telecommunications policy in the United States offers a case in point. During the past two decades, an active telecommunications industry and responsive regulatory actions have wrought significant changes. Both marketplace and regulatory regimes are now primarily characterized by pro-competitive conditions and policies, promoting further entry of new equipment and service providers, availability of a broader and more diverse range of equipment and service offerings, and greater choice for consumers.

The trend toward deregulation and competition in the United States has been evolutionary and can be attributed to a confluence of technological, economic, and regulatory factors, rather than to a single event or decision. In large measure, the series of events initiated by the telecommunications policy makers in the United States — the Federal Communications Commission, the executive branch, and the Congress

This chapter covers remarks made by the author and was not a regular paper presented at the second TIDE 2000 symposium.

— leading to the erosion of the de facto monopoly of AT&T have been undertaken in response to the combined pressures of technological innovation and consumer demand for new products and services.

The results have been dramatic. Twenty years ago, our common carrier industry was characterized by a small number of firms supplying chiefly basic and undifferentiated services, employing relatively stable technology, and subject to pervasive federal and state economic regulation. The telephone industry was also largely self-contained. The leading firms typically were vertically integrated, their manufacturing affiliates concentrated chiefly on satisfying internal corporate needs, and communications imports constituted a relatively small factor in the industry overall.

Today, however, there is throughout the United States a diversity of suppliers of virtually all common carrier products and services, except perhaps certain components of very basic local telephone service. Increased demand and reduced costs have stimulated the growth of traditional offerings and facilitated the introduction of new services, such as cellular mobile radios. AT&T has been restructured by the courts, and new market entrants have included other carriers, such as MCI and Sprint, as well as noncarriers, such as IBM and GM. Foreign-based telecommunications firms, mostly equipment manufacturers, have also entered the U.S. market. With this change, the U.S. equipment market has also become much more integrated with the world market, due to the increased participation of foreign-based firms in the domestic market and the growing importance to U.S. companies of market opportunities overseas.

As I have noted, technological innovation has been one of the principal forces behind the changing character of the U.S. telecommunications market. Substantial federal spending on the space and related high-technology programs stimulated the already rapid development of the communications equipment, aerospace, and microelectronics industries. Research and development efforts have yielded innovative transmission techniques (such as fiber optics and satellites), advances in the information sciences, and the benefits of solid-state electronics. In turn, these innovations have led to telephone plant improvements and the creation of new, more sophisticated services.

Let me briefly summarize some of these developments:

software-driven electronic switches, which have created a variety of new capabilities and reduced maintenance costs;

"out-of-band" signaling systems, which permit the linkage of electronic switches with signaling systems operating independent of the calling path;

improved performance and declining costs of logic and memory
   circuits have permitted both customers and carriers to incorporate
   computer processing power into their equipment; and
lightwave systems, which will increase transmission capacity.

Innovation is not only changing state-of-the-art capabilities, it is
also changing the manner in which existing services are provided
through expanded technical options. Consumer demand is developing
in at least four dimensions in the emerging marketplace, demonstrated
by demand for:

lower cost, greater efficiency, and improved performance of products
   and services already in the marketplace;
equipment and services that meet growing data communications
   needs;
technology to meet special user needs (e.g., private network facilities,
   voice/data integration equipment); and
a wide variety of products and services that satisfy basic telephony and
   sophisticated user requirements.

Both carriers and noncarriers alike are developing products and
services to meet these user needs. Equipment manufacturers are
introducing a wider variety of intelligent terminal equipment, which
offers such features as high-speed facsimile, integrated data and voice
capabilities, wireless telephony, customized dialing, and other call-
handling options.

On the services side, the increase in data communications has
stimulated the development of computer-based message systems, such
as electronic mail, packet switched services, and what is known as the
information services industry, comprising data base and data processing services. Demand for high-capacity communications has also been
met through satellite services and fiber optic communications, which
provides additional user options to both satellite and existing terrestrial
systems for communications at very high information rates. Finally,
evolution toward integrated services digital networks (ISDNs) is progressing rapidly. Such networks will permit the transmission of voice,
data, graphics, and eventually images, in digital form and in an integrated fashion. The regulatory response to the combined pressures of
technological advances and consumer demand for new, sophisticated
goods and services has evolved in piecemeal fashion, yet the following
chronology of decisions is indicative of the trend of federal
communications policy toward deregulation and the promotion of
competition in the U.S. telecommunications market where possible:

1968: Customer-premises equipment was permitted to be attached to the public-switched network, provided a protective coupler was used (Carterfone).

1969: Nontelephone-company private line microwave service was approved (MCI).

1971: Specialized common carriers were authorized to provide private line service. Telephone companies (except for AT&T) were permitted to provide unregulated data processing services through separate subsidiaries (First Computer Inquiry).

1972: Domestic satellite common carriers were authorized.

1976: Resale of domestic private-line service was authorized.

1977: Direct connection of registered customer-premises equipment was permitted without the use of a telephone company-provided protective device (Part 68 registration procedures).

1978: Specialized common carriers were permitted to provide switched long distance service (Execunet decision).

1980: Customer-premises equipment and enhanced services were required to be offered on an untariffed basis (Computer II Inquiry). Resale and shared use of switched network services (MTS/WATS) was authorized.

Thus, by 1982 much of the U.S. telecommuncations market was competitive. In January of that year, a negotiated settlement was reached between the Justice Department and AT&T to resolve the government's 1974 antitrust action against AT&T. The divestiture has served to accelerate the trend toward increased market competition, particularly in the areas of customer-premises equipment, long distance services, and telephone network equipment.

Other, more recent developments — such as the president's determination that alternative satellite systems were "required in the national interest" and the on-going Computer III Inquiry — reflect the continuing pressure for regulatory review, flexibility, and, potentially, revision brought about by the dynamism of the telecommunications and information industries and marketplace.

Although the U.S. experience with deregulation is fairly young — and in some cases still undergoing transition — some demonstrable benefits have accrued as a result. New enterprises have been made possible, aggregate demand for communications services has been stimulated, innovation and research have been fostered, and the range of reasonably priced communications options has greatly increased. U.S. industry has also streamlined itself to adapt to today's more competitive and challenging world marketplace.

Moreover, the U.S. experience demonstrates that competition in communications and other social goals can be accommodated. The goals of ensuring that firms and individual consumers continue to enjoy reasonable service at reasonable prices; ensuring that services critical to emergency preparedness, defense, and national security are available; and maintaining a strong, up-to-date, and responsive national telecommunications sector, and the objective of expanded customer choice produced by telecommunications competition, are not mutually exclusive. It is possible, for example, to sanction competition almost unreservedly in a number of communications sectors with little or no adverse consequence in terms of maintaining the technical integrity of the basic core telephone network. Nor is it necessary to undertake broad-scale restructuring of the telecommunications industry, as the United States has done, to capture the benefits of effective competition.

9

Issues in the Development of the International Information Economy: A View from the Southwest

NEIL PRIMROSE

BACKGROUND

Advances in information technology over the past decade or so have been dramatic. They have allowed structural adjustment in many industries and have provided for significant improvement in the cost effectiveness of certain others. They have also caused fear and resistance. The future is likely to be even more dramatic.

Before the technology now in the research laboratories becomes a commercial reality substantial engineering gaps must be closed. But although fiber optics appear to have the upper hand in the battle for the current communications market, "breakthroughs" in technology would tip the balance back toward satellites. The use of lasers for intersatellite (space-to-space) and satellite-to-earth links, for instance, would give satellites capacities similar to those of fiber optic cables. Over the longer term, the balance between submarine cable and satellite links may well be a seesaw in which the relative costs of both technologies emerge roughly even.

The same does not apply in all domestic applications. Although in Australia optical fibers are already finding application on the main trunk routes and elsewhere on the eastern seaboard, other terrestrial systems and satellites are likely to continue to dominate the infrastructure through most of the land mass.

AUSTRALIA'S SITUATION

The environment for the provision of communications services in Australia results from the interplay of a number of factors, including constraints imposed by the natural environment, the size of the country, population distribution, social attitudes, governmental policies, institutional arrangements, and responses to pressures for technological adaptation and innovation.

Particular factors that make up Australia's situation include:

A relatively small population (15 million) and hence a small economic base, making the export of goods and services important in seeking economies of scale.

Concentration of the population along the coast in a crescent from northeast to southeast (from Queensland to south Australia) and in the southwest corner of western Australia. Elsewhere the population is sparsely scattered over a vast area in which environmental conditions are harsh.

The spread of high-technology communications to rural and remote areas, not least to support the sophisticated needs of mining companies.

Social obligations and economic requirements have to be met over distances that for Europe and Asia are more related to international communications operations rather than domestic services.

Australia's small labor force is relatively highly educated and contains a high proportion of skilled personnel.

Australia's export trade has rested upon agriculture and mineral products, but with growth limitations in both those sectors it is now diversifying toward high-technology manufacture and the services industries.

Australia's heavy reliance on import of manufactures, services, and innovation is likely to remain a feature of the economy and will be an important foundation in developing the diversity of output noted above.

Internationally, Australia's economic heartland is situated at extensive distances from other economies and from other clusters of population, making the "hauling" of information expensive, satellite technology notwithstanding.

The ranges of temperature and humidity conditions that equipment has to be designed to withstand in Australia is extreme and means that much overseas-designed equipment needs to be modified. This adds impetus to indigenous design of equipment and software.

Australia's three telecommunications authorities — Telecom Australia, the Overseas Telecommunications Commission, and AUSSAT Pty. Ltd. — have served Australia well in providing a high-quality national communications system. This has been achieved inter alia by the development of an indigenous equipment manufacturing industry together with appropriate research and design work. Not least, Telecom's approach to the rural and remote areas problem through its Australian-developed terrestrial Digital Radio Concentrator System (DRCS) developed in Australia is a relatively low-cost system, which could be used as an element of other national systems facing similar problems of distance and isolation.

In Australia, a communications manufacturing industry of some 125 firms is dominated by eight major companies, seven of which are the subsidiaries of multinational companies. This has brought considerable technological innovation to Australia, but has tended to limit any emphasis on producing for export. This has been caused in part by franchise limitations and has, in turn, tended to diminish impetus for indigenous research and development.

The software and systems side of the industry comprises some 900 firms, many of them two- or three-person operations. The vast majority of information technology products used in Australia are imported or are assembled by foreign-owned companies. Local activity in the design and development of those activities is small but growing. Some fifty companies produce computer hardware (W. D. Scott and Company 1984).

THE ISSUES

The impact of the international information economy on Australia has given rise to various kinds of problems, some highly visible and others not as easily discerned although still real. The following discussion deals with some of the more significant of these issues under the headings of "The Bandwagon Effect," "Job Siphoning," and "The People Perspective." Each of those issues serves to highlight the particular pressures faced by the Australian public and private sectors in the business of finding a balance between advantage and disadvantage in grasping the prospects of the change noted above.

The Bandwagon Effect

For Australia, the ability of industry to join or gain a better seat on the bandwagon is of paramount importance but cannot be undertaken without regard for the cost.

Achieving industry growth requires significant import of technology as well as continuing development of indigenous sources. This has served Australia reasonably well in the past. This will, however, need to be on terms that allow local firms (including local subsidiaries of overseas companies) to build upon that base and export without restriction to any market in the world. Franchise limitations that would hinder such a strategy are likely to be resisted.

The financial sector is a prime example of industry restructuring assisted by information technology. Deregulation of Australia's financial markets has coincided roughly with the advent of technology for real-time dealing in the foreign-exchange market. Australian banks have particularly needed to diversify their operations offshore to take advantage of the rapid growth in the Western Pacific. The growth of services exported by Australian banks into that region has been from a small base and has needed to be complemented by long-established access to the substantial, though highly competitive, financial markets of the North Atlantic. Australia's very high credit rating and secure investment prospects were obvious points of strength. Distance supplemented by a heavily regulated banking system, however, was an inhibiting factor until the convergence of communications and computing technologies.

The result of restructuring in Australia has been a rapid growth in the strength and sophistication of the local financial industry. The range of services available to corporate and private customers has increased and significant expansion into overseas operations is in progress. As overseas banks begin operations in Australia, competition in the Australian financial sector is expected to increase further. As this leads to further expansion of services to corporate customers especially, every advantage is expected to be wrung by the financial institutions from information technology and the increasing capacity for transborder data flow.

The international airline industry is an example of this. The advancing technology of on-board diagnostic instrumentation, when matched to a data link, allows an aircraft to provide real-time information on the state of its systems to its maintenance base. Maintenance bases can thus be prepared for the arrival of an aircraft in such a way as to minimize nonoperational time. Most of the hardware and software is already available and the systems approach is now being marketed by Boeing, Airbus, and some of their equipment suppliers. As technology advances, an aircraft's systems may be linked directly to the manufacturer for resolution of more complex problems relating to, say, the engines. A remedy may be prepared and available at the maintenance base in time for the arrival of the aircraft. If reduction of inventories results, especially if this includes spare engines, then the costs of operation are reduced. An airline that does not keep up with such technology is likely to be less competitive. The point is especially important in Australia, where high labor costs and a centrally regulated wage system make concentration upon high technology a priority.

Efficiencies can also be reaped, as information technology develops, from quicker settlement of ticket charging within the airline system with the commensurate reduction of uncertainty of exchange rate movements and cost from capital tied up while the processing of settlements is effected.

Reaping the advantages from the technology bandwagon requires ready access to overseas markets through an open international trading system and a free flow of data. Other factors, however, argue for a balance between open access for international trade in transborder data flow and safeguards to prevent unfair trading practices or the detriment to national aspirations.

The crucial issue facing smaller players in joining the technology bandwagon is the concentration of control over transborder data flows in larger transnational corporations. Associated with this is the clustering of service industries around the headquarters of such corporations. Together, the processors of information, the sellers of information technologies and associated downstream industries create an environment of innovation and product efficiency that can gain significant self-generated momentum.

The falling price of both computing power and of data hauling may yet leave a place in the sun for smaller operations in economies separated from the major information clusters. In addition, in the same way that smaller manufacturers have not only survived in the world of transnational giants and cut-price foreign predators, but are currently seeing a resurgence as high-technology production techniques make specialized manufacture economic, so reducing costs and increasingly flexible computer technology may provide special advantages to smaller information operations. There are some signs of this happening in Australia, particularly in the software area.

Job Siphoning

One area of particular sensitivity, even to the major players, is the siphoning of skills and hence jobs from one country to another associated with companies hauling data for processing from subsidiaries in a host country to regional centers or to headquarters in another country.

Some industries are especially prone to such a siphoning of jobs and skills, particularly those involving significant information processing operations. A corporate strategy based on removing processing work from the host country will not only reduce the need for skills associated with performing the processing function at that spot, it will also decrease the need for servicing the computers that would otherwise be involved, diminishing the opportunity for the host country's market to share in sales and reducing the prospects of other downstream industries that would otherwise be employed. Of course, the skills and jobs created in the regional center or headquarters are a gain to those localities and are likely to be aggressively sought, especially in the case of large multinational companies whose economies of scale provide attractive arguments for hauling for central processing. The effect in the host country is likely to be a reduced ability to keep up with the technological bandwagon.

Australia does not currently have specific barriers to transborder data flows. In developing its own skills base in the information technologies, however, Australia would presumably be wary of an excessive imbalance between the inward and outward flows of skills in those technologies. At the same time, with prospects for developing exports in the information services, Australia will depend on a reasonably open international regime in that trade.

The issue is not academic. Already a variety of protective measures have been instituted by European governments in this area to prevent the siphoning of their national skills bases. If international companies wish the Australian situation to continue, sensitivity to national aspirations would seem to be desirable.

The People Perspective

Very little of the literature on information technology and transborder data flow deals with people. Yet the service industries generally are skill intensive, with a premium on imagination and flair. Transborder data flows no longer are merely the transport of data but are creative elements of the new economy.

The fear among many countries that they will be disadvantaged by change is well known. The reaction to U.S. initiatives on services in the GATT and the Group of 77 recourse to UNCTAD are cases in point. How this is reflected among interest groups within the countries concerned is less well documented. There is ample evidence, however, from OECD countries of the fear of change determining interest group reactions and pressures on governments. Barriers erected against the siphoning of the national skills base are an indication of such pressures.

It is clear that if the spread of protective barriers is to be resisted and the distortions from those already in place are to be reduced, then attention to the fear of change will be required.

In Australia, the greying of the workforce limits the extent to which industries can look to the younger generation of computer-literate people to move through the work force. Australia's highly unionized work force, reinforced by a centralized wage-fixing system, makes the extensive development of an alternative work force impracticable. Rather, unions need to be involved in the process of change. Reskilling and a positive approach to retraining of the existing workforce will be required to perceive the opportunities that exist in change and to be prepared to meet the personal costs of grasping such advantages.

A positive attitude to change also needs to be fostered in the young. Coping with information technology and making the most creative use of it requires computer-literate graduates of the education system. In some cases, this may involve change in the thrust of education curricula. This process and the issues associated with it need to be included in the information debate and given a high priority by corporate and governmental strategists.

One factor likely to contribute to a positive approach to change is the increasing internationalization of education, including in the western Pacific region. With increasing numbers of overseas students coming to Australia under aid and commercial arrangements and with the export of curricula and course materials published in Australia is the potential for barriers to trade to be eased and for demand for information to increase.

The prospects would appear to be promising for a significantly different environment for trade between nations to be created by the greater sophistication of businesspeople who have lived overseas as students.

FOR FURTHER CONSIDERATION

If escalation of regulation over transborder flows appears inevitable (Jussawalla and Snow 1986, 11), the most crucial issue for further consideration is the balance between regulation-for-order and the avoidance of regulation that distorts markets. Smaller economies especially will need assistance to remain open by avoiding the practices of foreign companies as well as governments that cause a defensive response. In this regard, corporate citizenship would appear to be as important an area for consideration as lowest-common-denominator regimes negotiated in multilateral forums. The latter should be seen as reacting to symptoms rather than as dealing with the causes of complaints. An open trading system involves not only access to markets, but also the opportunity for all players to be upwardly mobile.

Consideration needs to be given to the extent to which convergence of the information technologies has been accompanied by a convergence of the policy and regulatory regimes that earlier applied to disparate technologies. In Australia's case much of the regulation that now applies to the service industries is a function of their growth as domestically oriented industries. If they are to be effective in developing the export potential that many have, adjustments may need to be made. Achieving this is difficult enough within one *imperium*. To achieve it between competing *imperia* will be no mean feat.

In moving toward an international information economy, corporate strategies must accommodate national aspirations in host countries in order to reduce the erection of defensive barriers that may be counterproductive to one or both parties.

The people perspective needs to be included quickly in the agenda of issues to be resolved and pursued in the development of the international information economy. Attention to sharing the benefits and easing the costs will help ensure that interest group policies and activities do not hamper government and industry in grasping the prospects of change.

BIBLIOGRAPHY

Arnold, L., ed. 1985. *Education and Technology.* Report of the Australian Education Council Task Force on Education and Technology. Australian Education Council. Canberra.

Australian Law Reform Commission. 1983. *Privacy.* Report No. 22. Canberra: AGPS.

Crawford, M. H. 1982. *Competition, Cooperation, and Discord in Information Technology Trade.* Cambridge, Mass.: Center for Information Policy Research, Harvard University.

Department of Science (Australia). 1985. *A National Information Policy for Australia* (Discussion Paper). Canberra: Department of Science.

Department of Science (Australia). 1986. *National Information Policy Workshops* (Canberra December 3–4, 1985). Canberra: Department of Science.

Economic Planning and Advisory Council (Australia). 1986. *Technology and Innovation.* Council Paper No. 19. Canberra.

Feketekuty, G. 1985. "The Impact of Information Technology on Trade in Services." *Transnational Data Report* 8(4): 220–24.

Forester, T., ed. 1985. *The Information Technology Revolution.* Oxford: Basil Blackwell.

Hamelink, C. J. 1984. *Transnational Data Flows in the Information Age.* Amsterdam: Student litteratur AB Chartwell-Bratt.

Industries Assistance Commission (Australia). 1984. *Telecommunications and Related Equipment and Parts.* Report No. 352. Canberra: AGPS.

Jussawalla, M., and M. Snow. 1986. "The Impact of Information Technology on Trade Problems Covering Trade and Interdependence." Issue Paper 3 prepared for the TIDE 2000 Second Symposium, Institute of Culture and Communication, East-West Center, Hawaii.

Kane, V. J. 1985. *Communications Programs in Rural and Remote Australia.* Paper presented to the Second Communications Forum on Communications for Development, Tokyo. Unpublished mimeo.

Kirby, M. D. 1984. *The Morning Star of Informatics Law and the Need for a Greater Sense of Urgency*. Address to the Inter-Governmental Bureau of Informatics Second World Conference on Transborder Data Flow Policies, Rome, June.

Maitland, D. (Sir). 1984. *The Missing Link*. Report of the Independent Commission for World Wide Telecommunications Development. Geneva: International Telecommunication Union.

OECD. 1981. *Guidelines on the Protection of Privacy and Transborder Flows of Personal Data*. Paris: OECD.

OECD. 1983. *Telecommunications: Pressures and Policies for Change*. Paris: OECD.

OECD. 1985. *Declaration on Transborder Data Flows*. Press Release, April 11. Paris: OECD.

OECD. 1985. *Transborder Data Flows: Proceedings of an OECD Conference Held December 1983*. Amsterdam: North-Holland.

Robinson, P. 1986. "Legal Issues Raised by Transborder Data Flow." Paper presented at the Conference on Canada–United States Economic Ties, Cleveland.

U.S. Congress, Joint Economic Committee. April 1984. Hearing on the Service Economy and Industrial Change. Washington, D.C.: U.S. Government Printing Office.

W. D. Scott & Company (in association with Arthur D. Little Inc.). 1984. *Information Technology in Australia: Capabilities and Opportunities*. Vols. 1 and 2, Report to the Department of Science and Technology. Canberra.

III

INSTITUTIONAL CHANGES IN INTERDEPENDENCE: BANKING, FINANCE, AND TRADE

10

The Impact of Telematics on Financial Intermediaries and Market Interdependencies

Meheroo Jussawalla and Stephen Dworak

INTRODUCTION

During the post-war period many changes have occurred in the nature and operations of financial intermediaries, in the size and scope of financial markets, and in the regulatory policies and institutional structures that impinge on domestic and international processes of financial intermediation. Although many factors are involved in explaining and understanding these changes and their implications, even a cursory examination of them quickly reveals the important role that technological advances in telematics have played in their development. Financial intermediation is essentially an information industry, and, thus, changes in the ability to gather, process, store, or exchange information portend significant changes in the operations and markets of financial intermediaries. They also pose challenges to those charged with regulating these industries and to the framers of national economic policy, especially in the developed countries of the Organization for Economic Cooperation and Development (OECD) where this confluence of the financial and information industries is most prevalent.

This chapter will attempt to outline the conceptual, empirical, and political-economic background to the issues raised by the increasing use of advanced telematics by financial intermediaries, and will explore some of the key policy implications for the developed economies of the OECD. The second part reviews the general importance of information to the process of financial intermediation and the nature of technological changes that have taken place through the use of telematics. In the third section, some of the impacts on domestic and international financial markets brought on by the use of telematics by financial intermediaries are examined. The final section delineates policy issues that have arisen, and will arise, from these ongoing changes in financial intermediation and information technology.

THE IMPORTANCE OF INFORMATION IN FINANCIAL INTERMEDIATION

The reason information is so important to financial intermediaries is that financial intermediation is, in essence, an information industry, performing two basic informational functions: maturity transformation and risk diversification. The needs and desires of an economy's surplus income units (savers) are brought together with those of its deficit spending units (borrowers) in these mediating institutions, and information about both groups is required in order to perform that function efficiently. That is to say, information is a primary input into the production function of financial intermediaries. Additionally, in the process of mediating between these two groups, the financial intermediaries also provide information to market participants about the marginal rate of return that an investment must produce in order for it to be profitable, thus influencing decisions about the allocation of real factors of production through the information they generate. Information is a primary output of financial intermediaries. In modern market economies, financial intermediaries stand at the intersection of production and consumption and are the conduit through which information about these two most basic of economic activities is exchanged, both intra- and internationally.

Telematics Advances and Intermediation

The theoretical importance of information to financial intermediaries and their markets indicates that technological advances in the ability to gather, process, store, or exchange information would be quickly utilized by those trying to improve their profit/risk position, whether regionally, nationally, or internationally. Several prominent examples of this can be found in the history of financial intermediaries. The first newspaper in Europe was published by the sixteenth-century Augsburg banking family, the Fuggers. Banker Nathan Rothschild profited from the increased communicative speed of a private carrier pigeon service. The first telegraph link between New York and London, in 1866, led to increased financial market integration and reduced market price differences (Garbade and Silber 1978). The first telephone exchange, in Boston in 1877, had a bank among its first clients (Aronson 1977). Virtually every major advance in the information-related technologies has been put to use almost immediately by financial intermediaries.

It is not surprising, then, that in the post-war period, with its virtual quantum leaps in a vast array of telematics technologies, the financial intermediary industries in all countries have invested large amounts of time and money to make use of these technologies.

In addition, the period has seen such telematic developments in financial markets as FedWire, BankWire, CHIPS, CHAPS, SWIFT, Euroclear, Cedel, Reuters, Telerate, and recently Instinet, all of which are financial information exchange networks of one type or another, each involving large investments and high degrees of legal and political coordination. Information data bases have also developed, from which financial intermediaries buy information, including the U.S. Federal Reserves' Flow of Funds, the World Banks' World Debt Tables, the IMFs Balance of Payments and International Financial Statistics, Chase Econometrics Foreign Exchange, Reuters Economic Services, Standard and Poor's, and Moody's. Finally, there are the in-house communications networks owned or leased by most large banks and securities firms.

Regulation, Telematics Usage, and Financial Intermediation

The impact of technological advances in telematics on financial intermediaries and their markets has in some ways been a positive development, in that it has provided financial institutions with the ability to be more responsive to customers and markets and to offer a broader range of financial services and products. In other ways, however, the impact has been to reduce or alter the efficiency of some domestic monetary policies, to make it easier for those inclined to bypass legal and regulatory provisions, to blur and sometimes erase the traditional lines of distinction between banks and nonbank financial intermediaries, to permit low-cost access to speculative markets so that risk characteristics of financial intermediaries can be changed in ways undetectable by regulators, to increase the potential for the negative consequences of payment-settlement failure between institutions, and to strongly affect the transborder data flow debate and the related issues of nontariff barriers and trade in services. These policy cum regulatory issues are emerging in the most important features of the convergence of telematics technology and financial intermediation in all nations.

In a very clear and concise discussion of the relationship between technological change and the regulation of financial markets and their participants, Kane (1986) characterizes the situation as a "regulatory dialectic," a process of ongoing conflict and conflict resolution between opposing points of view and the economic, political, legal, and physical forces associated with each (i.e., as a continual and inherent conflict between regulators' attempts to regulate and the attempts by those regulated to lessen the burden of whatever regulations apply to them). For financial markets, this is exemplified by regulators' efforts to make financial intermediaries conform to a set of politically determined rules that were designed to achieve such objectives as economic stability, financial system integrity, efficiency, and equity; while the intermediaries being regulated are concerned with profit and utility maximization that leads them to seek exceptions or loopholes in the regulatory structure in order to reduce the net burden of the regulations applied to them. As Sparks (1980) so aptly put it, "The Euromarket is a paradigm of what happens when governments attempt to control the flow of capital in the new era of international communications." In the face of exogenous changes in technology, no permanent equilibrium is possible, for every seeming regulatory equilibrium contains the makings of its own undoing as regulators and the regulated pursue their own divergent interests.

IMPACTS OF INCREASING TELEMATIC USE
BY FINANCIAL INTERMEDIARIES

The consequences and implications of the increasing use of advances in telematics technologies by financial intermediaries, and the innovations in financial products and services thereby made possible, do vary between nations. This is primarily due to differences in the general structure of individual national financial systems and to the ways that the regulators and policy makers of a given country have perceived or responded to various developments. As the interdependence of national financial markets increases, the ability of countries involved to pursue particular monetary and fiscal policies is altered, and may in some instances be eliminated or produce undesired results when implemented.

Thus, it is apparent that a growing need exists for an improved understanding of the changes that the use and spread of telematics technologies are bringing to national financial markets and their participants. The experiences and actions taken in various countries may provide valuable information and insight for national policy makers and those charged with regulating, or reregulating, the financial intermediaries and markets of a given country.

Increased Diversity of Financial Products and Services

At the retail level this includes such things as "sweep" accounts, negotiable CDs, and money market accounts, and such new services as ATMs and home banking. And at the wholesale level, electronic funds transfer and cash management techniques are enabling corporate treasurers to invest idle funds aggressively and to have easy access to commercial paper markets. Telematics have also contributed to the tremendous growth in "plastic money" like credit cards and related cash and "smart" cards. But with these increases in available products and services has come a reorganization of intermediary pricing practices, with industrial services being priced independently, rather than the cross-subsidized price structures of the past. These costs may be prohibitive to lower-income groups. Additionally, this growing number of financial products and services can be bewildering to the nonspecialist, as the increased informational output of intermediaries is becoming harder to comprehend. This in turn is leading to an increased emphasis on the packaging of services by intermediaries and the trend toward one-stop financial institutions dealing in asset management, brokerage services, insurance, as well as deposit taking and loan making. Technology is at the heart of these developments.

Increased Competition between Banks and Nonbanks

As the capabilities made feasible by telematics have expanded, firms, not previously able, can begin offering products and services once the exclusive domain of banks. These firms can not only receive funds for deposit, they can pay close to money market rates, make loans, manage assets, underwrite equity issues, and sell insurance. As a result, banks are utilizing telematics to bypass or reduce the effects of regulatory limits on their operations to expand into these areas of financial services in order to remain competitive. Much of the pressure for financial market regulatory reform is a result of this competition. Although most of these rivalries are among domestic players, even national borders do not provide as much protection as they once did, because telematics permits rapid international flows of both data and funds. These increases in competition are healthy for consumers and beneficial to overall efficiency, but they do present some interesting and potentially problematic situations for regulators, because credit levels, money aggregate measures, and payments-system integrity are all affected by these changes in ways not wholly predictable.

Changes in Equity and Futures Markets

Securities and futures markets are making increased use of telematics in their operations. They have developed computerized trading systems, mechanisms for the electronic filing of required documents such as the SEC's EDGAR system (Electronic Data Gathering, Analysis, and Retrieval), and international links between markets based on telematics systems such as the CME/SIMEX link (Chicago Mercantile Exchange/Singapore International Monetary Exchange), the proposed link between the COMEX and the Sydney Futures Exchange, and the integration of the London Stock Exchange's clearing and settlement system, Talisman, with the major U.S. stock exchanges following London's "Big Bang." Technological advances allow price quotations, volume information, and other data to speed around the globe and enable traders to trade futures twenty-four hours a day.

Payments Settlement, Liability, and Risk Monitoring

The use of telematics technologies can lead to new vulnerabilities in national payments systems, because the increasing electronic links between institutions create the potential for payments-settlement failures to have far-reaching effects throughout the system. Either individual institutional failure or computer system failures (whether accidental or deliberate) could result in such situations, and this in turn raises questions about liability in such cases. Regulatory monitoring of risk positions is also affected by the capabilities of telematics. Low-cost and high-speed access to speculative markets can allow intermediaries to engage in risky behavior that may be undetectable to regulators. The use of technological capabilities by nonbank firms is also relevant and raises questions about access to national payments clearing mechanisms and the risks of opening the mechanisms to these less-supervised firms.

Three types of losses are involved in automated clearinghouse settlements: losses of principal, losses of interest, and losses resulting from foreign exchange fluctuations. Such losses may be caused by delay in transmission, the input of faulty information, or a participant's inability to settle the transaction on the day it was received. Hardware or software failures may cause the delays. There may also be fraud.

The question that arises in the allocation of liability in operating electronic transfers is, Should regulation of transfers be based on differences in costs associated with various payments systems or should it be based on the diverse degrees of risk involved in such funds transfers? Most legal experts believe that legal regulations should be based on the former. Although liability based on spreading risk was first evolved for products, the same principle is extended to cover services. Service providers are less able to spread losses. Electronic funds transfer (EFT) has both a service and a product component; it is a hybrid business that presents special problems to courts and to users and providers. It is difficult to discover how a particular error was caused and where it arose.

Efficacy of Monetary and Financial Policies

Several significant implications for national monetary and financial system policies arise from the impact of telematics in financial markets. The greatly increased speeds with which funds can be transferred increases the transaction velocity of money, and float times are reduced or even eliminated. These technologies also allow many assets that were previously illiquid to be easily liquified, as when lines of credit are granted against such assets as the equity in a home. This can result in monetary growth that policy makers may not desire or be able to completely take account of in monetary aggregate measures. Finally, telematic links between on- and off-shore branches of intermediaries may permit these firms to avoid the impact of given monetary policies and to gain access to off-shore sources of funds when domestic sources of credit are tight, thus reducing the effectiveness of intended restrictions on money growth.

International Aspects

The nature of international financial market relationships has been, and is, strongly affected by the technologies of telematics. These developments hold important implications for national financial markets, because the impact of foreign market developments on national markets is greatly enhanced by the informational connections between markets, and thus, particular policies may be rendered ineffective or may result in unintended consequences as intermediaries react to those policies.

Development of International or Euromarkets

Although the development of the Euromarkets was in large part due to various national regulatory restrictions, such as reserve requirements, interest-rate ceilings, and credit restraints, as well as the desires of some to avoid interference in the movement of their funds, it is fairly safe to say that telematics technologies have made this now enormous unregulated international financial market structure possible. As mentioned, these markets provide intermediaries with the means for avoiding the impact of certain domestic regulations. The result is that national policies must now be formulated with a heightened consideration of their international impact. The Euromarkets are in many ways like an international version of the U.S. federal funds market, and they may well be the most powerful agents for financial market integration, as intermediaries everywhere borrow and lend in the market to adjust their cash positions. International clearing and message systems like CHIPS, SWIFT, and Euroclear only enhance this process.

Increased Financial Market Integration

Telematic technologies and their use by intermediaries are increasing the number of both direct connections between national financial markets and indirect connections between national markets through the intermediary Euromarkets. As a result, national exchange rates and interest rates are increasingly determined by global forces rather than purely domestic ones. In fact, Walter Wriston (1987) has gone so far as to state that international financial market integration and the information links between markets have eliminated the effectiveness of past international structures such as the gold standard and Bretton Woods system and replaced them with an information standard, from which no one can resign and that makes policies and policy changes subject to instant judgment by traders who can react immediately to any changes. This internationalization of markets in banking and currencies is now also beginning in the equities markets, which should produce even more interdependence between national economies and allow capital to flow even more easily in response to differences in national financial market returns and policies.

Transborder Data Flows, Nontariff Barriers, and Trade-In Services

The interaction between the telematics industries and the financial intermediary industries has ramifications that extend beyond these two industries themselves and that can lead to both political friction and asymmetrical economic relationships among nations. The privacy, data protection, and national security and sovereignty issues on the political side, and the infant-industry, protection of regulated telecommunications monopolies, and balance of payments issues on the economic side, are of importance to the development of national policies regarding these industries. Efforts have been made to bring international information flows and trade-in services under the General Agreement on Tariffs and Trade (GATT) negotiations, but thus far arrangements between nations are for the most part on a bilateral or limited multilateral basis. This environment creates the potential for competition between nations in the amount and nature of regulatory restrictions on financial intermediaries and information flows, thus putting pressure on national regulators and policy makers to change or face the loss of intermediary business and the related benefits that complete access to world financial markets brings. Protectionist policies toward the financial or telematics industries could have significant spillover effects into other sectors of an economy. This is not to say that domestic concerns should be subsidiary to international ones, but that national policy formation must now develop with both domestic and international aspects considered if it is to have the effect intended. Domestic industries must devise courses of action that take into account the globalization of the world's economic structure. Telematics and financial intermediation are central to these developments.

SOME SPECIFIC DEVELOPMENTS IN OECD COUNTRIES

Although the impact of telematics advances on financial intermediaries and their markets is prevalent in all the developed economies of the OECD, specific structures in each country are unique to it by virtue of the different financial market systems and regulations that existed as these technological changes developed. Additionally, the responses of regulators and policy makers to these changes have varied in time and scope, often the result of necessity rather than planned action.

Japan

Deliberate government policy has long shaped the Japanese financial market structure, but noticeable changes are occurring. During the past few years, Japan has liberalized its foreign-exchange market, permitted a market in U.S. Treasury bonds to develop in Tokyo, allowed trading in new yen instruments like Euro-yen bonds, bond futures, and bankers acceptances, and began the process toward market-rate investment alternatives for individuals. Additionally, foreign firms were granted seats on the Tokyo Stock Exchange for the first time in 1985. These increases in competition and relaxations of financial market control are in part the result of impact of telematics on Japanese markets. For example, telematics assisted Japanese securities firms, led by Nomura in 1980, to begin selling market-rate funds dealing in government bonds, which in turn resulted in pressure to allow banks to issue market-rate instruments, and in late 1985 rates on large time deposits were freed.

On the domestic front, Japan has developed a nation-wide all-bank telecommunications system called the Zengin, through which credit transfers can take place between any two places in the country within an hour. Japan also has more ATMs per person than any other country, with nearly 320 per million. Not just banks have installed these electronic tellers; consumer finance companies, securities firms, and the postal savings system have extensive systems.

France

The financial system in France is heavily regulated, but, under the influence of market pressures and the efforts of reform-minded finance ministers, changes are evolving. Recent changes include moves toward privatizing state-owned banks, the removal of credit controls, the elimination of distinctions between various kinds of financial intermediaries, and the standardization of certain financial products and services. In many ways, these are the most significant changes since the mid-1960s, when branch banking was freed of restrictions and interest-rate controls on loans were abolished.

France leads the world in the development of a card-based electronic payments system. And, with the government, the banks are committed to a single national system for electronic funds transfer based on the chip card (another French development) by the late 1980s. France has also pursued the concept of home banking more intensely than other countries, with the French Post, Telegraph and Telecommunications (PTT) distributing nearly 1.5 million free videotext terminals to get the service started. The communications industry in France is unique among developed countries in the level of control and administration exercised by the PTT. This has advantages in terms of the universality of service, uniform rate structures and tariffs, and common technical standards for telematic networks, but it does not hinder the development of private financial intermediary communication systems that may be more cost effective for multinational institutions.

Due to the 1978 Nora-Minc Report, the French government has committed itself to the development of banking and finance data bases, so that U.S. banks would not have a monopoly on the organization of such files. French law established strict controls on such files, and their transmission, in 1978. The information-intensity of financial intermediaries necessitates the free flow of information, and French regulators must exercise caution so as to not impede financial market competitiveness. Nevertheless, the convergence of telematics and financial intermediation in France is well under way, and French policy makers will find the market forces for deregulation increasingly difficult to ignore.

West Germany

The West German financial markets have already experienced much deregulation. Restrictions on bank branching were dropped in the 1950s, along with credit ceilings, and interest rate controls were lifted in the 1960s. West German commercial banks have powers that extend to selling insurance and dealing in securities, so the primary sources of competition in German financial markets are from the savings banks and cooperative banks, and this competition is driven by market changes rather than deregulation. As a result, the savings banks are installing increasing numbers of sophisticated ATMs and balance-inquiry terminals, and the cooperative banks are fast becoming financial institutions of one-stop convenience for a variety of services.

One current area of contention does exist, arising out of telematics capabilities, and that is the desire of the savings banks to establish an on-line Electronic Funds Transfer at Point of Sale (EFTPOS) payments system, whereas the other banks prefer an off-line system based on the French microchip or smart card. West German banks are also fearful that their own abilities could be diminished if West German stock markets fall behind in the race to internationalize trading, and so they are encouraging the eight rather small regional exchanges to work together more cooperatively and to investigate possibilities of combining operations. In addition, the exchanges have recently agreed to collaborate in dealings with foreign exchanges and in the provision of market information. The tight control of the Deutsche Bundespost (DBP) over the telecommunications markets, however, does present some potential sources of difficulty for foreign financial intermediaries operating in West Germany, in that all communications must be routed through DBP facilities. Under the German Federal Data Protection Act of 1976, all private organizations with more than five persons involved in the automated processing of personal data must have a data-protection representative to maintain compliance with privacy regulations. These types of nontariff barriers may impede the development of internationalizing West German financial markets, though probably only marginally, because they increase operating expenses for intermediaries.

United Kingdom

The financial markets in the United Kingdom are exposed to innovations in financial techniques and technologies from both the usual domestic and from the existence of much of the international Euromarkets activity in London. British financial market regulations, as a result of these influences and the tendency toward privatization and freer markets in general under the Thatcher government, have been in a process of being considerably revised. In 1984, the first non-British bank (Citicorp) was allowed to join the clearing system, and by 1987 all banks and nonbank intermediaries meeting minimum volume requirements were allowed to participate in the payments system itself. Recently, tax laws were changed so that interest payments by the banks and their major competitors, the building societies, are treated equally. And in October 1986, the "Big Bang" occurred, and London's stock exchange was deregulated, eliminating minimum fees and allowing banks the ability to deal in securities through subsidiaries. Additionally, the London Stock Exchange has established electronic links with NASDAQ (National Association of Securities Dealers Automated Quotations) in the United States, and has begun negotiations to develop links with the New York Stock Exchange and other exchanges in Europe.

Britain was the first country to have automated cash dispensers and on-line ATMs, but other telematic developments in the domestic market, like EFTPOS and home banking, are less well developed. Information technologies are at the heart of the stock exchanges' new information system, and the increasing competitiveness of Britain's building societies in relation to the banks is in part due to the fact that they are developing telematics systems while older institutions must first write down their long-established manual-based systems.

United States

The U.S. financial markets have probably been the ones most affected by technology-related developments, because in many ways they were the most fragmented and circumscribed to begin with. Restrictions on interstate branching, interest rates, and underwriting securities have long checked the domestic growth of U.S. banks and were of considerable importance to their expansion overseas and into offshore centers. Telematics advances have been important in allowing greatly increased competition from nonbank financial intermediaries like Merrill-Lynch and Sears Roebuck, and in the development of money market funds that offered market rates of interest and NOW accounts that permitted savings and loans associations to offer checking services.

The allowance of onshore international banking facilities to stem the movement of bank operations offshore and the lifting of Regulation Q interest rate ceilings are two examples of deregulation trends. The big U.S. banks are among the most telematically advanced in the world, many having private or leased communication networks, centralized computer facilities and data bases, and subsidiary units involved with financial news analysis, software development, and the provision of information to outside firms. The number of ATMs has grown rapidly and so has the development of local, regional, and national shared networks. A number of multifirm consortia have been established, joining banks with corporations like IBM, AT&T, RCA, and CBS to develop a range of information services like home banking and news retrieval.

The securities markets in the United States are undergoing some equally dramatic changes due to telematics and the innovations they enable. And with the world's largest equity markets to monitor, the SEC is understandably making use of telematics, with its EDGAR system for document filing. The impact of such advances on the structure, size, and scope of U.S. financial markets can hardly be overstated.

POLICY ISSUES OF FINANCIAL INTERMEDIARY TELEMATICS USE

Financial intermediaries and their markets have been, and will be for the foreseeable future, undergoing many changes that are either direct or indirect results of rapid innovations in telematics technologies and the capabilities they endow. Formulating policy issues and courses of action with regard to these changes present serious challenges because the changes are occurring so rapidly and in such diverse directions that it is difficult for financial intermediaries themselves to anticipate what will eventually prevail, let alone for the often cumbersome and bureaucratized regulatory entities that are in place to monitor the intermediaries. Nevertheless, it is possible to discern some of the broad patterns likely to emerge and some of the important policy issues that national regulators can be expected to face in coming years, if not already. Policies alter market forces and the relative influences of the factors that determine price and product mix. The following are some of the more prominent issues policy makers will have to resolve.

The Distinctions between Banks and Nonbank Intermediaries

Most nations have long allocated specific functions to specific institutions. The combination of technological innovations in telematics and market forces, however, has significantly lessened the functional distinctions between types of institutions. Other financial institutions, and even nonfinancial institutions, are encroaching on activities once limited to banks. Policies of deregulation suggest that financial institutions could compete equally if barriers between various types were dissolved.

Payments Settlement, "Daylight" Overdrafts, System Integrity Issues

The technology of telematics is increasingly utilized in the processing of large sums of wire transfer payments without any real-time controls or limitations. The lack of such limitations has allowed banks that participate in these wire networks to in effect borrow funds intraday at zero interest cost. This is the so-called daylight overdraft issue. This creates risks of settlement failure if for some reason the institution fails during the day, or more importantly, if the telematically based transfer system should fail for some length of time, whether that failure is accidental or deliberate. Such risks could endanger the integrity of a nation's entire financial system.

Risk Monitoring of Financial Intermediaries

Technology can provide the impetus to improve diversification, but it can also permit low-cost access to speculative markets providing incentives for the intermediaries to engage in risk taking without being detected by regulators. Technology can, however, provide its own solution if it offers regulators a cost-effective mechanism with which to monitor intermediary activities continuously.

Monetary Policy and Related Issues

Much has been written about the impact of an increasingly globalized financial market structure on individual nations' abilities to pursue independent courses of action. Because telematics capabilities are at the heart of this development, and advances in both technology and technique are still occurring, these issues are likely to remain important and to include such essential areas as the measurement of money supplies, the setting of interest rates, and the determination of exchange rates. Regulators and national policy makers will have to grapple with these issues for some time.

Transborder Data Flows and Nontariff Barriers

Financial institutions and other types of enterprises have branched across national boundaries and depend heavily on the ability to move data freely and confidentially between offices in several countries. Some nations have passed laws limiting the collection and dissemination of data associated with individual accounts across their borders, whether for privacy or protection of trade interests or for national security reasons. Such restrictions could cause problems for some firms and could result in situations in which one nation's policies are established as a response to requirements from abroad. In addition, there is the concern that international data-processing centers concentrated in a few countries are vulnerable to disruption or destruction.

Electronic Theft and Fraud

The development of telematically based financial systems and the virtual explosion in the number of credit cards worldwide has opened up new sources of concern regarding theft and fraud. Computer theft is difficult to detect quickly, and counterfeit credit cards can be a source of significant losses to their legitimate issuers. The smart card, and variations on it, are contributing to the reduction of some of these problems, but policy makers and regulators will have to be increasingly on guard to keep ahead of equally sophisticated criminals.

Regulatory Design and Reform Efforts

The impact of telematics on the financial intermediaries and their markets is not a static phenomenon, but rather a continually evolving process of structural change as new advances in telematics and financial innovation occur. This presents national policy makers with the question of how to realign their legal and regulatory structures to make them more closely conform to the changing structure of the financial service industry. Should changes be made in an ad hoc, reactionary way, or should there be a complete restructuring and redefinition of legal and regulatory constructs?

CONCLUDING REMARKS

It is fairly apparent from the above sets of developments and issues that the impact of telematics on national and international financial markets, and the intermediaries that operate in them, create challenges for regulation and policy, for economic theory, for risk monitoring and management, and for the telematics industries themselves. These challenges stem from increasing international interdependence, which by its very nature is likely to reduce the power and efficacy of national regulation and domestic policies related to financial market developments. A terminal and a telephone are capable of eliminating the effects of time and space and of making all types of artificial barriers, like national borders or jurisdictional boundaries, increasingly irrelevant. In such a context the role of central banks as lenders of last resort becomes ambiguous. Is it possible for central banks to catch up with the technology and build a system of international supervision? Should the special responsibility for providing adequate liquidity rest with the host country or the parent country? How are solvency problems to be supervised? While twelve leading industrial countries have a network of regulators known as the Cooke Committee, it is better equipped to manage crises than to forestall them. And as the globalization of equities markets advances will there be even greater potential for financial flows disruptive to some countries? Are legal and regulatory frameworks now capable of coping with this increased scope of national equities markets? In order to ensure the credibility and security of national financial markets, and the global financial structure built upon them, research into these areas must be carried on, and policy makers in all countries must maintain a continually updated awareness of changes in telematics technology and its uses and applications by financial intermediaries.

BIBLIOGRAPHY

Aliber, R. Z. 1980. "The Integration of the Offshore and Domestic Banking System." *Journal of Monetary Economics* 6(3): 509–26.

Aronson, S. H. 1977. "Bell's Electrical Toy: What's the Use?" In *The Social Impact of the Telephone*, edited by Ithiel de Sola Poole, 15–39. Cambridge, Mass.: MIT Press.

Brimmer, A. F., and F. R. Dahl. 1975. "Growth of American International Banking: Implications for Public Policy." *Journal of Finance* 30(2): 341–63.

The Economist. 1986. "A Survey of International Banking." March 22. 54a–112a.

Flannery, M. J., and D. M. Jaffee. 1973. *The Economic Implications of an Electronic Monetary Transfer System.* Lexington, Mass.: D. C. Heath.

Garbade, Kenneth D., and W. L. Silber. 1978. "Technology, Communication and the Performance of Financial Markets: 1840–1975." *Journal of Finance* 33(3): 819–32.

Grubel, H. G. 1983. "The New International Banking." *Banca Nazionale del Lavoro Quarterly Review,* September:263–84.

Hamelink, C. J. 1983. *Finance and Information: A Study of Converging Interests.* Norwood, N.J.: ABLEX.

Herring, R. J., and R. C. Marston. 1977. *National Monetary Policies and International Financial Markets.* Contributions to Economic Analysis, Vol. 104.

Jussawalla, Meheroo. 1985. "Communication Technology and International Banking: Theory Versus Reality." Paper presented at the Nineteenth International Atlantic Economic Conference, Rome.

Jussawalla, Meheroo. 1985. "Global Banking at the Cross Roads: Technological Integration of Financial Markets." *TDR* 8(8).

Kane, R. L. 1986. "Technology and Regulation." In *Technology and the Regulation of Financial Markets,* edited by Anthony Saunders and Lawrence J. White. Lexington, Mass.: D. C. Heath.

Sparks, W. 1980. "The Flow of Information and the New Technology of Money." Address at the Conference of World Communications: Decisions for the Eighties, at the Annenberg School of Communications, Philadelphia, Pa. Unpublished.

U.S. Congress. Office of Technology Assessment. 1984. *Effects of Information Technology on Financial Services Systems.* OTA-CIT-202, September.

Veith, R. H. 1981. *Multinational Computer Nets.* Lexington, Mass.: D. C. Heath.

Wriston, Walter as cited by Paul Zurkowski. 1987. "Liberation: The U.S. Experiment." In *Intermedia* 15(6): 38.

11

The Impact of Information Technology on International Financial Flows

HANSJURG MEY

TECHNOLOGY AND BANKING

Bankers' Imagination Versus Technological Capabilities

Banks' operation and their range of services are interdependent with the technology applied. Let us look at past developments; there might be some lessons for the future.

Twenty years ago, general ledger bookkeeping and interest calculation with early EDP equipment was a courageous undertaking. The pace of development quickened, and soon banks were leading-edge users of EDP technology. The euphoria of the 1960s, including the cashless society and MIS-guided banks, soon disappeared when backbreaking job implementation was attempted. Yet the early pioneers of integrated customer information files, and online, real-time teller systems provided feedback, demands, and complaints to EDP suppliers, which spurred technological development. The yield has been reasonably reliable data-base management systems, communication procedures and equipment, and a large range of work-station equipment.

In some cases, technology influenced bank operations on an international scale. The Society for Worldwide Interbank Financial Telecommunication (SWIFT) was launched on the assumption that an airline reservation system's logic can be applied to international payments. It soon became apparent that a standard procedural logic, discipline, and binding legal rules were necessary complements to the technical equipment. The breakthrough was achieved because the commitment of the original underwriters of the venture was strong enough to make it a success. The lesson learned was that hardware alone wasn't sufficient; banks need automated functions (Witt 1985).

Market Orientation Versus Systems Orientation

There are two basic schools of thought in technology and banking. One is the market orientation of new technology in the form of ATMs or a magnetic strip–equipped card, which may support a new delivery system. Very often it is useful to generate more revenue for a bank or to reduce operating costs, and there is an abundance of small and larger opportunities to apply new technologies for such purposes; innovative steps abound. These developments may be implemented over a short term and can be adapted to almost any operational infrastructure. In a way they reflect the general trend of advancing technology; they scatter around the trend line but don't represent real breakthroughs into an era of vastly different banking techniques. They are singular, individualistic, marginal service extensions or cost-saving measures, and are not turning points in technology or banking.

The second school of thought is the systems orientation. Proponents of this school also see vast opportunities in the application of technology to banking. In view of the sizeable investments necessary for individual banks, they strive to avoid redundancies and short-lived marginal advantages to the longer term detriment of systems changes that go beyond the scope of an individual bank. Automated clearing houses, large scale electronic funds transfers (EFTs), common cash dispenser systems, chip in the card, and the like belong in this category.

New Demands and New Services

The left side of Figure 11.1 shows some general and some slightly more specific banker demands for improved automated functions.

A real breakthrough will only be achieved if on-line systems of sufficient geographical coverage come into existence. The mere communication capability will not mean much unless internal bank posting is on a real-time basis for the multitude of banking transactions.

FIGURE 11.1 — Bankers' Demands for New Services

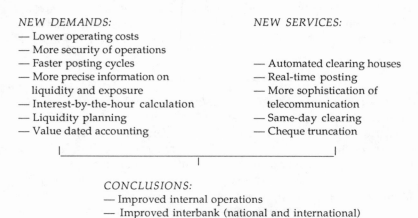

NEW DEMANDS:
— Lower operating costs
— More security of operations
— Faster posting cycles
— More precise information on
  liquidity and exposure
— Interest-by-the-hour calculation
— Liquidity planning
— Value dated accounting

NEW SERVICES:

— Automated clearing houses
— Real-time posting
— More sophistication of
  telecommunication
— Same-day clearing
— Cheque truncation

CONCLUSIONS:
— Improved internal operations
— Improved interbank (national and international)
  clearing facilities

ROLE OF INTERNATIONAL CORPORATE CUSTOMERS

Information Services

Large banks and some specialized smaller banks have always made great efforts to attract and retain large corporate customers (Revell 1985). Competition between banks for these customers is less likely to be hindered by regulations or agreements than it is in the retail sphere.

The position of the large customer is usually discussed in terms of preferential credit arrangements, but an especially strong form of competition takes place over the services to be supplied. Thus, customer relationships often depended on the ability of banks to make a profit on the services and giving a lower rate of interest on the loans in an effort to tie the customer to the bank. In all countries, banks try to develop customer relationships, in which a common feature is the "bundling" of credit and services.

The increased emphasis on fees and services has come at a time when new electronic methods offer banks increased opportunities for developing new services. One feature of these new services is that they are closely connected with providing information to customers: partly information that no other organization can provide and partly general financial information that banks are in a good position to acquire even though they have no monopoly of the sources.

Competition between Larger and Smaller Banks

Only those banks that can benefit from economies of scale in providing similar services to many customers will be able to prosper. For a time, the few larger international banks will meet competition from smaller banks, but eventually the smaller banks will have to provide the increasingly complex services with a franchise from the large banks or on the basis of a correspondent relationship. In this context the term *smaller banks* could well include the largest banks in smaller countries because the market is fast becoming an international one. In services of this type, banks will also face competition from nonbank providers, including computer bureaus, investment managers, brokers in various markets, and a wide variety of other kinds of organization.

Competition in services for multinational and corporate clients is likely to favor the largest banks on an international scale. It has been suggested that smaller banks would be forced to obtain access to them for their customers through a correspondent relationship, unless they are combined in associations with a central organization.

Role of Correspondent Banking

Probably only in the United States does there exist also a large network of correspondent relationships in the domestic banking market, although it works as a chain of relationships from small banks through larger local banks and regional banks to those in the money market centers. These correspondent banks provide a variety of services, such as clearing facilities, participation in loans, help in establishing ATMs, and practically any service that the small bank finds it cannot provide economically on its own. This sort of correspondent relationship, hitherto confined to the domestic market of the United States, may become more prevalent in international banking. There is also the likelihood of large changes in the networks of correspondent relationships in the new situation brought about by telecommunications facilities and the competition in computer-based services.

With the growth of same-day settlement and the general speeding of transfers brought about by EFT, it has been suggested that correspondents will be chosen in the future for their ease of access to the national bank telecommunications networks. Even if access to SWIFT, Fed Wire, Bank Wire and CHIPS through a correspondent bank that has no direct access or only the simplest of terminals may not, in practice, involve important delays, the bank that has direct and full access will still have the edge in marketing its services as a correspondent. A bank that emphasizes its links with the most modern techniques of transmission will have the competitive edge, and it may well acquire many more correspondent accounts.

SWIFT II

Formed in 1973 by 239 European and North American banks as a unique, cooperative, nonprofit venture, SWIFT was designed to provide an automated interbank funds-transfer message system. Originally needed to alleviate the pressure on existing paper-based methods, SWIFT has rapidly come to be regarded as the primary mechanism by which banks send their funds-transfer messages throughout the world.

Despite early doubts about SWIFT's overall potential, the confidence of its first members has been more than justified. From the start, the service provided by SWIFT was fast, reliable, and cheap. In addition, one of SWIFT's most important achievements was to produce a common set of standards for use in sending messages through the system. In one fell swoop, language barriers between banks in different countries were eliminated and all communication could be made using the common code of SWIFT.

Membership grew and today SWIFT boasts over 1,500 member banks in more than 50 countries. Transactions processed through the system now average 500,000 daily, nearly double the original volume anticipated. Geographical expansion of SWIFT is now reaching its limits, and the society has recognized that new members will only be encouraged to join if offered a greater number of services.

Conversion from SWIFT I to SWIFT II will take place during a cutover period of three years. Originally scheduled to begin in December 1985, the cutover was delayed due to delays in delivery of hardware from the manufacturers. For users, the SWIFT service will remain unaffected. During the cutover period, SWIFT I and II will be fully compatible with each other, and the enhanced function of SWIFT II will become available as each area is converted. Essentially, SWIFT II marks a departure from a centralized computer system to a decentralized one (Costello 1985).

Although SWIFT's track record has been good and no major breakdowns have occurred, there are occasions when lines are down and delays are experienced, causing a great deal of inconvenience to users. With SWIFT II, information can be stored in more than one slice network in different geographical locations, so that a malfunction in one area will not automatically lead to a loss of message information.

At the user end, the enhancements of SWIFT II are designed to give member banks more flexibility and greater control over the system. New software for the SWIFT terminals currently in use is to be provided in respect of the enhancements.

Improved retrieval facilities, in which information is stored on line for up to four months in SWIFT II, compared with only fourteen days at present, will help reduce the amount of time spent by bank staff checking out queries. Similarly, the ability under SWIFT II to trace a transaction directly by its reference number, rather than by the current procedure of having to retrieve the whole message containing the queried item, will improve the bank's response time to its customer.

SWIFT now has the technological capacity to offer users a good deal more than just a message-switching service. There are two schools of thought about this among the bank members: those who feel that the system was designed for the benefit of banks and should stay that way and those who feel that there should be some expansion of services to nonbanks as well as extending services to banks in areas such as cash management or multibalance reporting.

For SWIFT, the challenge of the 1990s may not be a technical one but a political one, which will ultimately determine whether it remains a servant to the banks or whether it becomes a powerful entity in its own right.

IMPORTANCE OF ELECTRONIC FINANCIAL TRANSFER

It is very difficult to estimate the actual percentage of electronic money transfer (on the total of money transfers) in the international financial flow. To give an idea on trends, we can demonstrate some statistics on bank-to-bank flows for national credit- and debit-transfer in eleven developed countries.

A number of methods are used in countries for transferring deposits from one account to another in the same or a different bank or depository. Table 11.1 distinguishes credit from debit transfers and paper from electronic authorization (Mitchell 1985).

TABLE 11.1
Percentage of Total Transactions, 1986

Country	Credit Transfers			Debit Transfers			Transactions per Inhabitant
	Paper	Electronic	Total	Paper	Electronic	Total	
Belgium	41	7	48	47	5	52	34
Canada	—	—	—	97	3	100	88
France	2	8	10	84	6	90	86
Germany	34	23	57	11	32	43	85
Italy	10	3	13	86	1	87	13
Japan	2	1	3	24	73	97	15
Netherlands	41	21	62	22	16	38	85
Sweden	n.a.	n.a.	77	22	1	23	64
Switzerland	54	34	88	11	1	—	94
United Kingdom	13	12	25	68	7	75	67
United States	—	2	—	99	2	—	159

REFERENCES

Costello, E. 1986. "SWIFT II: Who Calls the Tune." *Banking Technology*, April.

Mitchell, G. W. 1985. *Payment Systems in Eleven Developed Countries*. Washington, D.C.: Federal Reserve System.

Morelli, G. 1985. "Bank of International Settlements." *The World of Banking*, Nov.–Dec.

Revell, J. R. 1985. *Banking and the International Corporate Customer*. Bangor, Wales: Institute of European Finance.

Witt, H. J. 1985. "Technology and Banking in the Years to Come." *The World of Banking*, March–April.

Young, K. 1985. *How Banks Communicate.*

12

The Information Revolution and Financial Services: A New North-South Issue?

JOAN E. SPERO

Change in financial services has been driven in part by a parallel revolution in information technology. Thanks to rapid advancements in computer and communications technologies, there has been a sharp downward spiral in the relative costs of information processing, even as the technological possibilities have multiplied at an astonishing rate. Financial businesses have become heavily dependent on telecommunications and information technologies as an integral part of day-to-day operations and as the avenue for the development of new services and new products. And, of course, information has become a product in itself.

Although Reuters currently dominates the international information trading system, its competitors are increasing both in number and in sophistication. For example, Telerate is now the world leader in providing quotations on domestic U.S. money markets and fixed-income securities, and Quotron Systems is the leader in providing stock market quotations. Tymshare is another company involved in supplying financial information — in this case, information on precious metals and financial futures.

Furthermore, companies are expanding both geographically and in services offered. Reuters is moving beyond simply supplying information and has entered the business of arranging transactions. Large companies are beginning to expand beyond data supply into data analysis, and even smaller organizations are getting into the act, targeting specific market segments such as the professional or individual investor.

Even more interesting are the many ways in which these various pools of information are being consolidated and manipulated by users. A good example is commodities trading: walk into any trading room in London or New York, and you will be struck by the omnipresence of technology. In front of every trader sit several screens flashing data simultaneously from different sources — sources such as Telerate, Tymshare, and Quotron Systems. And next to each trader is a telephone that can instantly connect him or her to any part of the world by the touch of a button. Very soon, traders will need only one screen, on which they can call up and manipulate comparable bits of information from many sources.

This development is of crucial importance to the financial services industry, because information is the very basis for all financial activity. Information enables institutions to forecast interest rates and exchange rates, which in turn form the basis for asset and liability management. Information on differences in these rates creates new markets and new opportunities for trading, arbitrage, and hedging.

The availability of information such as this on a constant real-time basis is globalizing financial services markets. It is pushing the institutions offering financial services — especially commodities trading — into operating on a worldwide basis twenty-four hours a day. An institution can no longer afford to close its books at 4 P.M. in New York while trades are being made on new information in Tokyo, London, and Hong Kong. My own company, for example, has shifted to an around-the-clock, around-the-world system of trading commodities. There is also a movement to create twenty-four-hour securities markets in London, New York, and Tokyo.

The information revolution has implications, however, far beyond globalization itself. Because technology enables financial transactions to take place more frequently and more rapidly, there has been a sharp increase in the velocity of money, in the liquidity of markets, and in the magnitude of international capital flows. In the New York financial markets alone, dollars clear at the rate of $180 billion a day. That adds up to nearly $1 trillion a week, or $50 trillion a year. About $2 trillion of that is trade-related; of the rest, 96 percent is asset movements.

As another example, consider the interbank operations of SWIFT, the international banking user group. Despite the fact that SWIFT's role is decreasing in importance as the largest banks build up their own networks, the number of financial transactions processed by SWIFT has nevertheless tripled over the past five years — from 218,000 transactions per day in 1980 to an estimated 650,000 per day in 1985. The number of members has also increased dramatically, from 768 in 1980 to approximately 1,500 members currently — and, it should be noted, these members include developing-country institutions, as well.

Even in the area of consumer finance, technology is facilitating the growth of financial and information flows across geographic boundaries. For example, the development of electronic funds transfer technology now allows a U.S. tourist to gain access to funds in his U.S. account with an automatic teller machine in, say, Singapore.

As financial products become more information and technology intensive, the distinction between information products and financial products begins to blur. Even more confusing, the new technologies at our disposal have spurred creation of instruments so varied and complex that it becomes increasingly difficult to tell which products "fit" different types of organizations. Commercial banks, merchant banks, investment banks, and securities firms are all information suppliers and information processors; it is no longer possible to state definitively which product can and ought to be offered by which institution.

This process of convergence is particularly visible now because the regulatory structure in which it is taking place was largely created long before the coming of the information revolution. Consequently, as changes in information technology revolutionize the financial services arena, we find institutions pushing to the very limits of the regulatory boundaries — and beyond — in an effort to take maximum advantage of the new possibilities open to them. In a very real sense, technology is pushing us toward liberalization of traditional regulatory regimes, and this liberalization will enable financial institutions to offer their customers an even greater variety of services.

Finally, it is becoming increasingly necessary for the players in the financial services arena to compete on a worldwide basis. Securities firms, for example, now feel compelled to have offices in London and Tokyo in order to compete in trading markets around the world. As a result, these firms are opening offices even in the face of high competition, high costs, and low profit margins. They are acquiring securities firms in London and pressing Japan to step up deregulation of its securities industry. Ultimately, much of this is being driven by the technological changes that have revolutionized communications and globalized competition in financial services.

Of course, in the long run not everyone will be able to become a global player. Many will form alliances, and others will carve out market niches either domestically or regionally. However, the technology is certainly leading in the direction of globalized firms competing in globalized markets.

THE FINANCIAL SERVICES
REVOLUTION AND INTERDEPENDENCE

The full nature of the revolution in financial markets is only beginning to come into focus. Its impact is uncertain, and there is much about which we can only speculate. One effect of the revolution in financial services has already become clear, however, and that is the increased interdependence among the developed countries. Their financial markets, and the institutions and individuals that operate in them, are now linked as never before. This in turn means that national economies are also linked as never before. A rumor that Japan is tightening its monetary policy, for example, instantly causes bond prices to drop in New York. The link between the U.S. ability to manage its own monetary policy and Japanese savings and interest rates is also well documented.

What is less documented and far less clear is the impact of the financial-services revolution on the developing countries and on North-South relations. This issue raises many questions. Who will benefit from the revolution in information technology and financial services? Do these revolutions imply greater or less dependence for developing countries? Here I want to consider three questions in particular:

1. Who will have access to the new resources now available in the financial markets? Who will be the users?
2. Which institutions from which countries will be players in these new markets?
3. What policies should developing countries follow to maximize the benefits of the information and financial services revolutions?

I will state my overall conclusion up front: I believe that in the long run, information technology as applied in the financial services industry will benefit developing countries and will reduce, not increase, disparities between the countries of the North and the South. Developing countries are now important users in these financial markets, and in the future they can also become active players in the markets. In the long run, however, the ability of a country or institution to gain access to these markets depends heavily on the external policies it chooses to follow.

LDCS AS USERS OF INTERNATIONAL FINANCIAL MARKETS

Let me look now at the future of the developing countries as users of the international financial markets. It goes without saying that access to capital is critical to a country's economic development. It is therefore important to examine the degree to which less developed countries (LDCs) will have access to new pools of capital, new services, and new products created by the financial-services revolution.

As a matter of fact, developing countries are already major users of international financial markets. They became important users in the 1960s and 1970s with the internationalization of the banking industry. In 1977 the private debt of the developing countries totaled $167 billion; within five years it had more than doubled to $371 billion. At least in the period before 1979, borrowing on the international markets played an important role in promoting the developing countries' productive capacity and maintaining their economic growth.

Today, of course, the focus is very much on the problem of LDC debt and the related problem of continued LDC access to the international financial markets. Here, however, I think we need to look beyond the present debt crisis to consider long-term trends. I contend that, in the long run, many LDCs will again become important users of the world's financial markets, albeit in a different way than before. I believe this to be the case for several reasons.

First, the interdependence between developed and developing countries that has arisen via the financial markets may well contribute to the long-term solution of the debt problem. It is likely, although not inevitable, that developed-country financial institutions and governments will be successful in finding mechanisms for debt restructuring that will facilitate economic growth and the return of the LDCs to the international financial markets. In my view, the industrialized countries cannot afford *not* to find solutions.

I do not mean to minimize the mammoth task before us, but I believe that one force for a solution will be the new interdependence created by recent changes in the financial markets. These changes include the development of new secondary financial markets and various new mechanisms, such as interest-rate swaps. Furthermore, innovative financial instruments are coming into existence, partly as a result of new technologies, which should be attractive both to LDC borrowers and to their lenders. These innovations hold promise of a future in which developing countries seeking capital will have a greater variety of options available to them than in the past.

In the future, for example, securities market instruments can be expected to constitute an increasing share of new financing. This will happen because securities market instruments offer fixed interest rates and spread the risk among a much wider body of creditors than do traditional loans. There is also an active secondary market in securities that allows new credits to be realistically valued. Furthermore, the supply of funds to these markets is likely to rise rapidly as pension and life insurance funds in the developed countries swell in response to an aging population. In fact, one potential source for many of these funds could well be Japan.

Advances in information technology have an important role to play in providing access to new development funds for LDC borrowers. New markets are opening up in developing countries for investors from the developed nations, especially in the area of securities, and these new investment opportunities are providing the LDCs with fresh pools of capital. As an example of this development, the World Bank's International Finance Corporation recently disclosed plans for a $50–60 million mutual fund, the managers of which will trade shares on third world markets for about ten institutional investors from industrialized nations. American Express's banking division, Shearson Lehman Brothers, has created a fund to invest in Korean stocks, and Merrill Lynch is planning to launch a $10 million fund to invest in the Thai stock market.

With information so quickly and easily available in industrialized countries, and with larger pools of available capital, the competition in financial markets has become exceptionally fierce. The result has been shortened life cycles for financial products, because new instruments are quickly copied by competitors. Consequently, spreads (and hence profits) in the traditional capital markets have been falling. These developments have created an enormous appetite in the industrialized world for new means of investment and new markets in which to invest. Developed-country investors in search of higher returns are now ready to assume greater risks, and they are beginning to look with interest at possibilities in the developing world. As more and better information on developing-country markets becomes available through improved information technology, international investors will be in a better position to make decisions about investing in LDCs, and that means an influx of new capital into the very countries that need it.

LDCs AS PLAYERS IN INTERNATIONAL FINANCIAL MARKETS

What, then, about developing countries as players in the international financial markets? Which institutions from which countries will become players in the future? It is not enough for the developing countries to be recipient-users of financial information and services; they also want, and need, to become players themselves in the world markets to avoid being relegated to a dependent, second-class status.

Currently, it is true, the situation favors institutions from developed countries, which possess the necessary technology and capital. Information technology currently gives a competitive advantage to multinational institutions based in developed countries, which, because of the technology they possess, have certain advantages over the rest.

Will these advantages now enjoyed by multinationals based in the developed countries necessarily persist over time? My crystal ball tells me they will not, for several important reasons:

First, sources of information are increasing both in number and in geographic scope. For example, Tymshare and Telerate are moving into Asia, and smaller organizations are springing up to seize their own market niches. Furthermore, no matter how the technology develops, LDCs will still have the advantage when it comes to local and regional information.

Second, technology is moving in the direction of decentralization. For example, as the use of microprocessors spreads and as the costs of services and technology fall, there will be less advantage for those with private networks or in major financial centers. This means easier access to markets for everyone else. As we move toward computer interaction and away from face-to-face trading on exchange floors, financial transactions can take place as easily in Bombay or São Paulo as in New York or London.

At the same time, there are currently no major barriers to entry for LDC institutions wishing to use the new information technologies. This is significant, for while few LDCs are likely to be able to compete internationally in the supply of hardware, several already have the capacity to apply the technology and to engage in related activities, such as systems development and systems design — areas in which certain LDCs could well prove to have a long-run comparative advantage. Much of the systems designs for American Express is done by an Indian company, for example.

However, even if there are no technological barriers to entry now, such barriers could easily develop. If developing-country governments begin restricting the technology available to their domestic institutions, then one day there will be de facto barriers to entry, because those institutions will be so far behind the rest of the world technologically that the costs of catching up may well be insuperable. This is especially true in the financial services industry, which is highly sensitive to state-of-the-art communications technology, so that there is a very real danger in allowing oneself to fall behind technologically.

As we look ahead, we can see that the financial world of the future will be more complex than it is today. Most likely there will be a few full-service global superfirms, some of whom may be from LDCs. There will also be firms with strong geographic or regional bases. Finally, there will be specialty or niche firms providing customized services to a specific client base. And, of course, there will also be links between these various types of firms. In the midst of all this diversity, with the many possibilities for specialization, there will surely be a role for institutions from the developing world. They will not necessarily be the biggest, but they will most certainly have seats at the table — or, if you prefer, at the computer terminal.

POLICY IMPLICATIONS

Achieving these benefits also depends on important policy choices, which the developing countries themselves must make, and make now. Here I will focus on only one such choice: will LDCs cut themselves off from the international financial markets, or will they seek ways to achieve greater integration with them and reap the attendant benefits? Will they allow their domestic institutions to have access to the latest in communications technology and equipment and thereby become competitive, or will they shut their doors, dooming their domestic financial institutions to eternal obsolescence?

It seems to me that the developing countries have a significant stake in opening themselves to full participation in the world information and financial markets. Such participation means greater access to sources of capital, more efficient domestic financial markets, and eventually international markets for their own financial services. If the developing countries wish to promote economic efficiency, and if they wish their domestic institutions to become technologically sophisticated in order to compete in the international arena, then they will have to make needed technologies and services available to their financial institutions. Policies of protectionism in technology penalize the users of that technology, depriving them of the chance to become efficient domestically and competitive internationally.

The Organization for Economic Cooperation and Development (OECD) countries are primarily interested in freer trade in services among developed countries, but they also feel that if they are to open their markets further to manufactured goods from the developing countries, then it is only fair that the developing countries open their markets to services from the OECD countries, for whom services are now an important component of their national economies. This issue of including services in the General Agreement on Tariffs and Trade (GATT) has become the major sticking point between the OECD and a handful of developing countries. These countries fear that if they open their markets to services from abroad, their domestic institutions will be overwhelmed by the entry of foreign competitors.

I think that the point of view represented by those countries is mistaken. In my opinion, the developing countries have far more to lose from closing their doors to developed-country service institutions than from allowing them in. For one thing, it is reasonable to assume that in any future multilateral trade negotiation, the LDCs will be able to negotiate — as they have in the past — differential treatment that protects them from being overwhelmed. Second, it is highly unlikely that an agreement on services would provoke a flood of foreign entrants into LDC markets. Events would move much more gradually. Finally, it must be recognized that protectionist sentiment is growing in the developed world, and if the new round of multilateral trade talks at GATT should stumble because of LDC opposition to services, then we could well see an increase across the board in unilateral protectionist actions, which would only harm all of us in the world trading system.

CONCLUSION

To sum up: has the Information Revolution created a new North-South issue? Yes, it has, but this issue need be neither explosive nor divisive. The future of the world is greater interdependence among nations, North and South, and it will not be possible in this new era of advanced technology and internationally linked markets for any nation or group of nations to opt out of the revolution that is currently shaking the foundations of the world financial system.

There is every reason to believe that the information and financial systems evolving today will benefit the developing countries. The Information Revolution, rather than closing doors or widening the gap between North and South, has in fact opened doors that were previously shut and has given us the technological tools to bring markets and nations closer together. The only thing required of us is that we seize the opportunity while we can and that we develop forward- and outward-looking policies that will bring us together into the new information age.

13

The Strategic Importance of Telecommunications to Banking

EDWARD J. REGAN

The corporation I work for, Manufacturers Hanover Trust Company, is the fourth largest U.S. bank. I work in the International Banking Sector, which does business with multinational corporations and correspondent banks worldwide. The trends I will be discussing affect my bank's relationship with this top-tier customer base. But these trends are not simply affecting the way the big U.S. banks deal with the U.S.-based multinational corporations; these are global trends that are fundamentally changing the way the world's largest banks address the financial needs of their largest customers.

Before I begin my remarks I would like to acknowledge the great economic development Japan has experienced in the past twenty years. In particular, I want to note the predominant position of Japan's banking industry. As recently as 1979, only one Japanese bank was among the top ten banks in the world (ranked by size of assets). Today, there are five Japanese banks in the top ten in the world. Indeed, the four largest banks are all Japanese.

I will discuss the strategic importance of telecommunications to banking. However, I do not want to give the impression that banking's dependence upon communications is a recent phenomenon. Walter B. Wriston, retired chairman of Citicorp, has said that "sound banking business is and always has been based on good information received in a timely fashion." Wriston has also noted that "in the sixteenth century, Jacob Fugger built the preeminent financial institution in Europe on fast couriers bringing news from agents stationed in Spanish America, Mediterranean Africa, and the Orient." Communication has always been very important to banks.

My overall thesis is that the convergence of information and telecommunications technologies has enabled the creation of a "new banking" to service the needs of the top-tier corporate and bank customers. But before describing the "new banking" it is necessary to review what banking has been during the last twenty years.

Banking has been concerned primarily with lending money. The support of traditional banking services such as funds transfers, foreign exchange, and letters of credit has always been important, but very much secondary to the lending process. The straightforward reason for this was that the banker's lending business was his chief source of revenue.

There are now multiple marketplace forces changing the nature of banking. What I call the "new banking" emphasizes noncredit services and investment banking services, broadly defined. The lending business is no longer supreme. Large multinational corporations are simply not borrowing very much from banks. And with so much competition for the remaining business, the margins in lending are unprecedentedly low and the cushion of free or cheap balances in the funding of bank loans has eroded. Banks cannot be highly profitable by simply lending to large corporations. Consequently, in today's world it is becoming increasingly critical for banks to derive profits from their noncredit services and investment banking services.

With that thought as a subthesis, let me now state three observations.

First, the provision and delivery of highly profitable noncredit services is absolutely dependent on the use of state-of-the-art information and telecommunications technologies.

Second, banking's journey into the world of high technology is now beginning to have an impact that extends far beyond noncredit services. The global information and telecommunications systems banks have put in place are now changing the very credit process itself. Our ability to deliver information on demand worldwide is giving new meaning to such trends as the securitization of credit assets and the disintermediation of the lending function.

My third observation is that the demands on bank profitability, as measured by return on assets and return on equity, have created new imperatives with respect to pricing, customer selectivity, and the placing of technological bets.

Large corporations have become more sophisticated and demanding of noncredit services from their banks. Banks need to be able to provide state-of-the-art operations-based services at a profit to help strengthen existing relationships and lead to new relationships. Corporations are reducing the number of banks with which they deal. Banks that can only offer traditional credit availability are going to lose business to banks that can provide top-quality noncredit services.

Today, large corporate customers demand access to their banks' noncredit services from terminals located in the customer's office. Leading banks have invested millions of dollars to develop the information and telecommunications systems required to provide these customer terminal-based services. Banks that cannot offer their customers these sophisticated, high-tech services are losing market share.

These bank systems enable customers using a data terminal or a personal computer in their offices to:

Review every transaction posted to their demand deposit account the previous day.
Review same-day transactions posted to their account today.
Review their prior-day account balances in all currencies in all branches of the bank worldwide.
Access foreign exchange information.
Initiate electronic funds transfers.
Initiate letter of credit transactions.

Although these terminal-based services are very costly to develop, when properly designed they can be profitable and can provide a competitive advantage. For example, the leading banks in the provision of these services now place personal computers in their customers' offices. Proprietary bank software in the personal computers prompts the customer to enter transaction details in the precise format the bank requires.

When the customer subsequently transmits this data from his or her personal computer to the bank's computer system, it is received in a format that can be automatically executed. There is no need for bank staff to interpret the customer's instructions. Thus, these transactions that originate from personal computers at the customer's office anywhere in the world can be executed at computer speed as soon as they arrive at the bank. Not only does the customer get faster, more accurate service, but the bank can reduce its transaction-processing staff.

The global information and telecommunications systems that banks have put in place are providing more efficient ways of meeting the credit requirements of our large corporate customers. There are many structural forces that have led to this fundamental change in the credit process. But the most important would certainly include:

The globalization of financial markets of all kinds — now not just a nice concept, but an operating reality.

The integration of credit and capital markets, with commercial bankers acting more and more like investment bankers each new day.

The securitization of credit assets — the movement toward securities as opposed to loans, including loan sales, as distinct from loan participations.

And last, a whole new form of disintermediation — this time, the disintermediation of the lending process itself, as credit now flows more directly between the suppliers of funds and the users of funds.

There is one final overall force at work, one which gets me back to my second observation — namely, technology's impact in helping to facilitate the trends just described.

The securitization of credit assets and the new disintermediation I've been describing are particularly evident in the Euromarkets and can be seen in the rapid growth of Euronotes and Eurobonds and in the parallel, relative decline of syndicated loans.

The value of all new Eurobond offerings has been exploding over the past few years. Measured in billions of dollars, the total value of Eurobonds grew from $47 billion in 1983 to $80 billion in 1984 to $133 billion in 1985. And a preliminary report for the first quarter of 1986 indicates that this will be another record year.

On the U.S. front, securitization and disintermediation can be seen in the continued explosion of commercial paper. It can also be observed in the increased involvement of commercial banks in private placements. Private placements, of course, are not new. What *is* new is the development of a secondary market for private placements.

Trading and market depth are what allow markets themselves to intermediate the flow of funds and permit the development of new instruments that are securities, not loans. But trading and market depth are, in large part, a function of better communications and analysis — which gets us back to technology.

An example from Manufacturers Hanover Trust Company involved a Swiss franc capital-market transaction, which was then repackaged into a currency swap transaction with a number of Japanese banks in Tokyo — all for the benefit of a London-based British conglomerate that wanted to raise $60 million with a ten-year maturity.

What we did first was colead a Swiss franc, floating-rate issue that was sold in the capital market of Zurich. In other words, we ourselves both encouraged and facilitated securitization and disintermediation, because we knew — and, of course, the customer knew — that it could raise francs more cheaply in the capital markets than it could by borrowing from a bank.

But we then had to execute a currency swap. Because, for the company's own currency exposure and hedging reasons, it ultimately did not want a Swiss franc liability, but, instead, a dollar liability. We had to turn around and market pieces of a swap to institutions wanting a Swiss franc liability.

To locate such interested counterparties, we employed our own proprietary, global communications system, which we call GEONET, to mobilize our customer contact officers in our 100-plus branches and offices around the world.

In this example, the search for interested counterparties led us to banks in Japan. But it just as easily could have led us to counterparties in Jakarta, Hong Kong, London — or, indeed, almost anywhere in both the developed and the developing world.

But the use of high technology did not end with GEONET. Because, in order to properly price and arbitrage these transactions, we had to synthesize — on literally a minute-by-minute basis — what was happening in the foreign exchange markets, the money markets and the capital markets around the world. And thus, back in New York we were relying upon the timely financial information that came to us over our Reuters and Telerate screens.

Major commercial banks may ultimately prove to have a decisive advantage over investment banks as we move out still further into the brave new world of securitization and disintermediation. In fact, we may have three advantages:

1. A larger capital base;
2. Experience with credit, risk-assumption capabilities, and, therefore, positioning capabilities; and
3. Ability to communicate quickly and to execute quickly by virtue of the global communications infrastructures and the international branch networks we have put in place.

Thus, the new technology is certainly no longer a "back-office" issue — if, indeed, it ever was. Moreover, it is not even an exclusively noncredit issue anymore. Instead, a bank's information and telecommunications systems have become absolutely crucial to its ability to meet a broad array of financial requirements, both credit and noncredit.

Due to the massive investments required to offer state-of-the-art, operations-based services, new risks have emerged in banking. The first is spending money on a service the markets won't pay for or that a particular bank does not have sufficient volume against which to distribute its costs. But the second risk entails not spending money on the services a bank absolutely needs if it is to go where it wants to go within its chosen markets.

These risks are growing more evident each day. For while the new banking has brought new opportunities, it has also brought new pressures — new pressures on capital and, therefore, heightened pressures on the returns a bank must achieve on its equity base.

Assets volume and incremental aggregate earnings growth are no longer revered. Return on assets, return on equity, and return on sending are now the only games in town. And thus the penalties that can come from making the wrong decision in the field of high technology can be very grave.

Happily, however, there is a way to come to grips with this risk. It is to know one's market. It is to recognize that banks don't build systems for themselves anymore; they build them for their customers.

14

The Impact of Information Technology on Trade Interdependence

RAYMOND J. KROMMENACKER

INTRODUCTION

Is efficient trade — the buying, selling and shipment of goods and services — fundamentally driven by information technology? In other words, would more timely and better information create a competitive advantage for those who possess it and know how to use it?

THE ECONOMICS OF KNOWLEDGE AND INFORMATION

Trade theorists have not been much interested in the impact of information on international commercial policy and trade interdependence. A few writers have emphasized the degree to which the evolution of information technology will produce a society with greater emphasis on intellectual activities and knowledge-related industries. Among them, Fritz Machlup has extensively discussed the economics of knowledge and information and extended the capital theory to human resources (1980, 1984; see also Porat 1977).

In addition, Machlup (1980) considers that the easiest way to distinguish the three sites of knowledge and categories of capital is to trace the flows of benefits derived from their use.

Knowledge embodied in machines and similar material goods improves the performance and value of these machines, and the returns to the investment come in the form of sales prices or rental of the machines or differential rents included in the sales revenues of their products. Knowledge embodied in persons improves the performance of the knowledge carriers, and the returns to the investment come in the form of differentials in salaries and wages. Knowledge not embodied in persons or machines improves the performance of many or all productive factors, and the returns to the investment come either in the form of monopoly rents or, if the use of the knowledge is unrestricted, in the form of increased real income of consumers.

AN EVOLVING INFORMATION TECHNOLOGY ENVIRONMENT

The evolving information technology environment is characterized by cross effects among new services and technology innovations, telecommuncations and informatics or computer convergence, Integrated Services Digital Networks (ISDNs), digital satellite communications, wideband communications, and local area networks (LAN).

With respect to the underlying information technology dynamics that are driving telematics applications and markets toward trade interdependence, the complexity of the environment could be reduced to six fundamental themes. First, the increasing application of very large scale integration (VLSI) and the downward spiraling costs of digital and microelectronics is a driving factor in telematics technologies, systems, and architecture. The integration scale of VSLI components has doubled each year for the last decade and it is predicted that densities of 100 million component chips will be achieved in about ten years' time. These trends have resulted in digital technology enjoying economic advantages both in terms of capital cost and operations expenses over the analogue counterparts. Increasing functional density necessarily implies multifunction capabilities at the chip level. Integrated circuit chips and microprocessors are being used increasingly to implement code and communication protocol conversions and interfaces that are having the effect of dramatically reducing the cost and complexity of interconnecting dissimilar terminals, computers, switches, and networks.

Second, the telematics convergence results in information technology networks built from the base technologies of computers, digital communications, and software, and then tailored to meet specific use or provider communication needs. Considerable issues are raised by information networks that lead to a complete restructuring of social, economic, and political foundations. In many countries, this boundary blurring caused by the telematic convergence has not yet provoked a reexamination and redefinition of national industrial structure, international trade, and commercial strategies.

Third, major attention has been focused on a wide variety of new services. Although it is premature to suggest how distinctive these classes of services are — overlapping of applications and requirements may arise — a tentative listing of these new services may include new electronic household services, data base systems and access services, enhanced data transmission services, enhanced voice services, integrated data/voice goods and services, and services derived from the ISDN. Some countries are advanced in exploring the distributions of these new services directly to homes, but it is probably in the area of business communications equipment and services that the first major thrust in integrated services will be witnessed.

Fourth, the digital electronic information network will replace the existing analogue system not suitable for optimized multiple services. There are a variety of reasons why digital switches are certain to dominate the switching field in the future. These include, inter alia, the fact that

1. Architecture in a digital switch is independent of subsystems and modules such that advantage can be taken of new technologies without a complete system redesign.
2. Opportunities for new types of data services can be charged on a per-bit-transferred basis (or bit for second), and tariffs based on a bit-rate will be a profound change in international tariff structures.
3. Smaller size, weight, and power consumptions than equivalent analogue switches.
4. Technology advances and cost reduction will continue, giving digital switching an increasing economic edge (ITU 1985a, 1985b).

Fifth, the future of digital transmission of voice and data will be shaped by developments in the media. Optical fibers, terrestrial radio, and satellites will present new implementation opportunities and reinforce trade interdependence. Satellite communications, fiber optics, and digital communications are important.

Sixth, the technical and systems architecture concepts embodied in the ISDN will be the critical factors that shape information technology and trade interdependence (Kuwahara 1985). Other major factors will be the emerging new industry structures and the national and international regulatory policies and practices that will determine the nature and extent of the trade interdependence. None of these factors can remain static. Both current and evolving policy rules and standards must be adapted to this new area.

According to recent literature, the question of whether or not countries enjoy comparative advantages in services may not seem to be the most helpful inquiry. More relevant is the theory of the firm that specifies that to maximize the gains from trade in services, it is important not to restrict trade in any particular activity, and, above all, the priority for the firms is to respond to all challenges of the information technology; that is, to define investment priorities to turn the information technology to their competitive advantage. These authors contend that information technology is affecting the entire process by which firms create their goods and services. It is also reshaping the product itself, the entire package of goods and services firms provide, by making it possible to customize them. The main effect of these new combinations of goods and services in information technology as well as in space technology is the emergence of information or space generated, highly integrated goods and services (IGS), or complex packages of either goods, services, or a mixture of both, christened "compaks" by Albert Bressand (1985, 1986).

Information technology is changing the rules of competition in three ways. First, advances in information technology are changing the industry structure. New corporations are emerging that could be described as vertically disaggregated, relying on other companies for manufacturing and any crucial business functions such as marketing and distribution. Some authors think that these network, information technology–based firms that are working on a contractual basis with other firms may represent the future organizational model for corporations. If it is broadly adopted, this network model would in fact be only the third real innovation since the mid-1880s, when the vertically integrated firm was set up. The two following changes were the divisional structure, in which vertical chains of command for each operating division existed in parallel, and the "matrix" system, in which workers reporting to various supervisors, depending on the task they performed, made it easier to assemble temporary teams for big projects.

Second, information technology is an increasingly important lever that firms can use to create competitive advantage through lower costs, enhanced differentiation strategies, and changing scope. For example, information technology is at the core of growing interrelationships in financial services — in which the banking, insurance, and brokerage industries are merging — and in office equipment in which once-distinct functions such as typing, data, and voice communications can now be combined.

Finally, information technology is spawning completely new businesses by making them technologically feasible, by creating new businesses within old ones (Porter and Miller 1985; Business Week 1986; Forbes 1986). For example, in February 1986, the Credit

Commercial de France, a French bank ranked 117th in 1984 in the top 500 list of *Banker* magazine, launched an electronic service enabling customers to gain instant access to credit by using video terminals in their home. The service, called Libertel, is believed to be the first of its kind in the world.

A recent study by Juan Rada illustrates the consequences of the increasing transportability of services as one of the main effects of information technology on trade interdependence (Rada 1986, 98). According to Rada, these consequences, which are not mutually exclusive and, in most cases, are concurrent, are as follows: increase in productivity of service production, greater transparency of markets, blurring of borders between sectors, changes in the barriers to entry, and further internationalization of services. Some of the effects of information technology on services activities are listed in Table 14.1.

TABLE 14.1

Partial List of Services Activities and Some of the Effects of Technical Change

Service	Impact of Technological Change	Comment
Shipping (freight)	Partial substitution of transport of goods by services	Substitution of shipped printed matter by sending it through telecommunications
Other transport (air, rail, road, inland waterways)	As above	As above. Transport of mail is partly substituted by electronic mail. New logistic systems are emerging in which the goods themselves are transferred through telecommunications. This trend will be reinforced through cellular radio.
Travel (passenger transport) applications	Partial substitution, especially of business travel	The use of teleconferencing in specific applications is increasingly substituting for business travel in specific.
Tourism (counseling, advertising, tour operations, hotel/motel services)	Highly transportable	New systems incorporating videodisc and interactive routines are becoming available. Long distance and international toll-free services will be widely used. Hotel/motel and airline reservations will be far more computerized. The industry will be more internationalized. Some hotels are now offering teleconferencing services between their different locations. Videotex already allows bookings to be made directly for some services.

continued

TABLE 14.1, continued

Service	Impact of Technological Change	Comment
Insurance and reinsurance	More transportability	Customers will be able to order directly specific insurance through retailing points or terminals as is now the case in many airports, which offer flight insurance.
Banking and other financial services	More transportable	Automatic teller machines can reach many different places while providing 24-hour service. Telebanking is done now at corporate level and in some households. SWIFT will evolve into a worldwide trading network. Banks are also increasingly becoming information suppliers in finance, trade, and investment.
Brokerage	More and highly transportable	This service is heavily based on availability of information. It will become even more international in the future when it will be possible for nonspecialists to intervene through terminals, thereby eliminating middle-men in many cases, as already domestically available in the U.S.
Accounting	More and highly transportable	This was one of the first applications of EDPD and is used by many transna-tional companies on an international basis. Many small- and medium-sized enterprises will internalize this service rather than buy it from specialist firms. This is possible because of microcom-puter programs combining accounts, billing, and management reporting systems.
Advertising	More and highly transportable	This will be the case especially with direct satellite broadcasting due to start operations in Europe in 1986–87. Already operational in Canada and parts of the U.S. International regulations related to the satellite "footprint" when the signal goes across borders will slow down applications. The main concern is with cultural identity as well as the economic effects when advertising revenues are obtained by a company operating outside the national territory.

continued

TABLE 14.1, continued

Service	Impact of Technological Change	Comment
Films and T.V. features	Already highly transportable	Direct satellite broadcasting will increase transportability, while the existence of videotapes will make enforcement of copyright laws practically impossible. "National content" regulations will be difficult to apply except for national broadcasting services.
Wholesaling and retailing	Increased transparency of markets. Goods and services supermarkets	Easy access to price information and services could increase competition in this sector. Complex delivery systems are likely to be developed. In large supermarket chains, the trend is to offer also a "supermarket of services." Teleshopping is already used for a limited number of goods. This will evolve into a sort of "international mail order" catalogue with direct relationship between the consumer and main wholesaler or retailer.
Construction engineering (management, consulting, design/architecture)	More and highly transportable	The use of Computer Aided Design (CAD) systems and remote entry for calculations in centralized systems will increase transportability.
Professional services	More and highly transportable	Remote access is the key in this sector.
Legal	More and highly transportable	Large data bases, of a national and international nature (e.g., Lexis). People seeking advice might interrogate bases directly.
Economic	More and highly transportable	Large data bases, both national and international, already exist. This area will expand greatly. There is concern about sovereignty over national data as well as questions pertaining to individual privacy.
Medical	Transportable	Remote diagnosis for some types of illness is already in experimental stages. The results of medical exams can now be transmitted in some cases to specialist clinics within or outside the country. This is analogous to processing data abroad.

continued

TABLE 14.1, continued

Service	Impact of Technological Change	Comment
Technical	More transportable	Different technicians operating in distant places can work on the same problem as is now the case with the design of chips. Access to technical data bases has been possible since the late 1960s and developed rapidly during the 1970s. Specific technical data bases are being developed for new manufacturing processes such as machining.
Education	Highly transportable	This field is normally under nonmarketable services. The use of educational software, teaching machines, interactive programs, and videocassettes is converting a large proportion of this activity into a marketable service, at least as far as "instruction" is concerned. Technology allows the widespread application of the British Open University concept even at the high school level. High quality interactive teaching for remote locations becomes possible.
Repairs and maintenance	Highly transportable	Because equipment includes electronics and self-diagnosis, maintenance and interaction for repair can be over long distance, as well as by running recovery routines. Repairs as such have to be done in situ, but the instructions come long distance, unless redundancy capacity can be switched on. Modular repairs are increasing the self-service aspect of this activity.
Data processing	More and highly transportable	The key in this sector is the ease of data communications. Data can be processed within or outside a country.
Software	Highly transportable	Software can be developed and maintained by teams at distant locations. It can be marketed and distributed using telecommunications lines.
Remote data entry	More and highly transportable	There is a growing trend to use cheap skilled clerical labor for remote data entry, replacing keypunch operators.

continued

TABLE 14.1, continued

Service	Impact of Technological Change	Comment
Information services Newspapers	More and highly transportable	Telecommunications permits the *International Herald Tribune* to be edited in Paris and printed in Zurich, Paris, London, and Hong Kong. In turn, videotex will partly do away with hard copies.
On-line systems	Already highly transportable	Commodity, stock, and financial information. It will develop to provide a more analytic type of information with graphics included.

Source: Rada 1986, 64ff.

TRADE INTERDEPENDENCE

Four broad types, or stages, of cooperative arrangements can be distinguished among the members of an interdependent information technology community, taken in ascending order of closeness:

1. The first involves periodic international discussion about problems of common interest, reviews of developments in each member country, and explanations of the actions that have been taken. But each nation basically fends for itself. Broadly speaking, this is the type of information cooperation that started in 1982 at the Versailles Summit among the seven member countries and the European Communities, the program of work of which is contained in the 1983 report "Technology, Growth, Employment."
2. The second level of cooperation also involves periodic discussion of problems of common interest, but it goes beyond the first in requiring consultations on certain kinds of measures to be taken and in calling for international justification of policies involving restrictions on information technology transactions. Thus, the use of restrictions is subject to a greater degree of international supervision than at the first level of cooperation. In certain respects, this level of cooperation has already been reached by the OECD.
3. National policy makers may develop sufficient confidence in the policy judgments of their counterparts in other countries to make them willing to share mutual support. Such a common approach could be found in bilateral, plurilateral, or multilateral approaches for closer cooperation in information technology policies; e.g., the existing or tentative experiences between the United States and

Canada or Israel, countries in the Pacific region, or the proposed GATT trade negotiations (Krommenacker 1986b).

4. For regions that have close information technology ties in which capital, labor, goods, and services are supposed to move freely and in which there is a high degree of agreement on information technology objectives, close coordination of domestic information technology will serve to reduce one principal source of imbalance — divergence in these policies — and will guide the region as a whole to its global information technology objectives. This situation seems to prevail to a greater extent as time lapses in the European Economic Community, in which not only the twelve member states but also other countries like Canada, the United States, and Switzerland participate in the information technology developments within the Esprit, Eureka, and Race Programs.*

In judging the relative importance of trade interdependence and the impact of information technology, one should move away from a high level of abstractions to see whether the concept of interdependence remains vague and elusive or, on the contrary, whether researchers have been able to design a convincing way of measuring either the

---

*On February 27, 1986, non-European companies were invited to participate in the EUREKA high-technology program. The proposal appeared directed primarily at U.S. and Canadian companies. To participate, any outside company first must have had an agreement with a company within one of the eighteen participating nations. The projects under study included inter alia a European supercomputer, a new generation of tiny integrated circuits in silicon, extra-fast integrated circuits in gallium, a flexible automated production-line system for the factory of the future, a European software factory to develop new software tools, and a flexible, intelligent robot that would be developed over seven years. EUREKA was proposed by France in April 1985 as a non-EC-bureaucrats, pan-European research drive in advanced technologies. On February 25, 1986, the EC commission announced that affiliates of U.S.-based companies would be awarded research contracts in the EC telecommunications research program, known as RCE (Research and Development in Advanced Communications Technology for Europe). European affiliates of ITT, IBM, GTE, and AT&T were awarded research contracts in RACE, a U.S. $30 million program scheduled to run until 1991. The RACE program aims at developing the largeband integrated services digital network to allow a worldwide standardization of information, and therefore full compatibility between telecommunications and informatics devices. The 1984 ESPRIT (European Strategic Programme of Research and Development in Information Technologies) program of the EC commission has already begun to develop a standard computer architecture for automating factories. Such a system specifies how to connect factory computers and machine tools so they can communicate with one another even if they are made by different manufacturers. The project involves the two largest computer makers in the world: IBM and the Digital Equipment Corp.

level of interdependence or changes in the level. The structure of exports of information technology products (hardware), however, is subject for the time being to much closer analysis than its software content, which remains almost entirely "invisible." It is considered that in 1984 world trade in this field expanded by about 22 percent to $125 billion compared with 7 percent for all other manufactured goods. Japan enhanced its leading position in world exports of information technology products by increasing its shipments by one-third to $35.5 billion as compared to 1983. Exports of computers and electronic parts rose by more than 50 percent (GATT 1984/85; Kemp and Larroumets 1985, 7–34). In the meantime, the United States became a net importer of electronic products. The combined exports of the four major exporters of electronic products (Taiwan, the Republic of Korea, Hong Kong, and Singapore) increased by more than one-third to about $15.3 billion. This was more than twice their shipments in 1979 and exceeded the value of EC exports excluding intra-trade in 1984. These countries also rank among the twelve major exporters of electronic products in the world. More than one-half of the electronic exports are for the United States market alone.

CONCLUSION

An evaluation of the impact of information technology on trade interdependence must await operational experience. In the meantime, further research is required to establish clearly the precise mechanisms and the links between production and exchange of goods and services and how they are affected by new developments in information technology. Countries should also explore the means for more complete integration of information technology policy into a broader international trade policy agenda.

Currently, many procedural and operational questions and issues are left unanswered and, in several cases, are not addressed properly. Some of them will ultimately determine both the nature and extent of the trade competitive environment that is achievable and the magnitude of continuing regulatory involvement required worldwide. Thus, to a considerable degree, the trade competitive impacts and the impacts on the magnitude of regulatory involvement are interrelated and yet to be determined. Substantial analysis is needed about the combined effects or the long-term effects of (1) the simultaneous relaxing of the main restrictions in the information technology trade with (2) the emergence of new national and international regulatory principles and rules and (3) the rapid developments in information technology.

Ultimately, governments may find it difficult to keep pace with information technology changes. Governments tend to react to complaints from particular groups or firms, which are often based on past experience and rarely on future trends. Government policy reactions, therefore, especially their trade policy reactions, are usually adjusted to problems of the recent past, or the present, rather than to problems of the future. The challenge, then, is to reorient government policies toward the future rather than the past; to reduce emphasis in trade policy on adjustment resistance (that is, protection for old industries and out-of-date jobs); to stop trade nationalism that can only have the long-term effect of widening economic and technological disparities among countries; and to seek international agreements that open the way for worldwide benefits generated by information technology.

REFERENCES

Bressard, Albert. 1985. *Le Prochain Monde.* Paris: Ed. Seuil.

Bressand, Albert. 1986. Services, corporate strategies and GATT negotiations: A new challenge for Europe. Ditchley Park. Mimeo.

Bruno, Lanvin. 1986. *The Impact of Trade and Foreign Direct Investment in Data Services on Economic Development: Some Issues.* Preliminary draft. Geneva: UNCTAD.

GATT. 1984/85. *International Trade 1984/85.* Geneva.

ITU. 1985a. *Integrated Services Digital Network (ISDN).* Vol. III.5.

ITU. 1985b. *The Washington Round. Law, Regulation, Standards of Global Communications.*

Kemp, E., and V. Larroumets. 1985. *Les echanges internationaux de produits de haute technologie.* Paris: CEPII.

Krommenacker, R. J. 1986a. "Services and Space Technology: The Emergence of Space Generated, Highly Integrated Goods and Services (IGS)." In *Services Worldeconomy Series Number 1.*

Krommenacker, R. J. 1986b. *Services, Their Regulatory and Policy Framework in the Light of the Emerging "Integrated Services Digital Networks" (ISDN).* Honolulu: Pacific Telecommunication Council.

Kuwahara, Satoshi. 1985. "The Changing World Information Industry." *The Atlantic Papers,* No. 57.

Machlup, Fritz. 1980. *Knowledge: Its Creation, Distribution, and Economic Significance.* Vol. 1, *Knowledge and Knowledge Production.* Princeton: Princeton University Press.

Machlup, Fritz. 1984. *Knowledge: Its Creation, Distribution, and Economic Significance.* Vol. 3, *The Economics of Information and Human Capital.* Princeton: Princeton University Press.

Porat, Marc. 1977. *The Information Economy: Definition and Measurement.* Washington, D.C.: GPO.

Porter, Michael E., and Victor E. Miller. 1985. "How Information Gives you Competitive Advantage." *Harvard Business Review* pp. 149–60.
Rada, Juan. 1986. Information technology and services. Mimeo.

15

Trade Negotiations, Telecom Services, and Interdependence

JONATHAN D. ARONSON

BASIC PREMISES

Certain key assumptions about trade in services and telecom services pervade this analysis.[1] These include:

Technically, it is or soon will be possible to flash voice, data, and images between any two points on the globe.

Most international telecom arrangements were negotiated among national monopoly service providers: PTTs in most countries and AT&T in the United States. Technical standards were generally negotiated within the International Telecommunication Union (ITU).

Political, cultural, and security differences will delay the emergence of a single global integrated services digital network (ISDN) and slow the growth of a world information economy.

Trends toward deregulation, privatization, and liberalization in the national provision of telecom services will produce new bargains among key telecom actors and will make it necessary to develop new global arrangements for the management of telecom services.

New international arrangements among telecom firms and post, telegraph and telecommunications (PTTs) from different countries will continue to proliferate. The telecom market will grow more global, making it more difficult for national regulations to function efficiently.

These new global rules for telecom are more likely to emerge as part of trade negotiations in the General Agreement on Tariffs and Trade (GATT) than in the ITU or other forums.

Services, particularly telecom services, are becoming more tradeable. Investment is less necessary for selling services abroad than in the past. Therefore, the international sale of services is a trade and not just an investment concern.

GATT rules, procedures, and principles were designed with goods, not services, in mind. (The Uruguay Round started in 1987.)

There will be a new round of multilateral trade negotiations launched in the GATT, probably in late 1986.

Services will be one of the key items on the agenda of these negotiations. Telecom will be central to any negotiation on services.

The United States, the main initiator of these negotiations, has no set idea of what form a final agreement on services should take. If it had a clearer vision, others would fear, more than they do, that new negotiations are a U.S. plot. But without focused objectives, U.S. negotiators cannot hope to build and maintain corporate and congressional support during prolonged negotiations, and the prospects for significant breakthroughs will evaporate.

New trade negotiations will last longer and be more complicated than any of the seven previous GATT negotiating rounds.

Total success is unlikely, but considerable progress toward constructing a new regime covering trade in services, including telecom services, is possible.

INTERNATIONAL CORPORATE ARRANGEMENTS

Trends

International corporate arrangements (ICAs) in telecom and other areas are increasing in number and vary widely in scope and duration. To understand what form an international arrangement will take, it is necessary to understand the motivations and goals behind it.

Why do international alliances seem particularly important today? What forces are motivating firms to collaborate in this manner? Most generally, it appears that a number of structural changes in the international economy have led to the increased popularity of alliances. One factor was the decline in U.S. competitive hegemony and the growth of rivals from Europe and Japan. In today's more competitive environment, international corporate arrangements help firms keep an eye on competitors, establish "controlled competition," and maintain threatened market shares. International corporate arrangements also help firms gain rapid access by using the existing distribution networks of other companies or by coordinating cooperation among powerful foreign competitors in ways that no longer can be achieved by merger.

A second factor is that firms need to source and distribute products on a global scale. This has led to a number of alliances in the form of international networks to supply or distribute products. Third, rapidly changing technologies have meant that firms can neither afford nor generate state-of-the-art technologies on their own any longer. Fourth, the growth of nationalism and government-owned firms has meant that companies often must collaborate to fulfill local requirements or to avoid nationalization by spreading political risks. ICAs are increasingly taking place between private companies and government entities in many sectors from oil to telecom (e.g., NIT and IBM). In this light, ICAs can be considered second-best solutions that companies have chosen in new conditions.[2]

How are ICAs different today than in the past? Joint ventures across national boundaries have long been popular, but traditionally they consisted of one dominant company paired with a smaller company. Today, ICAs increasingly take the form of agreements between industry leaders from different countries. In addition, contemporary alliances appear to be much more fluid and evolutionary.

To simplify and summarize, three basic types of ICAs exist now. First, portfolio alliances are designed to spread risks over a number of distribution channels or sources of technology. These are the traditional form of most corporate alliances. Second, there are alliances that become part of a company's corporate strategy and hence part of its identity (e.g., Fuji-Xerox has shaped the strategy of both companies for over two decades). Third, there are tactical alliances designed to alter the competitive environment. It seems likely that changes in interdependence and the structure of the global economy will create more of the second and third types of alliances in the years ahead. This will be true in the telecom sectors (equipment, basic services, and value-added and information services), but also in many other sectors as well.

The policy implications of ICAs are potentially profound. The primary differences between international and intranational alliances may be the consequences they have for national and international economic policy. For example, the dissemination of proprietary technological knowledge among firms could take place in ICAs on a scale far beyond that considered in the current debate on issues such as licensing. There are also fiscal considerations, such as how much local nationals will benefit from R&D subsidies given to firms involved in international consortia, and how to control the process of transfer payments. In this context, the notion of a national government garnering benefits from such international involvements seems to be increasingly unrealistic. Can governments formulate coherent international economic policies in increasingly interdependent economies? Have multinationals raced ahead of governments by making policies on an international basis on their own? Should governments remove barriers that hamper the formation and operation of ICAs? Are U.S. firms protecting and promoting the national interest on their own by allying with competitors rather than risking the loss of current market shares?[3]

ICAs could also have significant impact on issues related to jobs, trade, and trade negotiations. ICAs may create, not export jobs (but heretofore jobs were not frequently a central issue in trade negotiations). A more significant issue may be the extent of the impact of ICAs on trade deficits and the willingness of governments to accept alliances as a substitute for imports and exports. Increasing global interdependence and the globalization of the research, production, and distribution of corporations will make it especially difficult for negotiators concerned with narrow national interests to formulate and conclude successful trade negotiations on goods and services during the coming round.[4]

In summary, international alliances are an increasingly important phenomenon in the 1980s in a manner unique from joint ventures of the past.[5]

Prospects

The ITU, International Services Organization (ISO), Council of European Posts and Telecommunications (CEPT), and other organizations work with governments and public and private telecom providers to set standards and protocols so that voice, data, and images can be transmitted between countries.[6] Technological advances have created the possibility that a wide variety of new telecom services can be traded internationally. Work is slowly progressing to develop the standards and protocols to permit the emergence of an integrated world information economy. At the same time, regulatory changes involving liberalization, privatization, and deregulation in some countries (e.g., the United States, Japan, and Britain) have disrupted the traditional system for establishing standards. Consequently, new rules and procedures need to be developed to manage competition between private telecom firms and government-owned or -controlled monopolies. In addition, private telecom equipment and service firms are actively forming new international corporate arrangements to remain competitive internationally.

Without government interference, corporations would elaborate their international alliances in all areas of telecom. For example, there are too many firms (particularly in Europe) creating digital switches and new megachips. The EC, through programs such as ESPRIT and RACE, are trying to encourage more intra-EC cooperation.[7] Notable examples include the agreement by Philips and Siemens to work together on new semiconductors (although Siemens subsequently also allied with a Japanese partner and struck an equipment deal with GTE) and the proposed collaboration between Plessey, CIT-Alcatel, Siemens, and Italtel to work on a new digital telecommunications switch. European collaborations with U.S. and Canadian firms are even more popular. AT&T's publicized arrangements with Philips and Olivetti and British Telecom's purchase of Canada's Mitel and its abortive effort to form a value-added services partnership with IBM represent only the tip of the iceberg. And smaller equipment firms such as Sweden's Ericsson and Canada's Northern Telecom and service firms such as Britain's Cable and Wireless can be expected to seek more formal ICAs in Japan, Europe, and North America.

Similarly, U.S. and European firms are seeking links with Japanese firms at an unprecedented rate. IBM and Nippon Telephone and Telegraph's (NTT) collaboration on value-added services is just the most prominent example. U.S. telecom firms can be expected to form links with Japanese firms outside of the traditional NTT family (NEC, Fujitsu, and Hitachi). U.S. computer firms might be expected to look more toward the Japanese telecom firms. And all of the proposed satellite consortia wishing to provide long distance services to Japan April 1, 1985, include U.S. partners.[8]

In short, the monopoly provision of services in large countries and internationally is eroding. The West German Bundespost is fighting an increasingly lonely battle to preserve its monopoly on the provision of basic services, to do away with flat rates on private leased lines, and even to extend its grasp to value-added and information services. The dangers with such a policy are that German users trying to compete internationally may be saddled with expensive and inefficient information service inputs that make it difficult for them to compete outside Germany and that foreign users may choose to locate their primary communication centers elsewhere.

In contrast, many countries are exploring liberalization and privatization along the lines pioneered by Britain and Japan (No country, even Canada, seems much interested in emulating U.S. deregulatory extremism.) Instead, it is likely that in the equipment, basic service, and value-added and information service components of telecom, a few key companies will emerge as national leaders.[9] These companies, to survive, are already creating a web of ICAs that will lead to greater global information integration. The lines between competitive groups is likely to shift over time and across sectors, but recognizable patterns of cooperation are likely to emerge. The politics and economics of the competition between these groups will lead to greater ease of information flow between countries, but the dream of a single integrated, broadband digital network is still far in the future.[10] There are likely to be improved conversion protocols to translate among standards, but no global ISDN standard is in sight.

THE REVOLT AGAINST INTERDEPENDENCE

Trends

The emergence of international corporate arrangements is but one facet of interdependence. Lines are blurring and borders becoming indistinct. For example, where do goods stop and services begin? What lines divide trade and investment in services? How can the line between computer, communication, and broadcasting technologies be drawn? What are basic communication services and what are enhanced services? Given these uncertainties, corporations are finding it increasingly difficult to define the dimensions of their business and to determine their priorities. National planning is no longer sufficient. Global planning is becoming essential for large firms. At the same time, government objectives and policy remain national in orientation. Examples of successful international coordination and harmonization involving monetary management and trade are the exception, not the rule. Erosion of consensus in the absence of hegemonic leadership is more common. This lack of coordination presents a major challenge because economic interdependence tends to make domestic economic policies less effective in the United States. The problem is magnified for smaller economies. Therefore, it is hardly surprising that the search for insights about achieving cooperation in international anarchy has become a major thrust of international political economy research.

In essence, governments have two choices. They can overcome their national jealousies, resolve tough questions of equity and adjustment across countries as they arise, accept the complexities of global interdependence, and plan together to deal with new issues that increasing interdependence among their economies will continue to create. Such an approach is extremely difficult and requires tremendous creativity, flexibility, and political courage. Or government leaders can revolt against interdependence and try to retreat from complexity. By turning back the clock and isolating their economies behind new barriers they can try to simplify their policy making tasks. They would in effect slow the natural processes of economic adjustment and change and trade the future growth and job creation that interdependence implies in return for improved control over their domestic economic policy.

Calls for protectionism in the United States and elsewhere and the rekindling of interest in mercantilist policies are a manifestation of this second path. The United States is not able and the majority of U.S. policy makers and citizens are no longer willing to support international economic regimes alone. The search for a "level playing field" for U.S. firms, the demand for fairness and burden sharing in international commitments, and the flirtation with conditional most-favored nation treatment in U.S. policy reflect U.S. unhappiness with the current situation. At the same time, U.S. policy makers sometimes recognize that the United States too often "shoots itself in the foot."

In effect, the United States has demanded that Japan, Europe, and ultimately some of the more successful NICs accept their responsibility to support the international economic system and stop acting as free riders. Otherwise, the United States will risk the fragmentation of the world economy and begin to act like every other country. Until recently, other countries did not believe that the United States would really take this step. But in November 1985, when U.S. trade representative Clayton Yeutter told a Senate committee that the United States would begin to negotiate deals with like-minded countries unless the GATT launched a new trade round, he was believed. The same reluctance of governments to accept interdependence also pervades the telecom issues. Protectionism is fungible. Countries found it convenient to reduce tariff barriers, but frequently these barriers were replaced by more far reaching nontariff barriers. Tariffs aimed at narrow service sectors gave way to non-tariff barriers (NTBs) aimed at telecom and other service sectors. Transparency was replaced by opaqueness.

Prospects

Technological advances and regulatory reforms are pushing governments toward greater information interdependence. Predictably, governments will try to slow and even reverse these developments and retain control over their own domestic information resources.

Modern examples of barriers to the flow of information abound. The United States wants to slow the flow of information that might have strategic value to the Soviet Union. Sweden passed the first of the privacy laws regarding data on its citizens (including corporations — so-called legal citizens). The Swiss banking laws are justly famous. Canada insists that banking data on its citizens be stored in Canada and curtails "border broadcasting" and promotes Canadian film and television to protect its cultural identity. Japan has limited the number of overseas computer facilities to which leased lines can be attached. West German regulations restrict the ability of private firms to offer enhanced services. The Bundespost will only provide international leased lines at a "flat" (nonvolume-sensitive) rate if the company involved assures the Bundespost that it is sending only *processed* data out of the country. Japanese government entities (but not private Japanese companies) are prohibited from procuring foreign satellites.[11]

In addition, the developing countries, fearing that the industrial world will gain an unfair advantage from information collected by satellites and other means and seeking to develop their own industries, restrict information and telecom equipment flows. The less developed countries (LDCs) attempt to shape a new world information order through UNESCO and Brazil's restrictive informatics policy receive the most attention. Other examples include Ecuador's quest to secure ownership of the geosynchronous arc 22,300 miles above its soil and attempts to assure that developing countries receive their equitable share of orbital slots and frequency spectrum. At the same time, industrial countries led by the United States complain that developing and socialist countries do not respect intellectual property rules (involving copyright, trademarks, trade secrets, unfair competition, and counterfeiting). In effect, they expropriate intellectual property from books to music, to software, to cable TV broadcasts without just compensation. (This has become a key trade issue between the United States and the NICs.)

My expectation is that over the next decade there will be progress toward integration of the telecom systems of the industrial and developing countries. Technology will push for liberalization; politics will slow the tide. Considerable synchronization of standards should prove possible in the GATT and ITU. Even where standardization proves technically or politically elusive, the push toward integration will continue, because conversion protocols will continue to improve rapidly. Attempts to impede transborder data flows are also likely to increase in the coming decade. Some of these efforts will be meant to protect privacy, cultural integrity, sovereignty, and security. Others will involve straightforward economic protection even if they are justified in other terms. These new barriers will restrict the types of services that can be traded internationally. They will also try to restrict the kinds of data that may be traded and the ownership of the network. The pricing and availability of leased lines will be a particular concern for conservative PTT authorities.

Ultimately, countries will probably find it too expensive and isolating to forgo being tied into the world telecom network. There will be strong economic pressure from domestic users for telecom authorities to provide international services at competitive prices. But many governments in developed and developing countries will respond by trying to limit transborder data flows and by controlling the networks.

TRADE NEGOTIATIONS AND TELECOM SERVICES

Trends

The United States has pushed for freer trade in services for a decade. Until 1974 services were never mentioned in U.S. trade legislation. They reached semantic equality with goods under the Trade and Tariff Act of 1984. Although services were touched only in passing during the Tokyo negotiations during the 1970s, they started to receive increasing attention in the Organization for Economic Cooperation and Development (OECD) and GATT after 1980. At the November 1982 GATT ministerial meeting, services reached the top of the agenda. They were one of the three most discussed and disputed issues at that contentious gathering. By March 1985 Japan, Canada, and the EC publicly supported the launching of a new trade round, agreeing that services should be an important agenda item. The industrial countries finally overcame developing country opposition led by Brazil and India in late 1985.

Many questions need answering before serious negotiations can proceed. For the purpose of negotiation, how should services be defined? Can more accurate data on the international exchange of services be collected? How should lines between trade and investment in services be drawn? To what extent should negotiations cover investment issues previously excluded from the GATT? To what extent should negotiations cover standards issues now handled in the ITU and ISO? To what extent should negotiations cover intellectual property issues associated with services now dealt with in the World Intellectual Property Organization (WIPO)? Which services should be covered under GATT negotiations; which should be excluded? Which services should be given priority? Should service negotiations be sectoral or horizontal in nature (or both simultaneously)? Should like-minded negotiators settle for conditional most favored nation (MFN) if developing countries do not negotiate in good faith?[12]

Even in this early stage of organizing negotiations, it appears that the United States will press for the centrality of telecommunications in the ongoing negotiations. The U.S. telecom industry has comparative advantages in many aspects of telecom services and seeks more open access elsewhere. In addition, many U.S. users led by the banking, insurance, and charge card industries hope greater competition in the international provision of services may drive prices of international services down.

Prospects

It is difficult to predict what shape trade agreements involving tele-com will take. The best place to look for hints about what might ulti-mately emerge will be the extension of the nonlegally binding Declar-ation on Trade in Services that was negotiated in conjunction with the U.S.-Israel Free Trade Area, which was signed in early 1985. The trade agreement bilaterally negotiated with Canada may serve as a model.

Debate will rage over what should be covered in regard to freer trade in telecom services during a new trade round. The key issues likely to be discussed and their possible resolution are briefly reviewed below:

Location of Telecom Service Negotiations

Just because the GATT decides to get involved with telecom services does not mean that other international groups will retire from discussions. The ITU, INTELSAT, ISO, WIPO, and others will continue to address their issues. Indeed, it is likely that conservative PTTs may try to develop ITU standards covering previously unregulated computer, value-added, and information services before the GATT can act decisively. Success in such ITU talks could undercut telecom service talks in the GATT.

Sectoral or Umbrella Service Negotiations?

Any umbrella agreement will necessarily be flawed, requiring numerous caveats and exceptions. But without such a basic understanding about common rules, principles, and procedures that bind together service industries, sectoral negotiations involving telecom or other service sectors will be hopelessly contradictory. Progress toward sectoral agreements, however, will be easier to negotiate than an umbrella agreement initially. Telecom might be the one service that draws enough user interest from various service industries to serve as a basis for service negotiations.

Scope of Telecom Service Negotiations

Negotiations could focus on basic services or on value-added and information services. Similarly, it could focus on common carriers that own their own networks, on resellers and value-added carriers that do not own their own networks, and on private networks. Negotiations will *not* focus very much on basic services provided by common carriers or PTTs. Every country will continue to regulate these services as they see fit. Negotiations will concentrate on value-added and information services and on the rights of resellers, value-added carriers, and private networks to operate, compete with, and be connected to public networks.

Defining Areas of Telecom Service Competition

Although already touched on indirectly, it is possible that countries might opt for a code of competition that would define the appropriate relationships between public and private firms and perhaps among common carriers, value-added carriers, and private networks. This could be modeled on GATT Article XVII, which deals with the appropriate behavior of state trading enterprises.

Reduction of Barriers to Trade in Telecom Services

The types of barriers that most disturb private telecom providers can be broken into four groups. First, there will be efforts to reduce obstacles to the trade in telecom equipment and software services. These issues will be addressed during the new round, but may be separated from the services talks. Second, discussions will focus on reducing restrictions that prevent the foreign provision of telecom services, particularly of value-added and information services. Currently, foreign carriers are often precluded from providing services in many countries, and corporations are forced to use the public network because they are prohibited from building private ones. These obstacles prevent the development of an integrated global information network. Considerable progress on procurement is probable as countries recognize that new international corporate alliances that span borders will be the major providers and that national champions are doomed unless they can also sell abroad.

The third type of obstacle, of which there are many varieties, limits and distorts trade in telecom services by limiting the variety of telecom services made available. Governments or their PTTs set requirements or take actions that prevent foreign telecom service providers from competing. Examples include: restrictions on the importation of necessary hardware or software not available domestically; local content laws that require domestic processing of data; mandatory use of domestic networks that do not provide cost-effective, specialized, or technically sophisticated services; limitation or prohibition of the use of leased lines; and discriminatory pricing schemes. Significant liberalization of procurement barriers and more competitive pricing seems within reach. Liberalization of the use of leased lines is inevitable in countries such as England and the Netherlands, but Germany may continue to fight this liberalization for a decade before accepting something like today's status quo.

Specific Telecom Priorities

Although the governments will give and take what they can get and no yellow brick road to successful negotiations is obvious through the jungle of complexity, the United States is likely to stress four specific negotiating goals. First, the United States will seek to clarify, expand, and guarantee the ability of private firms to offer value-added and information services. Second, the United States will take aim at restrictions that prevent private firms from connecting their equipment to the telecom network. Third, leased lines will be a focus of controversy. The United States will try to reduce limits on the use of leased lines, eliminate discriminatory pricing of leased lines, and eliminate restrictions that prevent the resale and shared use of leased lines. Fourth, the United States will want to increase the ability of firms to sell a wide variety of services (including accounting, advertising, architecture/design, consulting, education, health, legal, travel, and tourism, as well as other value-added and information services) internationally. Technological advances and increased competition that are resulting from moves toward liberalization, privatization, and deregulation will allow slow progress on each of these issues.

NOTES

1. The literature on trade in services, including telecom services, is growing rapidly. So far most of this work has argued that services should be on the agenda. Stated goals, however, remain sketchy and incomplete. See for example: Office of the U.S. Trade Representative, *U.S. National Study on Trade in Services,* prepared for submission to the GATT, December 1983; Jonathan David Aronson and Peter F. Cowhey, *Trade in Services: A Case for Open Markets* (Washington, D.C.: American Enterprise Institute, December 1984); Harald B. Malmgren, "Negotiating International Rules for Trade in Services," *The World Economy* (8)1 (March 1985); Helena Stalson, *U.S. Service Exports and Foreign Barriers: An Agenda for Negotiations* (Washington, D.C.: National Planning Association, November 1985); C. Michael Aho and Jonathan D.

Aronson, *Trade Talks: America Better Listen!* (New York: Council on Foreign Relations, 1985).

2.   The best popular introduction to the emergence of ICAs is Kenichi Ohmae, *Triad Power: The Coming Shape of Global Competition* (New York: Free Press, 1985). A more academic effort is David C. Mowery, "Multinational Joint Ventures in Product Development and Manufacture: A Survey," which is the introductory chapter in a collection of studies of joint ventures between U.S. and foreign firms in the microelectronics, robotics, telecommunications equipment, commercial aircraft, steel, pharmaceuticals, and automobile industries published by the American Enterprise Institute in 1986.

3.   Neomercantilists argue that over the long term, U.S. firms have exported their technological advantages too easily. Most strikingly see Robert Gilpin, *U.S. Power and the Multinational Corporation* (New York: Basic Books, 1975). More recently, arguments for "benign mercantilism" have proliferated. See John Zysman and Laura Tyson, eds., *American Industry in International Competition: Government Policies and Corporate Strategies* (Ithaca: Cornell University Press, 1983). For an even tougher statement of the dangers of U.S. corporate involvement in ICAs in regard to U.S. efforts to maintain its long-term technological edge, see Robert B. Reich and Eric D. Mankin, "Joint Ventures with Japan Give Away our Future," *Harvard Business Review* (March–April 1986): 78–86.

4.   See C. Michael Aho and Jonathan D. Aronson, *Trade Talks: America Better Listen!* (New York: Council on Foreign Relations, 1985), pp. 24–32.

5.   Jonathan D. Aronson and Peter F. Cowhey are preparing a book on international corporate arrangements as part of the Council on Foreign Relations trade project.

6.   George A. Codding, Jr., and Anthony M. Rutkowski, *The International Telecommunication Union in a Changing World* (Dedham, Mass.: Artech House, 1982).

7.   An excellent summary is M. English and A. Watson Brown, "National Policies in Information Technology: Challenges and Responses," *Oxford Surveys in Information Technology* 1 (1984): 55–128.

8.   "The World on the Line," *The Economist* (Telecommunications Survey, November 23, 1985).

9.   Even the various European ISDNs are incompatible in their various forms. The Japanese and U.S. ISDN developments also go in different directions. Nobody expects unified standards much before the late 1990s. Jonathan D. Aronson and Peter F. Cowhey, "Is Competition Contagious? Prospects for a Digital Pacific," Paper presented to the 1986 Pacific Telecommunications Council Conference, Honolulu, Hawaii, January 1986.

10.   Elizabeth L. Eisenstein, *The Printing Press as an Agent of Change: Communication and Cultural Transformation in Early Modern Europe* (Cambridge, Mass.: Cambridge University Press, 1979).

11.   Office of the United States Trade Representative, *Annual Report on National Trade Estimates: 1985*, as required by Section 303 of the Trade and Tariff Act of 1984.

12.   The difficulties of negotiating on trade in services are explored in Harald B. Malmgren, "Negotiating International Rules for Trade in Services," *The World Economy* 8(1) (March 1985), and in Rodney de C. Grey, "The Service Industries: A Note of Caution About the Proposal to Negotiate General Rules about Traded Services," in *Canada and the Multilateral Trading System*, ed. John Whalley (Toronto: University of Toronto Press, 1985), pp. 21–39.

16

The Use of Communications: A Vehicle for International Cooperation and Development

Arthur A. Bushkin

International trade issues are in the news these days, and one of the areas about which we hear a great deal is international telecommunications. Everyone will agree that international telecommunications has major economic consequences, but few people can agree upon what those consequences are. Indeed, it is difficult even to get people to agree upon what they mean by international telecommunications.

Are we talking about the provision by a supplier from one country of telecommunications equipment or services in another country for that second country's domestic consumption?
Or are we talking about the provision, through some form of cooperative arrangement, of a telecommunications service that originates in one country and terminates in another country?
Or are we talking about both?

To make matters worse, most discussions of international telecommunications issues immediately focus upon a small number of already familiar issues, such as access to foreign markets in the telecommunications equipment arena and potential competition to INTELSAT in the area of telecommunications services. The result is that we rarely have a chance to step back and look at the whole picture. We rarely get a chance to explore the true issues, focusing instead upon the arguments of the moment.

All of the issues that I have mentioned so far have something in common: they are all issues of supply. They are all concerned with who provides what telecommunications products or services at what prices and under what terms and conditions. In fact, as a general statement, the vast majority of international telecommunications policy issues — as well as the vast majority of international trade issues — deal with such questions of supply. That is, most international telecommunications policy issues are concerned with questions of market access. And not surprisingly, a great many (although not all) of the domestic telecommunications policy issues in most countries also deal with questions of supply.

When we limit our attention to questions relating to the supply of international telecommunications, we neglect a key point: namely, that telecommunications services can be layered. Once the underlying international telecommunications circuit has been established, it can be used by other companies to provide other forms of telecommunications and information services. In other words, the use of telecommunications promotes the supply of other services. This has important practical implications.

Policy makers must not, therefore, make the mistake of thinking that only the suppliers of telecommunications are affected by economic or trade policies relating to international telecommunications. Users of telecommunications, whether domestic or international, have a great deal at stake, as well.

By the same token, telecommunications suppliers can no longer worry about only their market share. They must also worry about their customer base. A barrier inhibiting the customer's use of telecommunications ultimately affects the telecommunications supplier as well.

The telecommunications and computer industries are simply the industries most visibly affected by policies relating to the use of international telecommunications. But other, less obvious, industries are also dependent upon telecommunications and information technologies for the products and services that they provide. The affected companies can be service firms that use telecommunications to deliver their service offerings, or they can be manufacturing or service firms that use telecommunications for their own internal corporate communications.

Just as divestiture in the domestic U.S. telecommunications arena had a significant economic impact upon a broad range of U.S. businesses, so too will any new international rules covering telecommunications services have a significant economic impact upon a broad range of international businesses. The obvious conclusion, therefore, is that satellite systems — and the telecommunications networks and services that they support and encourage — have an economic significance well beyond their own importance in the telecommunications sector.

The issue of who supplies what type of satellite systems under what terms and conditions must naturally be of concern to any country, developing or developed. By the same token, any country must be concerned with its own indigenous capabilities in the emerging telecommunications and information industries. It would be a mistake for any country however — and especially a country concerned with its own economic development — to focus upon these supply issues without attempting to ensure that it will also participate in the growing use of international communications systems.

It is, therefore, not surprising that the use of international telecommunications to affect international commerce has now become a major international trade issue in its own right. It goes by many names: transborder data flow, international information flow, and, most recently, trade in services. But the debate about this so-called trade in services is really a debate with two distinct components: (1) the debate about the noninformation-based service activities such as construction, shipping, and engineering, and (2) the debate about the information-based service activities such as communications, finance, banking, insurance, health, entertainment, news, and data processing. It is important to keep in mind that these services, especially the information-based services, are not only traded in their own right, but that they also support the activities of more traditional manufacturing enterprises.

So what does this mean in practical terms? Although the availability of orbital slots and competition with INTELSAT are certainly important questions, a country must also be concerned with a broader set of issues in its efforts to benefit from the use of satellites and other international telecommunications systems.

To illustrate that this is not a theoretical discussion, I would like to suggest several principles that might be appropriate as the basis of any new international agreement covering the use of international telecommunications to provide other information-based services. Although these principles address traditional market-access concerns, as well as some of the issues related to the use of services, their significance lies in the fact that they are intended to benefit both suppliers and users; they are not simply principles for telecommunications suppliers.

National Treatment: Foreign suppliers of both equipment and services should receive the same treatment as domestic suppliers.
Nondiscrimination: All foreign suppliers of both equipment and services should receive equal treatment.

Market Access: Foreign companies should not be subject to barriers to entry or demands for establishment. Foreign companies should enjoy a balanced group of rights to send and receive information internationally and to store and process information extraterritorially.

Assured Access: Countries and companies should have reasonable assurances that the extraterritorial storage and processing of information does not create an unacceptable risk to their future activities.

Transparency: Governments should make greater efforts to identify laws and regulations that affect international information flow.

Of course, we must also establish procedures for reconciling the international consequences of differing national domestic telecommunications policies. Furthermore, it is essential to avoid counting or measuring international information flows like a traditional commodity. Finally, we must take great care to discourage any forms of government monitoring or regulation of information flows.

The use of international telecommunications is now so widespread that it functions as a throttle that can either encourage or inhibit a broad range of international commercial activity. The use of international telecommunications and information technology has led us to the brink of a new era. We have the opportunity to bind the world together through the use of technology. I am confident that we are all up to the challenge.

I V

LEGAL ISSUES EMERGING FROM INFORMATION TECHNOLOGY

17

Informatics and Democratic Society: Beyond the Tokyo Summit

MICHAEL D. KIRBY

THE NECESSITIES AND DANGERS OF INFORMATICS

In May 1986, in Tokyo, Japan, the leaders of the world's most advanced democracies, also the most advanced industrialized nations, issued a communiqué that proclaimed their faith in technology. Hidden away among remarks about nuclear fallout and terrorism (items that captured the attention of the world's media) were comments on a more fundamental, lasting, and important force in society today, namely science and technology. The leaders were optimistic:

We reaffirm the importance of science and technology for the dynamic growth of the world economy and take note, with appreciation, of the final report of the working group on technology, growth and employment. We stress the importance for genuine partnership and appropriate exchange of information, experience and technologies among the participating States.

This is a chapter about some of the dangers and institutional problems for those societies whose leaders gathered in Tokyo and others like them. Although the chapter concentrates on informatics,

---

*This chapter is an adapted version of an address delivered to the Canadian National Forum on Access to Information and Privacy, Ottawa, Canada, March 6, 1986.

the other technological changes of our time are equally involved. As will be pointed out, what is at stake is nothing less than the preservation of the common features of the Western democracies and the capacity to retain and adapt their basic governmental institutions and social values in a time of profound scientific and technological change.

The features of the new information technology that endanger the value of individual privacy are now well known. The dangers derive from the following features of the technology in particular:

It transcends distance, darkness and physical barriers.

It transcends time, because of the capacity to collect and store massive amounts of data that can be retrieved whenever needed.

It is capital rather than labor intensive, because it is no longer necessary to have human intervention. The computer can analyze all.

It is universal in its application, decentralized, and triggers self-activating policing.

It has low visibility or even total invisibility.

It grows ever more extensive and covers larger areas of life, ever more deeply (Marx 1985).

These are trite statements about a pervasive technology that is overwhelmingly beneficial in its potential to release mankind from the millstones of routines and mindless drudgery. However, a poll conducted in 1985 by Louis Harris–France in eight industrial countries indicates that "invasion of privacy and unemployment continue to be viewed as two significant consequences of data processing" (Riley 1985, 1). In the United States, 68% of those polled agreed that it would be increasingly possible to use computer data banks to infringe on personal privacy. Knowledgeable people who are not Luddites, recognize that a hitherto important feature of our form of societies is seriously endangered by what is otherwise a beneficial technological development. Moreover, it is a development that has distinctly positive features for the enhancement of freedom. For example, the new information technology promises the improvement in cost-effective access to official information. In this way the public accountability of politicians and bureaucrats may be increased so that they extend far beyond the occasional visit to the ballot box, which was previously the theoretical occasion for enforcing the ultimate accountability of the executive government to the people.

In all of our countries three changes have occurred that promote the demand for privacy and freedom of information (FOI) laws. These are:

First, the significant growth in the role of the public sector, precipitated by the urgent needs of World War II and continued and expanded since. This phenomenon, and the panoply of agencies and officialdom thereby created, demolished many of the vestiges of the mythology of ministerial accountability. It has led to a rational insistence upon new institutions and rights that translate theoretical accountability into daily practice (Curtis 1985).

Second, the general advances in the education of the community that has had a dual impact. First, it has created an ever-expanding pool of well-informed citizens, impatient with the paternalistic notion that administrators necessarily know best. Second, it created, particularly in the educated middle class, a group of people willing to utilize new rights and to enforce them in the courts and in the protective administrative agencies.

Third came the new technology itself. As Marx and others have demonstrated, it presented novel problems, relevantly, problems of data protection and data security. But it also presented potential solutions. Keys, passwords, and inscriptions could be introduced to bar access to personal information, even to an inquisitive civil servant who, in the old days, might have had access to paper files. On-line facilities can assure the data subject, potentially, a right of access to data about himself or herself, in a way that the inefficiency of the old systems could not necessarily ensure.

Thus, the issue in a nutshell is one of thinking, as people in the United States say, positive: taking advantage of the remarkable and pervasive technology of informatics while, at the same time, acting with resolution to defend elements of individual privacy, deemed important for the liberty of mankind in the future — a future likely to be increasingly pervaded by the technology of informatics.

THE THREAD OF ARIADNE

The past decade or so has seen important legislative responses to informatics in all of the advanced English-speaking democracies. Freedom of information and privacy laws have been enacted in the United States and Canada (Canada, Senate 1983a; 1983b; U.S. Congress 1967). Privacy legislation has been enacted in the United Kingdom. But, although 57% of the British people last year told an opinion poll that they thought FOI would help protection of rights "a great deal" (Kellner 1985), the U.K. government seems to adhere to the old mythology of ministerial accountability, the Official Secrets Act, and the world of "leaks" that tends to accompany, nowadays, regimes of too much secrecy. The Ponting trial (*Economist* 1985) and the Westland helicopter affair all show what happens in secretive administrations in the age of the photocopier.

New Zealand has enacted an FOI law (New Zealand, Senate 1982). When I was there in February 1986, that country was looking at reform of that law and at the enactment of privacy legislation (Eagles and Taggart 1984). In Australia, a freedom of information act was enacted by federal parliament in 1982. It contained an important section for rights of access to personal information and for the protection of private information. Comprehensive federal privacy laws have been promised (Australia, Parliament 1982). But hand in hand with these developments comes a proposal for a national identity card to coordinate federal data banks as a suggested means of combatting tax and social security fraud (Australia, Department of Health 1986).

Recently, I had to offer a foreword to a publication, to be printed in Canada, on the problems and prospects of these information laws (Riley 1982). Looking through their reports, and the report on the Australian legislation offered by the late Senator Alan Missen, it became clear that a number of common themes were emerging. They chart the way ahead for those concerned about information law in the last decade of the twentieth century. To some extent, the themes are similar. They are illustrated by the workshops of this symposium. With differing emphasis, the authors call attention to concerns that will clearly affect the law and administrative practices involved in the exercise of privacy of FOI rights for years to come.

Two of the contributors, Inger Hansen and Harold Relyea stress the concern in Canada and the United States respectively that FOI is being used (or abused) to breach the legitimate expectations of business confidentiality. This confidentiality may sometimes be undermined by the revelation, pursuant to FOI law, of information supplied by business (usually under compulsion) to the government. How are these competing rights to be reconciled and the integrity of FOI maintained, while ensuring legitimate claims to business secrecy and candid supply of business data to government?

Concern is also expressed in the United States and Canada about the use of FOI to undermine, frustrate, and delay the processes of law enforcement. Particular anxiety is felt about the so called "mosaic" phenomenon, as a result of which, even where identifiers have been deleted, some material supplied pursuant to FOI can assist antisocial persons to identify public informers or to secure other information that public policy suggests should be kept secret.

Concern about cost of FOI is a theme running through all reports on the operation of information legislation. There is the suggestion that this is a luxury that, however desirable in principle, our communities simply cannot afford. There is also the suggestion that, depending as it does on the activities of enthusiastic individuals, our FOI and privacy laws are very much the guardians of the educated middle class. They provide little in the way of enhanced freedom for those people who are most dependent on and under the surveillance of government — social security recipients, veterans, hospital patients, and others whose very position of dependence often makes the enforcement of their information rights a matter of theory rather than practice.

In Australia, the concern about FOI and privacy laws has changed in the last decade. From the early debates about the numerous exemptions and conclusive ministerial certificates under the FOI Act, the concern today has shifted. So few ministerial exemptions have been claimed that the battle ground has moved. Now, the counterreformation comes from the bureaucrats who point repeatedly to the cumbersome and costly machinery to which they must devote scarce resources. And those concerned about spreading the impact of FOI and privacy access rights point to the narrow use of those rights, the widespread ignorance about them, their substantial confinement to the educated middle class, and the retreat from earlier public campaigns to promote general knowledge by media advertising, pamphlets, and the like (Australia, Attorney-General's Department 1982).

At this level of the debate, it would be possible to trace a thread of Ariadne through the controversies. Common themes undoubtedly exist. There is some evidence of a counterreformation, as attention is laid by bureaucrats and politicians in many lands upon cost and the various problems that the first decade of information legislation has disclosed.

Instead of taking this course, I have decided, with due modesty, to propound again the ten information commandments. It was said of President Wilson's fourteen points that he had divined four more than the Almighty. Being a more diffident type, I prefer to follow the Mosaic tradition. Hence the ten information commandments, which I am moved to hand down twice. Perhaps if Moses had done so, the original Ten Commandments would have been better known and more faithfully observed.

THE TEN INFORMATION COMMANDMENTS

1. *Contemporary technological developments endanger human rights and civil liberties and require responses from society — including the legal system.* The first "commandment" states the obvious. It is not confined to informatics. The most remarkable feature

of the late twentieth century is the coincidence, at one moment of history, of three important technological developments. I refer to nuclear fission, biotechnology, and informatics. Each of these developments has implications for human rights and civic freedoms. Information technology presents the problems, some of which have been identified already by Garry Marx.

Biotechnology presents quandaries that go to the definition of human life itself. Human cloning, in vitro fertilization, the growing of human body parts, and numerous other features of genetic engineering and biotechnology present major dilemmas to the philosopher, the lawyer, and the law maker. In the Australian Parliament, a committee is examining a Private Member's Bill designed to restrict and control many biotech developments, in some of which Australian scientists have made notable contributions (Australia, Parliament 1985).

Of nuclear fission, I need say nothing, except that unless the international community can bring this technology under effective international control, the long-run prospects of mankind's surviving accidents, mistake, or nuclear folly appear problematical. So the starting point, the beginning of wisdom, is a realization of the enormous challenge that technology presents to humanity in our generation. We need a Luther of jurisprudence to lead us to the legal solutions and political leaders of wisdom to lead our communities thoughtfully to the responses that preserve life and freedom.

2. *The fertile common law system, even as enhanced in some countries by constitutional rights, is insufficient to provide adequate responses to the challenges of technology. More legislation is needed.* Some people say that the common law, developed by the judges, will be adequate to defend our liberties, in the future as it has in the past. No doubt there is a role for the common law. It must surely respond to technological change. Benjamin Cardozo once said that the law, like the traveller, must prepare for the morrow. In the United States, with the famous language of the Bill of Rights and lately in Canada with the Charter of Rights and Freedoms, scope is offered to the judiciary to enhance the creative element that has always existed in the common law. But even in such countries, and still more so in countries such as my Australia, without such a catalyst for judicial creativity in the protection of rights in the modern era, more will be needed.

Shortly before my departure from Australia, the High Court of Australia reversed a decision in which I had participated. It was a decision relevant to information rights. The Court of Appeal had declared that, in modern circumstances, the common law of natural justice required the giving of reasons by public officials enjoying legislative discretions (Osmond v. Public Service Board of New South

Wales 1984; 1985). The High Court, referring to old authorities, many of them preceding the three developments to which I have referred, unanimously ruled that a right to reasons was not required by the rules of natural justice (High Court of Australia 1986). Development of the law here, it was said, was for the Parliament, not the courts. A signal was sent out cautioning against judicial creativity. It was said that in other countries of the common law, for example India, where a right to reasons is now established, constitutional considerations, in the form of fundamental rights, might explain and justify developments in the law. Perhaps in Canada the law will respond more readily to changing times and changing technology because of the facility provided by the Charter of Rights and Freedoms. But in Australia, as in New Zealand, England, and elsewhere, the judiciary since the nineteenth century and the reforms of Parliament has, with notable exceptions, preferred to emphasize the noncreative features of the common law. Yet a signal that calls for judicial restraint calls equally for legislative attention, in default of which the judges will be urged again to remedy wrongs and to provide defenses to freedom.

3. *In some cases, the technology itself demands or even produces legal reform.* This third rule refers to the tendency of modern technology to undermine current law or to render it irrelevant or ineffective. I have already mentioned the way in which the photocopier undermines excessive secrecy. Doubtless this is why photocopiers are kept under lock and key in the Soviet Union. The technology of photographic reproduction and on-line linkages reduces the capacity to keep things secret. The selfsame technology that presents the problems of privacy promotes the flow of information that tends to enhance accountability both in the public and private sectors. But in the field of informatics, the results can be surprising. One case is well known and is called to attention by Professor Jon Bing of Norway (Bing, Forsberg, and Nygaard 1983, 59ff). A social scientist in Norway sought on-line access, under United States FOI law, to NATO deployments in Norway. Such information was a state secret under Norwegian law. The social scientist was prosecuted in Norway. Information technology with its international applications reduces, by transborder data flow, the effective operation of the sovereign laws of domestic jurisdiction.

4. *The people are not always the best judges of their own interests. Informed observers have a duty to identify dangers of freedom.* One of the chief arguments that the minister proposing a computerized national identity card in Australia continually refers to is that public opinion polls show that nearly 70% of Australians favor a national identity card with photograph (Blewett 1986). In a democracy, it is

natural for intellectuals to bow to the corporate wisdom of the people. If the people want an ID card, why should they be denied such a facility? Especially if it would help combat welfare and tax fraud? The answer, sadly, is that the public is all too frequently willing to participate in the destruction or erosion of its own liberties. It is to informed people (particularly lawyers conscious of our long constitutional history and the famous struggles for freedom), that there falls the sometimes unpopular function of holding out against the popular tide.

Opinion polls may persistently favor the reintroduction of the death penalty. They may favor the return of flogging and, who knows, even transportation to a faroff place such as Australia. But such opinions may be based upon false impressions or ignorance of the available data. They may ignore the statistics that show the ineffectiveness of such punishments. They may ignore the statistics that show the fall in jury convictions where capital punishment is available. They may be based on ignorance of the countervailing effects of such punishments. So it may be with a national identity card. It may be based on a desire of people without access to gold American Express cards to have a nice plastic card, as other people have. It might be based on the notion that "if you have nothing to hide," the card can do no harm. It might conjure up the memory of the occasion when proof of identity would have been useful. But it remains for those who are aware of the special relationship that exists in countries of the common law between authority and the citizen to point to the dangers.

A dentist who survived Auschwitz may declare that the best thing of living in Australia (it could equally be the United States, Canada, or England) is that he is never liable to be stopped on the corner by someone in uniform with the demand, "Papieren!" Yet provide a universal computerized ID card and the risk exists that the data base will be enhanced and that more and more officials will seek access to it, in the name of efficiency, and that in the course of time carrying the card will be obligatory. And producing it will become a commonplace and ultimately, in response no doubt to some outrage, obligatory. In the space of a few years, an important principle that marks off the intrusion of officialdom into our lives could be quite easily demolished. The intrusion might not be just physical. It might go on behind the scenes — intrusion into the data profile where more and more decisions affecting the subject may be made without the slightest knowledge of the data subject.

Lulled by a trivializing diet of soap operas, cowboy westerns, and Manhattan gun battles, our people become indifferent spectators to or even conspirators in the erosion of their own freedoms. Should we care? Should we who are aware of the long battles for freedom also surrender, acknowledging that some erosion of privacy is inevitable as a product of the new information technology? The Fourth Commandment teaches that we *should* care, and that it is the responsibility of politicians, and those who advise them, to work even in the face of popular indifference or opposition for the preservation of hard-won freedoms. For once they are lost they are rarely regained.

5. *The costs of information rights must be counted. But so must the intangible benefits.* In the jargon of the economist, it is important for lawyers who talk of liberty and freedom to take into account the incremental costs involved in the externalities to decision making. The protection of freedom and the assurance of fairness certainly have a cost. It involves the assignment of scarce resources. A recent decision in Canada requires hearings for refugee immigrants. It was a blow for administrative fairness, but clearly the cost of providing this facility will run into millions of dollars. The provision of the facility to the persons affected will necessarily result in the denial of benefits to others. That is nothing more than the simple consequence of the economic problem (Bouchard 1986). So it is in information rights.

There is now a great deal of talk, particularly in Australia, concerning the costs of FOI and privacy rights. There is a similar debate in the United States. Whereas the U.S. FOI legislation is now a robust adolescent, the same cannot be said of the equivalent laws in Canada, Australia, and New Zealand. The combination of talk about cost of the provision of information rights, the inevitable concern of politicians about skeletons they would rather leave in the computer cupboard, and the hankering of not a few public servants for a return to the "good old days," all present the danger of the Information Counterreformation. It is a danger that supporters of information rights must repel. They must work with special vigor in countries such as Canada and Australia because of the relative ease with which governments, dominating the legislature, could secure the rolling back of legislative entitlements to information, whether public or personal. The rolling back of such rights can be done by frank legislative amendment and repeal. But it can also be done, in practice, by the introduction of or increase in charges. These may effectively bar some of the more deserving people from exercising their rights. Or it can be done by cutting back in publicity about the existence of the rights, so that they remain (in practice) the province of the media, of corporations, and of educated middle-class citizens.

It is natural that in more difficult economic times governments should be concerned about the costs of information rights. The direct costs include not only the administrative staffs and bureaucratic time.

To them must be added the provision of courtrooms, judges and tribunal members, shorthand writers, and so on. As well, there are the opportunity costs — the other facilities and benefits foregone by virtue of the decision to stick with information rights.

These concerns have led government ministers (e.g., see Walsh 1985), and the leader of the opposition, in Australia to foreshadow the possible winding back or limitation of review mechanisms for the enforcement of information rights. This is sure to be an important issue in the decade ahead. It may be that corporations and others who are major users of such rights should pay a differential fee in recognition of the fact that they can pass such business expenses on to consumers using their products. It may also be that attention needs to be given to the more cost effective way of delivering information: avoiding the cumbersome, expensive, and dilatory machinery of courts and tribunals. But when the public costs are added up, so must be the public benefits. And the relativities must be considered. They include the well-known statistic that the cost of FOI in the United States is less than the upkeep of lawns on golf courses for overseas defense personnel. And as Dr. Relyea points out, against the cost of providing information that people want to know must be considered the cost of official government information services that nowadays pour out thinly disguised propaganda, repeated through media handouts, concerning what the government *wants* people to know. The former may be a healthy corrective, on occasion, to the latter.

6. *Information laws must be developed flexibly because of changing technology and the rapidly changing perceptions of the problems.* Not to devise and implement adequate privacy laws, in the inadequacy of the common law and current legislation, is to make a decision. It is to stand quietly by while the technology itself erodes hitherto valued rights. But the counterpart of this principle is that inflexible laws can outlive the understanding of the problem they have been introduced to solve. This is why Professor Simitis has said that data protection laws are now at a "turning point." An illustration of this truism can be given. Many of the laws already put in place rely heavily on the right of individual access as a means of protecting individual privacy rights. But the effective utilization of this most beneficial right depends upon large assumptions. It depends upon knowledge by the individual that there is something to be concerned about. Yet if there is no notification that you are in the system, decisions may be made, vital to your life. Yet you may be blissfully ignorant. Similarly, the right of access makes large assumptions about individual initiative and enthusiasm. Realism might well raise different considerations. Apathy, resignation, or a feeling of

powerlessness may necessitate other solutions, if true data protection is to be afforded beyond the powerful and articulate who exert their rights. There is a tendency in our kind of society to slip into legislative mythology. It is an easy and convenient myth to believe that accountability is provided by a right of access and that information rights are thereby protected. In fact, such facilities should be seen as the start of a long journey — not arrival in the Promised Land.

7. *Information rights must extend from the public sector (where they have been developed) to the private sector.* So far, comprehensive information laws have concentrated on the public sector. This is natural, for it is in that sector that critical information affecting all citizens exists. But increasingly important in our lives, and often insusceptible to national control, are large corporations, including transnational corporations. People in the private sector tend to be foremost in asserting the right of accountability by public officials and access to public data. But the selfsame principle has relevance to the private sector, as well. Its full relevance is yet to be worked out. Of course, there is already much accountability by the private sector, including in the market. But information rights concern individual power, and power exerted in relation to the corporate state may be equally applicable in relation to dealings with private enterprise. Voluntary guidelines, such as compliance with the Organization for Economic Cooperation and Development (OECD) privacy principles, may provide a starting point. But it is scarcely likely that this will be adequate in the long term.

8. *Information technology presents international issues that require international solutions.* The need for transborder solutions to information rights is self-evident in federations such as Australia, Canada, and the United States. But there is a wider international stage. The technology itself is virtually universal. The problems presented necessarily transcend state borders. The OECD guidelines were developed in the hope of stimulating consistency in legislative and administrative approaches to information rights in the context of privacy. Other international agencies are now endeavoring to develop rules that can facilitate common approaches. UNESCO has just embarked on a major informatics program. The intergovernmental Bureau for Informatics in Rome has established a commission to promote a dialogue on data law and policy between the advanced countries of the OECD and the developing world. The technology must interface. Gross inefficiency will result if legal regulations are enacted that are incompatible and yet must be complied with by transborder flows of data. Data havens may destroy the effectiveness of information rights. The three technological developments of our time, nuclear

fission, biotechnology, and informatics, require of us that we should lift our sights from parochial and purely nationalistic approaches to the law. Until now, law has been very much jurisdiction bound. International technology imposes on us the need for international approaches to legal regulations. That is why forums such as this have a special utility. We in the developed world must become more conscious of the needs and concerns of those less rich. They follow the caravan of the information economy.

9. *Legal responses to information rights must attend to real problems and not content themselves with myths and mere symbols.* The ninth principle has already been foreshadowed. The easy thing for law makers to do is to establish a bureaucracy with attractive titles, set up with fanfare announcing that information is free and privacy is henceforth guaranteed. But what is important is the fine print. It has always seemed to me that the value of the OECD guidelines lay chiefly in the formulation of a short list of relatively simple principles for information practices. If these became well known and generally accepted as a bible of fair information practices, much would be achieved. Sanctions and advisory mechanisms are needed to deal with the problems that arise. But most people at the work place simply require a series of simple rules, ultimately backed by the law. The simpler the rules and the fewer, the more likely that fair practices will result. In the field of FOI, rights of access will not promote effective accountability unless they are reinforced by community rights of access to the public media. The concentration of the media in few hands may undermine the effectiveness of official information laws, because they prevent vital information from flowing through to the community at large. Thus we should be concerned with the reality of information rights, not the mythology. Laws that talk of "the consent of the data subject," for example, sound fine. But to an unemployed pensioner seeking a social security benefit or a hospital patient seeking treatment or an employee seeking information that does not result in dismissal or destroy advancement prospects, it may sometimes be necessary to go beyond reliance on the courageous individual. Information laws that depend exclusively on individual motivation for enforcement are much better than nothing. They are a step in the right direction. But they fall a long way short of providing effective protections against all of the implications of the new technology.

10. *Democratic values must be preserved, and it is at least questionable whether our democratic institutions can adequately respond to the challenges of technology.* This brings me to my last commandment. I approach my conclusion on a somber note. Those who look at the history of parliamentary democracies in this century, at

least in our countries, may be generally optimistic about the future. Despite many challenges, the institutions have survived. The alternative systems are infinitely less flexible and uniformly more oppressive. But the problem for parliamentary institutions, posed by rapid technological change, is the problem of keeping pace. If nothing is done, a decision is made. Yet the very technicality of the changes make it difficult for the lay politician (and indeed those advising him or her) to comprehend all of the ramifications. Furthermore, many of the changes are highly controversial, as debates about the privacy of children against their parents and debates about biotechnological experiments clearly demonstrate. In the face of such complexity and controversy, there is a natural tendency for parliamentary inaction, which is understandable. But it is dangerous. It is especially dangerous if it coincides with the disinclination of the judges (themselves often scientifically illiterate) to mobilize the creative machinery of the common law. There are at least some signs that this is what is occurring. It is most likely to occur if the executive, which dominates parliament, loses enthusiasm for information rights. That loss of enthusiasm may be dressed up in the name of economy and cost/benefit analysis. But it may simply disguise age-old issues of power: where power is to lie. In my country, there is much evidence of the institutional incapacity to respond. Only one state (Victoria) has enacted an FOI law. In others it is repeatedly promised, but nothing comes of the promises. Only one state (New South Wales) has a general privacy law, and that is of limited effectiveness. The federal privacy law is a long time coming. And there is much more vigor in pressing on with a national identity card, despite the dangers it poses for privacy, than in embracing privacy protection laws, limited as they may be. In the field of information rights, public lethargy now conspires with unsympathetic noises both from government and opposition quarters.

CONCLUSIONS

What is the result of this analysis? Is it that late twentieth-century man and woman, lulled in the global village into an intellectual haze by a constant diet of media trivia, has lost concern about real political accountability? Or are they indifferent to (and even conspire in the destruction of) privacy rights? Political accountability becomes little more than three yearly television wars between competing electoral jingles, with political parties sold like soap powder to a people programmed to watch personality politics, devoid of concern with the large issues and obsessed by the parochial.

You might say that if 70% of the people want the introduction of a facility used in other times and other places to destroy liberty, then governments and politicians must bow to the superior wisdom of the people and their assessment of their information rights.

But that wisdom ultimately depends on knowledge. And it is up to those who have the knowledge and who can see the problems to act responsibly and courageously. I remain incurably optimistic. But in darker moments of contemplation is a lingering doubt. And even more than its concern about the survival of political accountability and the persistence of privacy in the age of informatics is the institutional concern. In such a time of rapid change, complex science, and high controversy, can our law-making institutions cope? That is the question that transcends even the privacy and freedom of information issues discussed. They are in a sense a microcosm of a larger problem. For if our parliamentary democracies falter here, they admit their incompetence to govern us in the twenty-first century — whose watchword and engine will be science. Accordingly, we must remain optimistic about our capacity to adapt our institutions and laws to rapid technological change. A loss of confidence or heart, and a breach of the commandment of optimism, is a surrender to the nagging doubt that technology is inherently elitist and autocratic and that democracy, with all its inefficiencies, can not survive into the twenty-first century. We must make it our business to ensure that this prophesy of gloom proves wrong. But the responsibility for rational optimism is ours.

REFERENCES

Australia. Attorney-General's Dept. 1985. "Freedom of Information Act 1982." *Annual Report 1983–84*. Canberra: AGPS.

Australia. Department of Health. 1986. "Towards Fairness and Equity? The Australia Card Program."

Australia. Parliament. 1982. *Freedom of Information Act*. Ss 11, 48.

Australia. Parliament. 1985. *Human Experimentation Bill*.

Bing, J., P. Forsberg, and E. Nygaard. 1983. *Legal Problems Related to Transborder Data Flows: An Exploration*. Canberra.

Bouchard, M. 1986. "Administrative Law in the Real World: A Canadian Perspective." Unpublished paper presented at the New Zealand Legal Research Foundation Seminar on Judicial Review of Administrative Action, Auckland, Australia, February.

Canada. Senate. 1983a. *Access to Information Act*.

Canada. Senate. 1983b. *Privacy Act*.

Curtis, L. J. 1985. "Administrative Law Reform — Impact on Public Sector Management." Paper presented at the National Government Accounting Convention, University of Adelaide, Australia, February 21.

Eagles, I., and M. Taggart. 1984. *Report on Reform of Official Information Act.* Prepared at the direction of the Hon. G. W. R. Palmer, Minister of Justice and Attorney General (Australia). Mimeograph.

The Economist. 1985. February 16.

High Court of Australia. 1986. Public Service Board of New South Wales v. Osmond. Unreported.

Kellner, P. 1985. "All So Wrong about Rights." *The Times* (London). July 1.

New Zealand. Senate. 1982. *Official Information Act.*

Osmond v. Public Service Board of New South Wales. 1984. 3 NSWLR 447.

Osmond v. Public Service Board of New South Wales. 1985. LRC(Const) 1041.

Riley, T., ed. 1982. *Access to Government Documents: Some International Perspectives and Trends.*

U.S. Congress, 1967. *Freedom of Information Act.*

Walsh, Senator P. 1985. In *Commonwealth Parliamentary Debates (The Senate)* (of Australia). April 17. Canberra: AGPS.

18

Computers and Law

JAN FREESE

One of the most important changes in the transformation of society from the industrialized period into the information era is a loss of legal stability. Legislation has long been the stabilizing skeleton of the social body. The loss of legal stability has not yet been as fully recognized as it needs to be.

Rather early, however, legislators paid attention to human rights and the need to examine the protection of privacy in a computerized society. Today, special privacy protection acts have been passed in Austria, Canada, Denmark, the Federal Republic of Germany, France, Hungary, Iceland, Israel, Luxemburg, Norway, Sweden, and the United Kingdom. In some federal countries such as the United States, besides some rudimentary federal rules to control federal authorities' information processing there is legislation in several states. As early as 1970, however, the United States introduced the Fair Credit Reporting Act, providing control over a branch of business that already at that time was rather extensively computerized. In Switzerland, where legislation exists at the canton level, national legislation is expected soon. There is a queue of countries standing on the threshold of legislation, for example Belgium, Italy, Portugal, and the United Kingdom. Legislation in Spain is believed acceptable enough to enable Spain to ratify the Council of Europe's Convention for the Protection of Individuals.

Even if most countries that have already passed data protection legislation or are in the process of doing so have followed two recommendations from the Council of Europe's Convention Article 8, 1975; Australia's Data Protection Act of 1978; and France's Data Privacy

Act of 1978, the different laws do not and will not look alike. The Danish legislation is close to the recommendations, with separate laws for the public and the private sectors. In Norway there is just one law, which also covers the credit information business, whereas Sweden has a data act concerning both the public and the private sectors and a separate credit information act.

Even some developing countries have legislation. Brazil is one example, but the Brazilian law focuses on other concerns than just privacy. It protects national development, the labor market, knowhow, and sovereignty. In the People's Republic of China a data-inspection board is operating, but it is concentrating on data security.

Some existing laws look more farreaching than others, but it is impossible to compare them without a deep-sea dive into other legislation. Of great importance to the privacy protection standard is, for instance, the influence of constitutional rules, secrecy legislation, procedural laws, penal codes, and administrative rules — which together make up the control guarantees of free public access to information, for example, which can make privacy protection both stronger and weaker.

Although privacy legislation was an early point of focus, computer technology in a more general way has not been reflected to an acceptable extent in other parts of national legislation. In some countries the penal code has been amended both to protect privacy and to meet other problems. In Denmark, the penal code was amended early in the 1970s, the Data Protection Acts were passed in 1978. In Sweden some sections of the data act also cover nonpersonal data. Section 21, for example, deals with "data trespassing," which means that hackers and other trespassers can be sentenced for unauthorized use of computerized information. This section is subsidiary to the rules in the penal code, which does not deal with all kinds of computer crime or, usually more accurately, computer-aided or computer-related crime. In many countries the penal codes need to be amended to deal adequately with crimes of today and tomorrow.

It is possible to patent computers — both how they work and methods of processing — and production processes. It is also possible to protect programs by patents or other intellectual property rights, such as copyright. It is, however, often impractical and in any case not an easy task to do so or to maintain the protection. WIPO (the World Intellectual Property Organization) and UNESCO have been fairly active in the attempt to establish an international convention on the legal protection of programs, but until now without success, partly because of discrepancies in the views on these questions in developed and developing countries. This is one part of the debate on a new world information and communication order. There is also discussion between the developed countries in the Organization for Economic Cooperation and Development (OECD) about the legal protection of international data flows. Even in the "marketplace" of the OECD's Committee on Information, Computer and Communications Policy, problems of this kind are not easily solved.

It is among other things a problem of much money. The turnover just on programs for small computers (those in a price range under U.S. $10,000) in the United States alone in 1983 was more than $2 billion. One problem in the legal protection of programs is their short lifetime compared with earlier protected products. Programs are often mayflies.

Intellectual property rights border on rules in the labor market and working conditions — for example, both the employee's and the employer's rights to knowhow. The problems in this sector are made still more complicated by the extended use of consultants and their rights and responsibilities. A consultant in this field is usually involved in all steps of computerization, from a pilot study to the testing of a complete system, and has a different kind of responsibility from an employer.

The example of the programmer who changes jobs is also a problem of intellectual property rights. The discussion in circles close to WIPO shows a striving to keep these rather modern rights, in their traditional forms in the future, as well. Already, the photocopier and the tape recorder have partly killed such rights and the computer may very well finish them off. Copyright is no doubt the first intellectual property right to be in danger, but patent rights, design rights, and the like are also threatened.

Contract law is sometimes in trouble, as we are not used to all the changes computerization brings. Too much has become unforeseeable. Disputes between contracting parties are becoming more and more common, concerning both sales and services and both in court and in arbitral procedures.

The world is not only growing more and more cashless (bank and postal systems started the cashless trend), but it is also becoming signatureless. For example, until recently, in Sweden, when you withdrew money from your bank, two clerks signed this "agreement" between you and the bank. Nowadays, you agree on your withdrawal with a banking machine in the street and get a printed receipt; and there is very little practical evidence if, which happens, a technical failure or someone's abuse has affected your statement of account. This is not new. The problem is the same when we agree by word of mouth, but the dimensions today are of another kind. The signatureless society sometimes concerns big business. Banking is just one sector.

Still, central banks and political decision makers believe that they have a grasp of international money transfer through their national rules. You need not believe Alvin Toffler's *The Ecospasm Report* to disagree. Electronic funds transfer systems of different kinds are day and night moving money all around the globe, even outside the central banks' office hours. The international electronic funds transfer systems are probably typical examples of what will demand international conventions in the near future.

SWIFT (the Society for Worldwide Interbank Financial Telecommunications), one of the biggest international money transfer systems, coordinates transfers between 1,700 banks in about forty countries, amounting to half a million international and domestic transactions a day. To be precise, what happens is not the transfer of money but the registration and transfer of data.

Another legal problem is posed by the services offered by Teletex and other huge new data bases. They will no longer just border on more traditional media such as newspapers and radio and television broadcasting, which are already being regulated, they will also take over many of the traditional media functions and therefore require corresponding legal regimes.

In the 1960s and early 1970s, some people warned that computers would make the human being transparent. This problem has extended to companies, for two reasons. One is the increasing integration between the public and the private sectors. More and more information about private companies is collected by public authorities. This transfer of information is usually regulated, but not in order to protect the company. The traditional, official secrecy acts protecting information of this kind, as well as information concerning national security, do not work very well in a computerized environment. This may soon lead to an increasing understanding among businesspeople concerning the privacy protection problem, as it is a problem of exactly the same kind.

The growing lack of adequate legislation shows that sometimes it may be better to have no law at all than an obsolete law. The lack of competence on the part of the legal authorities makes the problem still worse, and perhaps this is one of the most serious questions in most countries that are entering the information society surfing on the Third Wave.

A real problem is the legislators' belief about how the laws they produce are used. Laws are still made in traditional ways and the legislators still think that new rules are taken care of by skilled lawyers who carefully practice the rules in case after case. In reality, it is not unusual for the rules to be taken care of by programmers who transform them into technical terms, whereupon they are used for several hundred thousand decisions a year, based on computer processing. In such an environment it is no wonder if some prophets believe in the need for new constitutions, as they guess that the future will demand a new type of democracy.

Computer technology in its marriage with telecommunications does not care about national borders. It is therefore rather natural that so many international organizations are involved in the legal discussions — e.g., the United Nations, the Council of Europe, the European Community, and the European Parliament, as well as the OECD and the Intergovernmental Bureau for Informatics.

National legislation is itself a slow procedure. In the international field the process is still slower. The Council of Europe started its discussion about privacy and computers as early as the end of the 1960s. In the OECD the subject was discussed for the first time a few years later. Not until September 1980 was a Council of Europe convention drawn up. At the same time, the OECD passed the goal post with its guidelines governing the protection of privacy and transborder flows of personal data. These two international standards have more or less the same content.

The Council of Europe convention has been signed by about fifteen countries and ratified by five. Five countries must ratify for the convention to enter into force, which happened October 7, 1985. The OECD guidelines have been accepted by the member countries. But even if these two international agreements are not bad goals, they still leave many problems unsolved; for example, the question of conflict of law.

The Council of Europe's Convention and the OECD guidelines were not born without resistance from the business community, which saw the rules as new international bureaucracy. But the critics are wrong. If they were right, the consequence should be a demand for abolition of all "traffic rules" governing international transport at sea, by road, and in the air. The result would then be great difficulties in getting an aircraft off the ground. The rules are meant to be a help, not a hindrance.

19

Privacy, Security, and Transborder Data Flow: A European View

JEAN-PIERRE CHAMOUX

International trade is based on free-flow principle. The Common Market has been developing faster than have national economies, probably because of its free-trade tradition, which has been ruled by the founding treaty. The Common Market has had a great influence on member states during the last twenty-five years, but it has not covered all fields of information-intensive industry.

The power of the states to control and dispatch the flow of information going in and out of the country has been much greater than its right to control the flow of goods and other services. This is true worldwide. It applies in the European Economic Community (EEC).

Although the customs and currency administrations have not hindered the free flow of goods and services all over Europe, the information business and the communication business are more strongly controlled by public authority than any other businesses. Laws are settled as if it was more important for the states to control information than any other product that is allowed to flow in and out of the country.

But our world is changing. Information technology has become vital to all multinational businesses and the free trade market may be jeopardized by the constraints imposed on the information flow that underlies business (i.e., orders, inventories, accounting). Similarly, technology bypassed the borders of national information systems, bringing an international perspective on most media, favoring a wide transmission of news all over the world, and forcing management to deal with worldwide problems.

These are some reasons for looking ahead with a new eye, keeping in mind the expectation that information technology will enhance the necessity for a drastic change in the international governance of communications and media. But in the meantime, transborder data flow is of concern to many trade operators, worried as they are about the consequences of the data-protection laws enacted in many countries.

DATA-PROTECTION IMPLICATION FOR SOME TECHNOLOGIES

It is worthwhile to state the typical data-protection problems raised by the technologies of information and communication that are developing quickly in several European states.

Electronic Funds Transfer

Anything dealing with banking and money is confidential in nature, but systems handling bank notes or enabling the user to transfer money from one account to another draw the attention of criminals and are subject to the menace of robbery. There is no question about the necessity of protection against fraudulent use of such systems, for which security devices are essential.

Technical devices may play an important role in lessening the risks raised by electronic funds transfer, particularly in the fields of authentication and certification of messages.

Personal Minicomputers

The question raised by data-protection laws is whether or not to apply prescription of the laws to all computers, including personal computing and text processors. Some countries may follow the Swedish example, which makes difference between professional users (required to follow strictly all legal procedures) and home users, who are released from most formal obligations (licensing and declaration to data inspection board).

With a few exceptions, small computers do not carry serious threats to privacy, unless they handle highly confidential data (e.g., credit scoring, church affiliation). Security measures on small computers are not essential, unless they belong to a network.

Interactive Videotex

Interactive videotex meets privacy in several ways. In home applications, banking transactions are made possible through videotex terminals. For other customers' applications of videotex, such as electronic mail ordering, a minimum security level is required, but privacy issues are less significant.

Broadcast Videotex (Teletex)

For this new medium using TV broadcast to bring specialized information to a wide public, there is generally no privacy issue, because the information sent on the air is public by nature (weather, news, and the like).

Security devices, however, have been specifically designed to cope with the problem of granting access to the broadcast information. The decoders branched on TV antennae bear a read-only memory, able to read the signal sent on the air. This system is using the smart-card system in the pay TV ANTIOPE in France for the purpose of billing. This is a typical security device involved with teletex.

Teletex and EMS

Just like videotex, the electronic mail services (EMS) require some protection of confidential information for public service, of course, but also for private, "confidential" services. With a few exceptions, the teletex message does not require a top-secret level of security, but mail privacy is considered essential.

Cable TV

The cable systems have been a substitute for broadcast TV in some countries. The Belgian network is probably the most versatile cable network operating in a European country. Some states (Germany, France, England) are developing networks that may have interactive capacity for video communication and two-way transactions. But little or no data protection problems were raised on these programs because little service is available with interactive capacity.

The experimental interactive program developed in Ohio with the support of WARNER AMEX Co. is well described in literature. It has basically the same features as interactive videotex and should probably be analyzed on the same grounds. A consciousness of the data-protection implications of two-way cable TV is developing in the

United States, with laws enacted in several states and proposals put before the federal authorities (see, e.g., Westin 1982). All analyses presented in Europe agree that the data-protection level of cable TV shall be quite different according to whether or not full interactivity is possible on the line:

With classic one-way systems, billing information is the only data considered sensitive. This requires some level of data protection. U.S. laws relate mainly to such billing information.

With two-way interactive systems, privacy and security questions become very similar to the ones quoted above for interactive videotex. Precautions should thus be similar.

Remote Sensing

Telemonitoring of empty homes, either through a telephone line, a cable system, or a high-frequency radio, are typical applications of remote sensing requiring a top level of technical security. The same will go for medical surveillance, elderly alarm systems, and the like. Few privacy issues may lie in this technology.

Sweden gave the start in 1973 to privacy protection and has been somewhat the leader of the European doctrine. The protection of privacy and individual freedom was the only objective of the early legislations enacted n Europe, following the path marked out by Sweden. The state laws of Germany, notably the one from Hesse, the Federal Republic Statute, as well as the French national legislation are based on the same ground: a widely accepted social objective to ensure that the citizen has been effectively warned of the places in which he or she is registered on computerized files. When the records have been settled in a foreign country, a regime monitoring TBDF was established by law. Very few TBDF cases are brought up, however.

It has often been said that the "omnibus" approach of privacy is typically European. As a matter of fact, the "common core" of these legislations was designed by a small group of experts of several nations within the Council of Europe, the Organization for Economic Cooperation and Development (OECD), and European parliament.[1]

One of the noticeable distinctions between the first laws enacted and the more recent ones concerns the protection of data connected with the nonphysical person; that is, data on companies, on associations, on groups of people, whether these groups may be considered as legal entities or not.

The laws of Norway, Luxembourg, Austria, and Denmark state the same protection for legal persons as for individuals. But the

U.K. parliament considered only the protection of personal information.

In terms of principles, the physical person is entitled to privacy protection whenever mentioned by name in a register held on a computer file. On the other hand, companies and legal persons have a very different legal claim to control and be aware of the information held upon them by a third party. This should not be based on privacy, which has no meaning for a company. Commercial and legal persons may wish to specify the protection system to be granted. A protection of that kind should be based on competition, not on privacy. But this has not yet been enacted in the existing bodies of European data-protection laws.

The interaction between privacy rules and transborder data flows in Europe is thus very limited for the time being.

IMPACT OF TELECOM POLICY

The communication tariffs are based on the International Telecommunication Union (ITU) conventions, signed by most countries in the world, including European states. These conventions were stated at a time when foreign trade was much less significant than it is today. During the 1960s and the 1970s, the core of international trade regulations changed widely.

Unfortunately, no similar evolution happened in the field of communication. On the contrary, the authorities kept the original structure of tariffs perpetuating a very complicated system, with no sound economic ground (Chamoux 1980).

This regulatory system has the following consequences:

Any national carrier has a wide degree of freedom in determining the price of telecom services paid in national currency.
The final-user telephone bill has very little to do with direct cost to the carrier.
There might be a significant difference in price between tariffs at either end of a given link, which induces strange behavior for some users: "call me back" to get a lower overall cost of communications.

The European scene has begun to move. Awareness of business has become clearer,[2] and a few companies have installed telecom audit procedures. An analysis of the costs with international comparison is done in many headquarters. It has been clear, for instance, that it was cheaper to settle the European terminal of a transatlantic line in England than in Germany, because of the tariff discrepancies between these two countries.

Our book *l'information sans frontiere* (Chamoux 1980) was asking for a quick move of the French PTTs. The French PTTs have also simplified the rate structure, unifying the whole country to one zone. Forecasting and auditing telecom expenses is much easier now, as a result of new tariff structures.

New devices like encryption are supplied on those broadband links that guarantee data protection. For the time being, a new competition is underway between the British and the French PTTs. We have been asking for the emergence of deregulation in Europe since 1979, hoping that a "Mr. Laker of telecommunications" will enter the game. Competition on prices has started for the benefit of the big user. This will continue for several years (Chamoux 1980).

As useful as it may be for the large user, this competition on broadband tariffs does not benefit all transborder flow users in Europe. The smaller users and individual citizens have no real benefits from this deregulation, for the telephone remains fully controlled by national monopolies. But this is another story.

Besides tariffs, there has been no move from PTT authorities to deter the transborder flow among and from EEC member states. But it is feared that the variety of regulations and tariff structures from one country to the next slow the flow of information between member states. Taking this into account, EEC directorates are calling for a harmonization of the European telecommunications policy and practice. The impact of telecom regulation may be more significant on transborder flows than the one of privacy regulation.

NOTES

1. Taking advantage of the 1973/74 decisions of the Council of Ministers, the European convention was drafted by the Strasbourg delegates, most of them being directly involved in their national legislations.

2. This move was remarkable in the French PTT administration since 1978 and in British Telecom since late 1980.

REFERENCES

Chamoux, J.-P. 1980. Communication to OECD/ICCP Special Meeting, Paris, Sept.
Westin, A. 1982. "The New Privacy Debate." *Datamation*, July.

20

Economics of Intellectual Property Rights in the International Arena

YALE M. BRAUNSTEIN

The economic arguments for the existence of rights in intellectual property often follow the arguments for the clear definition of property rights in general. Coase (1960) has argued that market failures are often due to inadequate definition of property rights. He shows, therefore, that a clear definition of property rights can reduce the possibility of market failure and the need for government intervention. The second line of argument relies on the Schumpeterian view that the existence of patents and copyrights stimulates creative activity; this is done by enabling creators of new works and processes to receive rewards that would ordinarily by denied them because of free-rider problems inherent in the disclosure of new products and processes (Schumpeter 1950; Braunstein et al. 1977).

THE CURRENT SITUATION

Nations have adopted a variety of laws to provide for ownership of intellectual property. In the United States these laws are codified in the federal copyright (17 U.S.C., Sec. 101 et seq.) and patent (35 U.S.C., Sec. 101 et seq.) statutes and in the trade secrecy laws of the individual states. (In the United States trade secrecy is based on state statute or common law; therefore, it varies across the states; see, e.g., Bender 1977;

"Economics of Intellectual Property Rights in the International Arena" is an earlier version of the article "Economics of Intellectual Property Rights in the International Arena," Yale M. Braunstein, Journal of the American Society for Information Science. Reprinted by permission of John Wiley & Sons, Inc.

Milgram 1976.) Recent debates have focused on the appropriate form of domestic protection for computer software, data bases, and microchips. As part of its 1978 final report, the National Commission on New Technological Uses of Copyrighted Works (CONTU) compared copyright, patent, and trade secrecy as alternative protective mechanisms (see Table 20.1). The U.S. copyright statutes were amended in 1980 to make explicit the applicability of copyright to computer programs (17 U.S.C., Sec. 117), and a special law protecting the masks used to make microchips was enacted in 1985 (17 U.S.C., Sec. 914).

TABLE 20.1
Characteristics of Protective Mechanisms (United States)

General Considerations	Copyright	Patent	Trade Secrecy
National uniformity	Yes	Yes	No
Protection effective upon	Creation of work	Successful prosecution of application	Entrance into contractual relationship
Cost of obtaining protection	Nil	Moderate	Moderate
Term of protection	Life plus 50 years or 75 years	17 years	Possibility of both perpetual protection and termination at any time
Cost of maintaining protection	Nil	Nil	Significant
Cost of enforcing rights against violators	Moderate	Moderate	Higher
Availability of:			
Statutory damages	Yes	No	No
Attorneys fees from infringers	Yes	Yes	No
Protection lost by	Gross neglect	Unsuccessful litigation	Disclosure
Software Considerations			
Consistency with other copyright areas	Yes	No	No
Availability for some programs	Yes	Unclear	Yes
Universal availability	Yes	No	No
"Process" protectable	No	Yes	Yes
Suited to mass distribution	Yes	Yes	No

Source: Commission on New Technological Uses of Copyrighted Works. 1978. *Final Report.* CONTU.

Since 1980, at least eight countries have explicitly extended copyright protection to compute software. Table 20.2, adapted from Bigelow (1986) summarizes the state of legal protection of software in thirty-seven countries. But the situation remains both complex and changing. The question of whether or not the best approach is to use copyright law, patent law, or a special law clearly continues to be debated in several countries. For example, in Japan, two possibly competing approaches have been proposed. In 1983, a MITI-sponsored subcommittee recommended the adoption of a new law for the protection of software that would draw on Japanese industrial property law and patent law (MITI 1984). Shortly thereafter, a Ministry of Education subcommittee recommended revision to the copyright law to make more explicit the protection of computer software under that statute (Copyright Council 1984).

There are many bilateral and multilateral agreements whereby countries have extended protection to intellectual property created by citizens of other nations. In the copyright area, the two major multilateral agreements are the Berne Convention and the Universal Copyright Convention (UCC).[1] The Berne Convention has been in force since 1886 and was most recently revised in 1971; the UCC was negotiated in 1952 and was revised, parallel to the Berne revision, in 1971. The fundamental provisions of the two conventions convey the same protections to works created by nationals of member states as exist for works created by citizens of the home country.[2]

TABLE 20.2
Legal Protection for Computer Programs (Selected Countries)

Nation	Copyright	Patent	Trade Secrecy
Australia	yes*	unclear	yes
Brazil	some+	no	limited
Canada	yes	some	yes
France	yes*	unclear	unclear
Germany (FRG)	yes*	possibly#	yes
Hong Kong	unclear	—	—
Japan	(see text)		
Taiwan	some*	—	—
United Kingdom	yes*	some	yes
United States	yes*	some	yes

Notes:
  *Special legislation
  +Domestic preference
  #If in processes

THE ECONOMICS OF CONSISTENCY AND COOPERATIVE ACTION

There are three possible approaches relevant to the question of whether or not one might gain from establishing barriers to the use of foreign works and from establishing consistent mechanisms for property rights — the economics of international trade and customs unions, the theory of clubs, and the economics of compatibility.

Valuable insights can be drawn from each of these approaches. For example, in the international trade literature, economists have analyzed whether or not tariffs or other trade barriers are economically justified and have computed the gains and costs of bilateral and multilateral reductions in any barriers that might exist (see, e.g., Bhagwati 1964). The principal findings of interest to the intellectual property-rights issue are that protection can be economically justified if there are distortions in the domestic economy (such as economies of scale in the production of the goods being protected), and that jointly reducing tariff barriers with one or more trading partners does make the members of the union better off, but an even greater increase in welfare can be brought about by alternative actions.

With its focus on gains from joint ownership and consumption, the theory of clubs includes as a variable the degree to which ownership and consumption rights might be extended over differing numbers of individuals (Buchanan 1965). There is an optimal sharing group with more than one, but less than an infinite number, of members. Within this framework, one can both model the decision of whether to join the club or undertake consumption alone and compute the efficiency gains from group action.

In the technical compatibility literature, the user prefers to consume or sample from a "portfolio" of products or services. Braunstein and White (1985) have constructed positive models of the likely behavior of unregulated decision makers confronting the choice between producing a product that is either compatible or noncompatible with others in the marketplace. The social gains from compatibility are due to the avoidance of costly translation devices or the creation of duplicate stocks in a variety of languages or formats.

ECONOMIC MODELS

The models I develop in this section are primarily based on those in the theory of international trade, although they also draw on the theory of clubs and compatibility literature. An important assumption of each model is that imported works are not available unless there exists some mechanism for the enforcement of property rights. In other words, the possibility of one nation unilaterally declaring works produced by foreign creators to be in the public domain is assumed not to exist.

The Rights Mechanism as a Barrier to Trade

I shall start by assuming that a particular country, A, wishes to guarantee property rights to domestic creators of a new category of intellectual works, such as computer software. This is irrespective of whether the works are considered primarily creative, industrial, artistic, or whatever. The question is the extent to which the laws and institutions in A related to these rights will require creators (rights holders) in other countries to incur costs if they both wish to protect the rights to works that they have created elsewhere and wish to sell in A. Whether it is in A's interest to design its property rights mechanism (laws and institutions) to impose barriers on foreign creators will depend on the existence and nature of distortions in A's economy. This can be illustrated with a model similar to that developed by Meade (1955) to determine the optimal tariff in the presence of such distortions?

Note the following definitions:

Country A consumes three goods, X, Y, and Z. It produces X and imports Y; Z represents all other goods, which can either be produced domestically and/or imported. X and Y can be either substitutes or complements.

P_X and P_Y are the domestic prices of X and Y in A.

d_x is the rate of distortion in A in the production of X (e.g., from economies of scale, monopoly power, taxation, in the X industry).

t_y is the additional cost (as a fraction of the international price, say in country B) imposed on the consumption of Y in A because of A's rights mechanism.

Note the following: the marginal cost of X in A is $P_X / (1 + d_X)$; the marginal cost of Y in B is $P_Y / (1 + t_y)$

It can be shown that economic welfare will be maximized when the cost, t_y, of the rights mechanism satisfies the following equation:

$$t_y / (1 + t_y) = d_x / (1 + d_X) \qquad \text{(an expression with elasticities and} \qquad (1)$$

(an expression with elasticities and
cross-elasticities of demand and
the elasticity of domestic supply).

This result can be applied to three scenarios.

First Scenario

If identical software (X and Y) can be produced both in A and abroad, Equation (1) becomes:

$$t_y / (1 + t_y) = d_X / (1 + d_X) \times 1/1 + (e_d / Ge_s),\qquad(2)$$

where
  e_d is the price elasticity of demand for X and Y in A;
  e_s is the domestic elasticity of supply of X; and
  G is the proportion of total supply of X and Y satisfied by imports.

Therefore, an optimal rights mechanism would impose costs on the imported works that, on a percentage basis, were somewhat less than the relevant distortion in the domestic software industry. There are two caveats that are important in the interpretation of this result. First, the barrier must be one that adds costs to each unit of the imported good sold. If the barrier merely raises a one-time fixed cost to sell any of the product, it is simply a deadweight loss to society. Second, this is a "second-best" optimum that comes about because of the assumption that one can not correct the distortion in the domestic economy. From the point of view of maximizing economic welfare, it is often more efficient to correct this distortion by direct means such as subsidy. (Of course, domestic subsidies can have adverse foreign trade and political repercussions, but that is beyond the scope of this chapter.)

Second Scenario

If domestic software (X) and software produced abroad (Y) are less-than-perfect substitutes, again the second-best optimum occurs where there is a barrier. In percentage terms, the barrier should be less than the magnitude of the domestic distortion in X; the greater the degree of substitutability between X and Y, the higher the optimum barrier.

Third Scenario

Now let A produce hardware (X) domestically and import software (Y). Because X and Y are complements, both the cross-elasticity of demand and the expressions in parentheses in Equation (1) become negative. This leads to the optimal value of the "barrier" (t_y) being negative; i.e., country A should not only reduce the costs of foreigners protecting their software but should encourage imports by means such as subsidies.

It is worth noting at this point that the economist's concern with maximizing economic welfare may not be shared by policy makers. The results in each of the three scenarios above will change if there are other objectives. For example, if the objective is to attain a given level of domestic production of the importable good, either a trade barrier, a production subsidy, or a combination of the two can be the efficient mechanism, depending on whether there are changes in the terms of trade (Corden 1957). Similar results obtain when the objective is a specific reduction in the volume of imports (Johnson 1965).

Advantages of an International Agreement

When a nation extends property rights in certain works to foreign creators (rights holders), it can utilize one or more of the following options: unilateral action, bilateral agreements with other nations, and multilateral agreements with groups of nations. As noted above, there is widespread reliance on multilateral agreements (conventions) in the copyright and patent fields.

The following model draws on the analyses of customs unions in the trade literature: Country A trades with countries B and C, although there are barriers to trade in intellectual property due to the expense a national of one country must incur to secure property rights in the other countries. (B and C can be groups of countries.) A and B agree to a mutual reduction in barriers to works of each other's nationals, but this reduction is to be discriminatory; i.e., it does not extend to the works of C's nationals.

At first the agreement seems to make economic sense, so long as the costs of entering and enforcing the agreement are less than the gains resulting from the lowered barriers. The cooperative action of A and B will tend to divert trade such that imports from C will be, at least partially, replaced by imports from the other member(s) of the cooperative arrangement, even if the costs of production are lower in C. Secondary effects may include price reductions in the exports from C and increases in bargaining power A and B each have when negotiating future reductions in the barriers that exist in trade with C.[3]

But again the action is not first best. In fact, A and B can obtain greater increases in their economic welfare by reducing the barriers to imports in a nondiscriminatory manner than they can by granting mutual preferences to each other. If the amount of the nonpreferential reduction in barriers is designed to result in the same levels of consumption and domestic production as would result from the mutual, restrictive action, then there would not be the possible diversion of imports from low-cost producers to higher-cost members of the cooperative arrangement.

Optimal Number of Members in an International Agreement

Buchanan's result that there is a finite optimal size of a club depends on his assumptions of decreasing per-member costs with increases in the membership of the club and a concave benefit function that first increases with the size of the club and eventually decreases (Buchanan 1965). The first assumption is certainly valid in the case of a cooperative agreement reducing barriers to the exercise of rights in intellectual property, because of the relatively low marginal cost of providing additional copies of the works. But the second assumption does not hold. This can be seen by applying the logic in the case above: additional benefits accrue to each importing country from any, even nonmutual, reduction in barriers that raise the costs of obtaining works produced elsewhere. Even if the benefits to an existing member do not increase as new members join the agreement because of, say, a lack of demand for the foreign works, the benefits do not decline. Because costs will decline as the fixed component is spread over larger numbers, the optimal size is infinite.

Which Cooperative Agreement to Join

If nation A has the option of joining one or more cooperative agreements that mutually reduce barriers to the exercise of intellectual property rights, the logic above argues for A to join as many such agreements as makes sense when evaluated on an individual basis. But what if the agreements are mutually exclusive? For instance, this could arise if one agreement was patterned after copyright law and required disclosure and another was based on trade secrecy and forbade disclosure. This model combines the approaches of the technical compatibility and customs union literature.

Assume countries A, B, and C produce 50 percent, 30 percent, and 20 percent, respectively, of the world's intellectual works of a certain type (such as, software) and that there are higher barriers to trade in any direction. Country A wishes to choose between a barrier-lowering agreement with either B or C, but there are mutually exclusive mechanisms for the provision of property rights in those countries. What is the desirable course of action?

If there is specialization such that the only demand in A is for the works of just one of B or C, then A should seek a cooperative agreement on a low-barrier, possibly common, property rights mechanism with that one country, regardless of whether or not that country produces more works than the other country. But if the demand in A is for a "portfolio" of works originating from other countries (say, roughly in proportion to their output), A should seek an agreement with whichever partner for whom the product of the volume of trade times the per-unit savings from the lowered barrier is greater. As the coalition adopting a common mechanism grows, it will put increasing pressure on other countries to join the dominant coalition (Braunstein and White 1985, 345–47).

CONCLUSION

I have shown that economic models based on the international trade, theory of clubs, and technical compatibility literature can provide insights into the rationales for using property rights laws and agreements to create or reduce barriers to the use of works produced by foreigners. The principal findings are that the optimal size of these barriers depends on (1) the degree of substitutability between domestic and foreign works; (2) the degree of complementarity between intellectual works and other goods (such as computer hardware); and (3) the magnitude of any distortions in relevant parts of the domestic economy. International agreements to mutually reduce barriers to the use of foreign works can improve the welfare of the agreeing nations. Broader action of this sort, however, even if unilateral, can result in an even greater increase in welfare. I have also shown that there is no finite limit to the optimal size (in terms of number of members) of an international cooperative agreement to reduce barriers through the adoption of common property rights mechanisms. The choice of which of competing agreements a nation should join depends on the pattern of demand for imported works in that nation, the volumes of works produced by the members of the agreements, and the size of the potential reduction in any barriers. The growth of a coalition adopting a common rights mechanism can, in itself, put pressure on additional nations to join that coalition.

REFERENCES

Bender, D. 1977. "Trade Secret Software Protection." *Computer L. Ser.* 3.

Bhagwati, J. 1964. "The Pure Theory of International trade: A Survey." *Economic Journal* 74: 1–84.

Braunstein, Y. M., and L. J. White. 1985. "Setting Technical Compatibility Standards." *Antitrust Bulletin* 30: 337–56.

Braunstein, Y. M., et al. 1977. *The Economics of Property Rights as Applied to Computer Software and Data Bases.*

Buchanan, J. M. 1965. "An Economic Theory of Clubs." *Economica* (February 1965): 1–14.

Coase, R. H. 1960. "The Problem of Social Cost." *Journal of Law and Economics* 3.

Copyright Council. Sixth Subcommittee (Japan). 1984. Tokyo: Government of Japan.

Corden, W. M. 1957. "Tariffs, Subsidies and the Terms of Trade." *Economica* 24.

Johnson, H. G. 1965. "Optimal Trade Intervention in the Presence of Domestic Distortions." In *Trade, Growth, and the Balance of Payment,* edited by R. E. Baldwin.

Meade, J. E. 1955. *Trade and Welfare.*

Milgram, R. 1976. *Trade Secrets.*

MITI. Subcommittee for Improvement and Strengthening the Foundation for Software for the Industrial Structure Council Information Industry Committee. 1984. *Aiming towards Establishment of Legal Protection for Computer Software.* Tokyo: Government of Japan.

Schumpeter, J. A. 1950. *Capitalism, Socialism, and Democracy.* New York: Harper.

NOTES

1. The World Intellectual Property Organization (WIPO) is secretariat to the Berne Convention for the Protection of Literary and Artistic Property, and UNESCO is secretariat to the Universal Copyright Convention. The United States is a member of the UCC but not of the Berne Convention.

2. See, for example, Article II, Clause 1 of the UCC: "Published works of nationals of any Contracting State and works first published in that State shall enjoy in each other Contracting State the same protection as that other State accords to works of its nationals first published in its own territory."

3. The conditions under which these results obtain are discussed in Meade 1955, Ch. 32.

21

Information Technology and Legal Issues

TOSHIHIRO ARAKI

The impact of recent and anticipated advancement in information and communications technologies on the existing legal framework is an important issue. In the second Conference of TIDE 2000, the following topics were considered by the participants: privacy protection, protection of intellectual property, trade rules, unfair trade practices and monopoly, and computer crime and security.

PROTECTION OF PRIVACY

On the protection of privacy, intensive work has been done by the Organization for Economic Cooperation and Development (OECD). A model code, of a nonbinding nature, was drawn up by a working group chaired by Justice Kirby in 1983. Most of the OECD countries have since adopted their own privacy protection legislation. Periodic review of progress in OECD countries has been conducted by the same organization, because protection of privacy is important not only for the protection of the individual's basic human rights, but also for the free flow of technology and information. If uniform legislation is not possible, then at least a harmonized regime is desirable.

PROTECTION OF INTELLECTUAL PROPERTY

Information and communication technologies have changed industrial protection to a great extent. Newly emerging industry and already developed industry with new production and distribution systems are in need of a new legal framework to ensure appropriate returns on their research and development costs. Protection of intellectual property becomes an issue of urgent importance. The intellectual property issue is not only limited to information technology, but to the entire structure of technological change. The obvious concentration of technological changes in this sector, however, makes the information sector the leading promoter for new legislation.

Involved in the discussions are industrial property (which is chiefly known as patent, trademark, and so on), as well as copyright. The patent system is not the main concern for policy makers, at least for the moment, although the protection of the knowledge accumulated by an employee of a high-tech company could become a center of concern.

This issue is known as the protection of trade secrets. The difference in approach to trade secrets between the United States, Europe, and Japan might cause a major problem in the near future. The European and Japanese approach to the issue is to apply laws covering unfair competition, whereas several states in the United States have legislated specific trade-secrets laws. As software assumes crucial importance in industry, trade secrets protection will become a central issue.

Another issue is protection of computer software. Most of the OECD countries have adopted the copyright-protection method. Several newly industrialized countries (NICs) have also done the same. With the growing concern for the protection of software, and several issues such as idea/expression dichotomy (scope of protection), protection criterion, and protection period, and with the differences of national legislation, copyright protection has become a preferred idea in the majority of countries.

TRADE RULES

Information is a peculiar commodity distinguished from other economic commodities. Information is inexpensive to copy and its value difficult to measure. Given these characteristics, the increase in the trade in information or information-related goods would increase the concern of the information industry about the protection of their proprietary rights over their information products. Recent lawsuits between computer giants in the United States and Japan over rights on computer software and reported settlement fee after mediation is one particular example. Small software houses in Taiwan, Italy, and some Latin American countries are causing serious concern to the U.S. software producers. In each case, the money involved would exceed a billion dollars.

New trade rules are under consideration within the framework of the Uruguay Round of the General Agreement on Tariffs and Trade (GATT) negotiations. The GATT has started its approach to the intellectual property issues after the Tokyo Round was initiated in the field of trade in counterfeit goods. The modern rationale for the GATT compatibility to the issue should be found in the trade-restrictive aspects of the intellectual property rights and the consequent hindrance to market access.

When the Paris Convention on the protection of intellectual property was negotiated and put into effect about a century ago, no one realized that there would be a North-South problem. Despite the efforts of member countries, the World Intellectual Property Organization (WIPO), the administration of the convention, has been incapable of unifying member countries' legislation. Some argue that industrial promotion should be the utmost goal of intellectual property-rights protection, whereas others take inventors' protection as the task of the system. Whichever is most important, it is a fact that WIPO has been sterile in its mediatory role function.

To solve the immediate problems of trade, GATT is best suited, as it can provide dispute-settlement procedures. Unification of national laws could be continued in WIPO, but GATT must be able to solve trade disputes. Although it is difficult to predict the negotiations of the Uruguay Round, certain conditions for contracting parties to observe and procedures to be followed for dispute settlement could be the core of the possible agreement.

An existing draft of the counterfeit code should also be worked out, but it is not necessary that the new code should include anticounterfeit and antipirate-trade clauses. The anticounterfeit code is an agreement of the border and domestic law enforcement, whereas an intellectual property code would not be able to restrict itself to law enforcement.

UNFAIR TRADE PRACTICE AND UNFAIR COMPETITION

During the Industrial Revolution, the industrial property rights system served to promote industrial research and development, as well as industrial application of new technology. The question to be addressed is the appropriate balance between the rights of the inventor and the industrial application at large. Industrial property rights, namely patents, were made public in return for the right of the inventor to exclusively use that innovation.

Protection of computer software by copyright law or any other special legislation similar to copyright must be reviewed at some point of technological development from the point of view that the protection should never function in the degressive way in terms of technological development. The recent trend to protect software-related ideas as trade secrets might go too far if it is legally adopted by the majority of nations, because trade secrets can never be defined in the way the legal system requires to protect all the people's rights.

Another problem is the necessity to strengthen unfair competition legislation and enforcement. It is often the case that traditional criminal law cannot be applied in a straightforward manner, as can be the traditional concept of the theft or embezzlement. Unfair competition legislation could therefore solve the gap between the shortfalls of existing criminal law and rapidly advancing technology.

COMPUTER CRIME AND SECURITY

The more our society is integrated into an information network, the more the role of the computer increases. There have been cases in which accident to or malfunction of a telephone exchange caused serious damage to economic and social activities. Physical protection of the computer systems is also an urgent issue for society.

A more serious problem is the protection of computer systems from terrorism and crime. Computer hacking has been increasing, not only in the United States but also in Europe and Japan. Transborder hacking is also seen not only on the North American continent but also between Europe and Japan. In the traditional sense, crime can be committed in a given place, but with information technology crime can be committed from a remote place, accelerating the problems of crime prevention and legal jurisdiction. These problems are perceived vaguely as assault or kidnapping, but the consequence of the computer crime could be far wider.

V

SOCIOCULTURAL ISSUES RELATED TO INFORMATION TECHNOLOGY

22

Impact of Information Technology on Education, Training, and Employment in European OECD Countries

Walther Richter

The introduction of any new technology requires a period of adaptation and then results in some new socioeconomic equilibrium. The adaptation period is the time during which some or all of the old technology is phased out, new skills are acquired to master the new technology, and socioeconomic changes take place in the course of which a relocation of production facilities may occur, efficiency may improve, employment patterns may change, and so forth.

Consideration of the societal impact of information technology (IT) thus requires a twofold approach: first, what are the effects of the necessary adaptation to IT, and second, what will be the resulting socioeconomic equilibrium? The two questions are not independent, but are distinct enough to merit separate consideration.

HISTORIC ENVIRONMENT

Telecommunications in some archaic form was probably applied very early in the development of mankind. The earliest example from a European Organization for Economic Cooperation and Development (OECD) country would seem to be Greek and Roman signal fires (Morgan 1986) and, about a millenium later, the construction of castle towers on the rim of the Alps in Austria, overlooking the Hungarian lowlands, so that an observer on one tower could see signs given from a neighboring tower.

Our environment changes — we do not speak Latin in Europe any more — but basic human behavior has hardly, if at all, changed since early historic times. Olympic games attract, relatively, as many spectators today as more than 2,000 years ago, just to give one example. If one acknowledges the behavioral steadiness of mankind as described in connection with society by Tepperman (1985), it is well worth looking back in history to learn from the effects of impacts of technologies similar to the impacts of IT that we are now experiencing.

INFORMATION TECHNOLOGY AND EDUCATION

Education at school has meant an education for a stable life, based on a firm, well-established knowledge base, for hundreds of years. Latin, literature, mathematics, history, and so on formed the basis. The lifestyle, which forged this educational pattern and for which it was a prerequisite, was determined by heavy reliance on traditional values, slow changes in production processes, very limited travel, and little trade beyond the national boundaries. Why learn foreign languages? Why bother about changes? Moreover, political changes were numerous, and more changes would have been hard to bear.

Another factor in the Federal Republic of Germany and Austria which contributes to this profound attitude toward stability in life, contrary to the United States, was a relatively early fabric of social and economic security. Government employees were assured of jobs for a lifetime; large families, which had lived for quite some time in the same area, supported their members; the church did its part; and social security was the great achievement of the early union movements. The need to fight for one's economic well-being with the threat of going down the drain otherwise was not as strong as across the Atlantic, where entrepreneurship and innovation is clearly more necessary to survive.

But, the basics of the educational system had not changed, despite all political changes, despite the wars, despite the boom of international trade and other cross-frontier relations. The social changes within society provoked thinking, whether or not the existing schools were still adequate for their time.

The new technologies (and IT is in the forefront of them) have changed society and continue to do so. This urgently requires an education that prepares for those changes, both in technology and in society. Today's requirement for many involved in economic processes, and in particular for young people entering a professional career, are personal stability, willingness to take responsibilities and risks, open mindedness, and faith in one's future. People today must realize and accept the facts that they are involved in a dynamic process and that there will continually be new challenges to be accepted. We need people with initiative, engagement, and an active attitude toward life.

It can be said that IT necessitates a fundamental change in the principles behind the educational system, at least in the Federal Republic of Germany and Austria. The former, very traditional approach, as well as recent trends to put more weight on the development of a child's individual characteristics, proved inadequate for the needs of the information society. Not all, but some, of the youth unemployment problems can be attributed to this fact.

THE ROLE OF IT IN THE PROCESS OF EDUCATION

Children in industrialized countries learn early that to run a car one needs petrol, a battery to start it, a steering wheel, traffic rules, and so on. Computers are not yet as widely used as cars, but they are on the way to it, and so the politicians in charge of setting up the school curricula thought it justified to teach "Informatics" at school. As this is quite a special field when considering education, it is mostly voluntary in general schools and compulsory only in engineering and business administration establishments. The purpose of teaching is to familiarize the children with the new tool, the computer, and to teach them its usefulness and limitations in its various applications. The Minister for Education and Science of the Federal Republic of Germany states this in the following way: "This is the task of education policy of our time: We must enable the people to recognize the available new possibilities and to make responsible use of them" (Wilms 1986).

Computers, or rather the way they are used, offer a truly new method to train the intellectual capability of youngsters. Only those who know programming themselves can appreciate from their own experience how mind forming it is to learn to describe and write down a simple process, say how to look up a word in a dictionary, such that it could be performed by a computer. Each process, as simple as it may seem, has to be first divided into its most simple elements. These are then put together in a structured, logical way.

IT AND PROFESSIONAL TRAINING

The breathtaking pace with which IT develops makes one thing obvious: Anybody dealing with it has to develop his or her knowledge accordingly, otherwise he or she is outdated and threatened in his professional career.

Looking at the influence of IT on the composition of jobs within an economy, one realizes that primarily the contents of production and clerical jobs are affected. New requirements widen the scope of the work, calling for ever greater flexibility. Second, traditional occupations (e.g., mechanics or sales) do find entirely new areas of work, such as the maintenance of robots or sales of text processors. In these cases, the type of work stays more or less the same — there is little basic difference in repairing a clock or a robot or selling cars or computers, except the field in which one is active. Only a relatively small group of jobs is really new, mainly those in data processing proper.

People need not, therefore, be afraid of having to learn a new profession every five years or so. A few may decide to switch — hopefully for a lasting career — to one of the new jobs, again another few may require retraining (Sullivan 1985), but the overwhelming majority of jobs will need a widening of their job content in the direction of a higher degree of understanding, oversight, and responsibility, best perhaps summarized as "more competence." That the information professional will need lifelong continuing education is true because the information-handling tools have developed dramatically during the last thirty years, and there is no sign that this development has come to a standstill. Actually, quite a large percentage of people who are engaged in economic activities need a continuous expansion of their competence to be able to absorb the development of IT and the change of the work content that IT brings with it. The German daily *Frankfurter Allgemeine* reported in this context on February 4, 1986, that a meeting of European trade unions had requested appropriate training programs for the members so that they could acquire the necessary qualifications.

A joint project organized by the German authorities and Siemens A.G. (the largest German manufacturer of electrical and electronic products), tries to teach unemployed persons, especially from the teaching profession, some skills so that they can be gainfully employed (Schlitzberger 1986). The majority of them are trained in communication and data processing technologies. The success rate so far is promising enough to allow one to forecast a continuation and extension of this project.

Apprenticeship proved to be valuable because it provided the economy with badly needed skilled labor. It will continue, however, to attract capable and qualified young people if they can be assured of continuing training during their professional lives and, as a result, some prospects for a career. IT will be a major area in which professional training will be required and offered, and thus will continue to attract, and challenge, a continuously better-qualified work force for an improved output and higher efficiency.

Economic theory, from whatever school it emanates, tells us that microeconomic studies are interesting and do have their place but that they are not up to the complexity of the economic reality, with all its linkages and feedback mechanisms. Thus, studying the macroeconomic effects and trends is indispensable if one wants to come to some deeper understanding. Different schools of economic thought do have distinct opinions about this subject, however.

Ricardo (1821), a classical economist, wrote that the economy does not immediately adjust to the introduction of new machinery and that structural problems arise during and after the shift from a primarily labor- to a capital-intensive way of production.

Neoclassical thought did not regard the structural problems during transition as very stringent. It was assumed that the adjustment would cause less severe problems, if only the prices were flexible enough.

Keynes did not write about the effects of innovation on employment. Unemployment would result if there was insufficient investment — but Keynes did not investigate whether underinvestment in traditional or innovative sectors had different effects.

Schumpeter (1939) and other structuralists saw it again differently. Introduction of new technology was regarded as the engine of economic advance. Whereas, previously, one had agreed that innovation was more or less a byproduct of growth, the structuralists introduced a causality into this relationship.

No one seems to question the importance of structural adaptation to innovative technology, but because it is difficult to describe the effects of these changes, not all studies agree on them, nor on the optimal methodology for studying the adaptation process.

CAPITAL NEEDS FOR IT INVESTMENTS: AN EMPLOYMENT BOTTLENECK?

Information technology does not come free of charge, obviously. It is said, as an example from R&D, that the development of one of the modern, large, digital telephone exchanges costs on the order of one billion US$. Robots, office computers, and other equipment are not cheap for those who need them. Does this pose a problem for employment?

IT equipment represents a relatively high investment, allowing then a higher productivity, or equivalently, a lower production cost per unit. The alternative to investing in IT is not to invest in it; that is, to save the initial outlay at the expense of higher relative production costs later on. A simple discount analysis would show when the financial break-even point is reached; that is, when it is uneconomical not to have invested and when jobs are threatened due to diminishing competitiveness.

This is no secret and is well understood in the business world. The optimal approach would be to invest in IT (like any other technology), when the expected rate of return is a maximum. But this requires a lot of capital, often more than is available. In such cases it may very well become true that due to lack of investment in IT jobs are jeopardized in the long run. To the author's knowledge, this concern was first analyzed in detail at the University of Sussex at the TEMPO project (1980–1984).

REFERENCES AND BIBLIOGRAPHY

Eliasson, G. 1982. *Electronics, Economic Growth and Employment — Revolution or Evolution.* Booklet No. 131. Geneva: IUI.

Freeman, C., and L. Soete. 1985. "Information Technology & Employment, an Assessment." Unpublished document. University of Sussex.

Morgan, P. F. A. 1986. "Highlight in the History of Telecommunications." *Telecommunications Journal* 53 (3): 138–48.

Pastre, O. 1984. "L'information et l'Emploi." In *Editions la Découverte,* 2d ed. Paris.

Ricardo, D. 1821. "Principals of Political Economy and Taxation" (3rd ed.). *The Works and Correspondence of David Ricardo,* edited by P. Saffra. Vol. 1. Cambridge: Cambridge University Press.

Schlitzberger, Hans. 1986. "Neue Technologien und ihre Auswirkungen im Unternehmen und in der Gesellschaft." *Informationen/Argumente* (Siemens) 20.

Schumpeter, J. 1939. *Business Cycles: A Theoretical, Historical and Statistical Analysis of the Capitalist Process.* 1st ed. New York: McGraw-Hill.

Segal Horn, Susan. 1985. "The Human Implications of New Technology." *Management Services* (United Kingdom) 29 (11): 9–12.

Sullivan, B. C. 1985. "Economics of Information Technology." *International Journal of Social Economics* (United Kingdom) 12 (1): 37–53.

Tepperman, Lorne. 1985. "Informatics and Society: Will There be an 'Information Revolution'?" *Journal of Business Ethics* (Netherlands) 4 (5): 395–99.

Tonn, Bruce E. 1985. "Information Technology and Society." *Information Society* 3: 241–46.

Wilms, Dorothee. 1986. "Was uns bewegt." *IBM Nachrichten* 36: 281.

Wilson, R., and J. Whitley. 1982. "Quantifying the Employment Effects of Microelectronics." *Future* 14 (6): 357–75.

23

Information Technology from Social Impact to Social Input: A European Perspective

GÉRARD POGOREL

In a long-term perspective, debates related to information technologies have followed those conducted in the 1970s about the "limits to growth." They have proposed answers to the search for energy — and commodity-saving activities.

The first hopes, however, derived from these providential newcomers have been moderated by the deteriorating employment situation. The dramatic increase in unemployment in Europe in this period has provoked short-sighted, conservative reactions and has very often delayed the introduction of new technologies. As a consequence, innovation in processes, as opposed to product innovation, has prevailed on a very large scale. As a matter of fact, the first category of innovation is an immediate condition for the survival of companies exposed to international competition. But for employment to catch up with the evolution of the labor force, for jobs to be created, new products and new services have to be imagined.

The social concerns are exacerbated by the feeling of a decline in the role of Europe in the world economy. In the electronics industry (Electronics International Corporation 1986), Europe accounted for 26 percent of world production in 1980 and only 21 percent in 1985. The United States has maintained its position (46 percent in 1980, 47 percent in 1985), and Japan has gained 5 points of market share (from 15 percent in 1980 to 21 percent in 1985). Europe's trade deficit with Japan has increased from 3.9 billion dollars in 1979 to 8.5 in 1984, and with the United States it nearly doubled from 5.6 billion dollars to 10.8 during the same period. Europe imports 29 percent of the electronic goods it consumes (the United States 20 percent and Japan 9 percent).

Imports of Japanese products in Europe mainly consist of TV sets, VCRs, and other consumption goods, whereas the flow of computers from the United States is twice larger. In fact, the main technological and financial gap for Europe is not with Japan but with the United States. U.S. companies account for 75 percent of computer production, and IBM alone for 43 percent. Europe has failed in designing at an early stage a properly cooperative policy in the field of electronics as it has done in the aerospace and defense industries.

CHANGING CONCERNS WITH IT

To achieve the necessary change in perspective, the effects of information technology (IT) should not be thought of any more as an outside transformation of existing activities. The major in-depth effects are still ahead: during the last decade issues pertaining to new information and communication technologies have been addressed mainly from an industrial viewpoint. The prevailing approach has been the analysis of innovations and their diffusion; experience curves showed the exponential increase in performance and decrease in costs. The emphasis was on the impact on productivity in industry and services, on equipment goods, and in a period of economic crisis; the debate focused mainly on quantitative, employment-related issues. Shifting away from the exclusive search of cost reductions, the coming of the information age still requires an intensive effort. Technological breakthroughs will have to be mobilized to overcome the limits to growth of the manufacture-based economy. For initial, massive investments to be recouped, the pace of diffusion of "new technologies," the pervasiveness of the market was essential. That is why in their early stage of development new products feature only few really new functions. A stage has now been attained in which computers are present in all companies, from medium and small to large ones. But information stocks and flows are still highly underutilized. IBM-France, for instance, estimates that 90 percent of its operational system (production and marketing) is now computerized, but only 25 percent of its management system and a very minimal part of its decision system. For intercompany operations, a longer way has still to be made, the rule nearly systematically being a double processing on both sides for each transaction. The tendency now is to provide all employees with microcomputers or workstations and to let them communicate and gain access to company data organized in data banks.

Communication has long been associated with consumption. We know that the medium is the message, but the message was one way. But now communication is becoming explicitly interactive. Consumer choices are conveyed deep into the production process, at the earliest stage of product design, and into the manufacturing process, orders being immediately transmitted and executed. The limit between production and distribution is blurring and the ultimate horizon is their full integration. Home terminals are partaking in this evolution. We get closer to what Roland Barthes once called the "Empire of signs": communication is everywhere, as in a theater where everyone plays his role. No surprise, the empire Barthes was referring to was Japan. In this context, new entrants get involved and traditional producers and distributors have to improve their skill. Competition is growing between old and new, specialized and multipurpose, uni- and multimedia networks.

CHALLENGES TO THE SOCIAL AND ECONOMIC BALANCE

Ultra-large-scale integration (ULSI), artificial intelligence (AI), and computer-aided intelligence (CAI) all combined will make our dreams come true. What do we dream of? As Groucho Marx once said: We have answers, but what are the questions?

The European continent has not yet built an open, united information space, and it is now engaging in an effort to cooperate in mastering information technology. The political and economic aspects of this effort (ESPRIT, RACE, EUREKA) are well known. Let me stress some of the cultural ones.

Oddly enough, despite the establishment of the Common Market, the basic trend in the latest years has been toward more scattered European countries. Reactions provoked by fears of cultural and industrial dominance by foreign countries had been purely national. The way the first wave of information technologies had been implemented has even contributed to it. Governments had seen television programs and standards, as well as telecommunications policies, from a purely national viewpoint. They have seen the interconnection of technologies and networks as an opportunity to enhance national control on information systems. In Europe, standards, languages, educational systems, and markets have to be made closer, but governments are still choosing divergent regulation paths — in telecommunications, for instance. It is essential, however, that a global information market should be built, not only because industry needs economies of scale, but because its scope can no more be restricted to national borders. National IT innovations have to be stimulated by international competition. In the field of IT, an open European space means: designing a common legal framework for information goods, concerning copyright of telecommunications; and setting common standards, not only for network interconnection, softwares, electronic components, and computers.

But the harder side concerns the practical process of market unification. Very specific national cultural patterns maintain the scattered markets. Cultures travel in sometimes very curious manners, defying political wills. Good examples can be found in movies and TV programs. They show that the internationalization of this type of information is proceeding along patterns of cultural pervasiveness, highly indifferent to political orientations.

Educational institutions are summoned to train not only people with a skill corresponding to specific needs in the industry, but also to develop entrepreneurial qualifications. In fact, the economics of education had their heyday in the 1960s. A period of heavy doubt has followed. This is a paradox, however, because knowledge is evidently the basis for the development of all activities, and its transmission is essential. We cannot but put the question: Is our present educational system up to this challenge? Steps have been taken in European countries to introduce information technology in schools, colleges, and high schools. But a lot more has still to be done. Education is very costly, but the educational system is a major factor of international competitive advantage. The effort concerning the psychology of learning, training, and pedagogical methods should be renewed in order to achieve higher productivity and efficiency. What would be the nature, the cost, of an education deriving all potential benefits not only from fake interactive programs, but from all the existing tools of computer-aided transmission of knowledge, and computer-aided intelligence. This will imply, too, new insights into the relationships between natural intelligence and artificial intelligence.

This implies also a new attitude toward knowledge and its scattered fields. It has only recently been understood that the development of information technology involved not only some branches of mathematics and applied research, but also linguistics and physics, logics and neurosciences, psychology and cognitive sciences. The division between basic and applied research is no longer valid but it has been prevalent too long.

IMPACT ON INTERNATIONAL AWARENESS

Do people in various countries feel a stronger solidarity when they read the same news, watch the same TV programs, share common interests in art and literature, and share ideas in international conferences? We would have liked to say, definitely yes! But shouldn't we be a bit conservative? We should be aware of two points.

First, even when and where people are made closer by partaking in common economic systems, including information systems, traditional solidarity bonds not only retain their strength, but even give shape to networks and technologies themselves. The fundamentals of living and living conditions are not changed, only their surfaces.

Second, a failure has to be recognized in international efforts regarding developing countries. Despite the heavy bias in the new international information order debate, fears of a growing gap in the use of information technology have to be considered seriously. If developing nations feel they are not included in the scope of international economic development, fractures will be open to serious conflicts.

SOCIAL SCIENCES AND THE FUTURE OF IT

Social sciences provide two major interpretations of the present phenomena. The analytico-Frankfurtian synthesis results from a junction of the British-U.S. analytical tradition and of the Frankfurt school. Its most famous exponent is Jurgen Habermas (1985b). He welcomes the increase in information made available and in communications as a positive factor in the history of mankind. New information and communication technologies are considered a great help to "modernization" in Max Weber's sense, in that they substitute equal relations between human beings for traditional, authoritarian ones.

A first danger is seen, however, in the growing autonomy of bureaucracies and the uncontrolled marketplace that tend to colonize the real world that they come from. A second danger, closely linked to the first, is the loss of the mythical/religious basis of social bonds, which modern, economic relations cannot fully replace. The latter are, however, the only rational basis for the establishment of acceptable social bonds. Endeavors to refer nostalgically to ideologies that have lost their ground and are no more acceptable by the largest part of the society are dangerous reactions. A common language, which involves communication, is called for to substitute the lost authority of myths. The principles of knowledge and social interactions can no more be imposed from above. They can and they should be defined through enlightened debates. Democracy in its essence sticks to rationality, and this is the condition for the freedom and autonomy of the individual.

The postmodern movement questions the possibility of qualifying the sense and direction of the movement of the society, the existence of a "great, continuous tale," and thus the significance of "modernization" itself. It emphasizes the weakening of the moral basis and even the loss in legitimacy of socialization systems, provoked by the melting of morals and ideologies. It stresses the necessary enlarging of innovation and creation processes to larger sectors of the national and international society, to prevent the development of dangerous and uncontrollable movements. The highest attention should be devoted to a large access to information, including electronic access, in order to avoid exclusions from information channels and networks.

This difference in emphasis leads us to put the following questions:

Shall we, as individuals and as a world society, be able to imagine a project large enough to take advantage of all the possibilities offered by information technologies? The empire of signs is now so largely open to our imaginations that we can hardly fill it. Shall we always rely on massive, government- (and mainly defense-) oriented, programs to launch initiatives and give impetus to our minds?

Will moral progress keep pace with our technological knowledge and capabilities?

Will we be able to elaborate a legal framework up to the necessary international level?

Shall we open the field for initiatives and entrepreneurship, and manage at the same time to keep in mind and in fact the necessary solidarity inside national societies and, internationally, between them?

REFERENCES AND BIBLIOGRAPHY

Centre de Prospective et d'Evaluation. 1985. "Innovations technologiques, innovations sociales." *Actes du Colloque,* Paris, May.

Commission des Communauteés Européenes. 1985. Communication de la Commission au Conseil et au Parlement relative à l'évaluation des premiers résultats d u programme ESPRIT. COM (85) 616 final. Brussels: Council of Europe.

Dawson, J. A. 1983. "Information Technology and its Effect on the Distribution Trades." University of Sterling (United Kingdom), Dept. of Business Studies, Working paper 8301.

Electronics International Corporation. 1986. "L'électronique dans le monde."

Ergas, H. 1986. "Technology Policy and Industrial Structure in Seven OECD Countries." Paper presented at the National Academy of Engineering of the United States, Washington, D.C., February.

Fondation Européenne pour l'Amélioration des Conditions de Vie et de Travail (FEACVT). 1985. "Nieuwe technologien in Supermarketen, rapport de synthèse."

Fondation Travail-Université. Les effets structurants de la télématique sur les industries. 1986. FTU-FAST/COM 52, Bruxelles, February.

Forrester, T. 1985. *The Information Technology Revolution.* Oxford: Basil Blackwell.

Giannini, C. 1985. *L'offerta di lavoro in Italia? Tendenze recentie e previsioni per il periodo 1984–1993.* Roma, Servizio Studi della Banca d'Italia.

Habermas, J. 1985a. *Der Philosophische Diskurs der Moderne.* Frankfurt: Suhrkamp Verlag.

Habermas, J. 1985b. *Theorie des Kommunikativen Handels.* Frankfurt: Suhrkamp Verlag.

Lyotard, J. F. 1979. *La condition post-moderne.* Paris: Minuit.

Lyotard, J. F. 1984. *Tombeau de l'intellectuel et autres papiers.* Paris: Galilée.

OECD. 1981. Les activités de l'information, de l'électronique et de technologies des télécommunications-Incidences sur l'emploi, la croissance et le commerce.

Pogorel, G. 1985. "Les échanges Européens: la dégradation." In *L'Europe et les technologies,* edited by F. de Lavergne and G. Pogorel. Paris: CESTA.

Wellmer, A. 1985. *Zur Dialektik von Moderne und Postmoderne.* Frankfurt: Suhrkamp Verlag.

24

Information Society and Democratic Prospects

Majid Tehranian

THE PROBLEM OF INFORMATION SOCIETY

The explosion of a great diversity of information technologies and their diffusion around the world during the past two decades have given rise to hopes for accelerating global development and democratization. What some liberal theorists have considered the dawn of a new postindustrial, information society, however, Marxist theorists have generally viewed as the increasing commoditization and privatization of information in the worldwide expansion of monopoly capitalism. By contrast, a third and emerging school of thought, called here "communitarian," considers the same processes as an example of the dual effects of information technologies — the harbinger of new possibilities for increasing levels of participatory democracy as well as new possible threats to individual freedom, social and information equality, and cultural autonomy and identity.

The liberal theorists have taken their cue largely from a tradition of research focusing on the technologically propelled changes of social structure. The transition from natural sources of energy (muscle power, wind, and water) to the steam engine and internal combustion clearly marks the beginnings of the First Industrial Revolution. The liberal theorists have considered the new information society as the

This chapter is drawn from the author's forthcoming book, *Technologies of Power: Information Technologies and Democratic Prospects.* The author is grateful to UNESCO and the Social Science Research Institute of the University of Hawaii for their support of this project.

harbinger of a Second Industrial Revolution, characterized by the application of information technologies to production, distribution, and consumption processes, thereby transforming the old industrial social and economic structures, eliminating the need for routine and repetitive jobs, providing greater opportunities for leisure and cultural creativity, and breaking down sociocultural differences and inequalities. Others in the liberal school of thought are urging the developing countries, which missed out on the First Industrial Revolution, to make efforts to bridge the widening gap between themselves and the more technologically advanced by leapfrogging, in order to take part in this Second Industrial Revolution.

The literature of the information society is vast and expanding, but the origins of the concept date back to Colin Clarke's celebrated analysis (Clarke 1940) that, due to sectoral differences in productivity and the increasing demand for social services (health, education, recreation, consulting, and so forth), the labor force in the industrial societies will move increasingly from manufacturing to service sectors. This observation has been borne out by the historic trends, elaborated upon later by Fritz Machlup (1962; 1980–84), Daniel Bell (1973) and Marc Porat (1977). Although Machlup has focused on the production and distribution of knowledge as a key to the understanding of the new economic structures and processes, Bell and Porat provide a broader historic view to suggest a new stage theory of development, a movement from agrarian to industrial and information societies. These transitions are analyzed particularly in terms of the U.S. economy, wherein massive statistical evidence suggests a clear shift from predominantly agricultural to manufacturing, service, and information occupations and employment (see Table 24.1 and Figure 24.1). To quote Porat, "In Stage I (1860–1906), the largest group in the labor force was agricultural. By the turn of the century, industrial occupations began to grow rapidly, and became predominant during Stage II (1906–1954). In the current period, Stage III, information occupations comprise the largest group" (Porat 1978, 7).

Although the historic evidence offered can be challenged on statistical grounds, depending on how we define *information*, some more recent analyses of contemporary trends by Jonscher (1984) and others suggest that we may be witnessing a reversal or at least a stabilization of the shift toward service and information industries. Nevertheless, the scientific theories of the information society have given rise to a more popular version serving as a new ideology for unabetted capitalist growth. Alvin Toffler (1970, 1980) and John Naisbitt (1982) have provided perhaps the most imaginative and far reaching of such popular visions of "information society,"

TABLE 24.1
Typology of Information Workers and 1967 Compensation*

	Employee Compensation ($ Millions)
Markets for information	
Knowledge producers	46,964
Scientific and technical workers	18,777
Private information services	28,187
Knowledge distributors	28,265
Educators	23,680
Public information disseminators	1,264
Communication workers	3,321
Information in markets	
Market search and coordination specialists	93,370
Information gatherers	6,132
Search and coordination specialists	28,252
Planning and control workers	58,986
Information processors	61,340
Nonelectronic based	34,317
Electronic based	27,023
Information infrastructure	
Information machine workers	13,167
Nonelectronic machine operators	4,219
Electronic machine operators	3,660
Telecommunication workers	5,288
Total information	243,106
Total employee compensation	454,259
Information as percentage of total	52.52%

*Based on 440 occupational types in 201 industries. Employee compensation includes wages and salaries and supplements.

Source: Computed using BLS occupation by industry matrix and census of population average wages. See Porat.

focusing particularly on the democratizing effects of the new information technologies. While Toffler is profoundly ambivalent about the prospects such a society might hold for democracy and human happiness, Naisbitt is enthusiastic. The corporate world of telecommunication and computer industries have, in turn, found some of these concepts congenial to their own interests and views.

FIGURE 24.1 — Four Sector Aggregation of the U.S. Work Force by Percent, 1860–1980

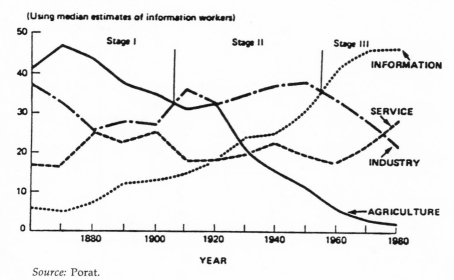

(Using median estimates of information workers)

Source: Porat.

By contrast to the liberal theorists, the Marxist critics of the information society and its corporate futurologists have generally pointed to the rising tide of dualism at national and global levels, creating islands of riches and information abundance in a global ocean of poverty and information scarcity (Schiller 1981, 1985; Mosco 1982; Smythe 1985; Hamelink 1983). They have suggested that the new technologies have generally widened the existing gaps, mainly through the privatization, concentration, and exploitation of information resources by the transnational corporations (TNCs). To avoid increasing dependence and vulnerability, they have argued, the developing world is well advised to pursue a strategy of dissociation, national self-sufficiency, and collective self-reliance.

The two schools clearly represent the increasing stratification of the world into centers and peripheries of wealth, power, and information. But the communication technologies that have contributed to this stratification have also created a global interdependence whose future depends vitally on cooperation rather than confrontation. Furthermore, international trade and cooperation in the field of information — perhaps more than any other field — depends on a clear understanding of the nature of this unique resource and its role in the historic transformations of our own era. The following critical questions might be therefore well worth considering:

Does the increasing abundance of information also mean increasing levels of *data* (relevant information), *knowledge* (interpreted data), and *wisdom* (contextualized knowledge)?

Or, conversely, is the explosion in the sources and varieties of information leading to information overload, future shock, and intellectual confusion?

Are the technological and socioeconomic advances of the information age creating greater information equality or information gaps and dualisms between the information rich and poor?

Does the phenomenal growth in channel capacity, brought about by the introduction of cable television, direct satellite broadcasting, teletex, videotext, and fiber optics, imply greater political freedom and participation, cultural pluralism, and enrichment, or centralization, political surveillance, cultural domination, and impoverishment?

Are the processes of automation, implied by the application of robotics and computer-assisted design and manufacturing (CAD-CAM), leading to greater leisure and cultural creativity or increasing levels of structural unemployment and waste of human resources?

Will the worldwide extension of the new technologies lead to the diffusion of a universal, modern, scientific, and technological civilization, or cultural backlash against the onslaught of modernization?

A more balanced view of the possible impact of information technologies on society should perhaps begin with a critique of the concept of the "information society" itself.

To proclaim the dawn of a new "information society" as the unique hallmark of our own age, as some theorists and publicists have, is to confuse information with the commoditization of information. In advanced capitalist societies, information has been increasingly commoditized to provide an expanding infrastructure of on-line information networks and transborder news, data, and currency flows for a new international division of labor. Such peripheries as the southern states in the United States and the new industrializing countries have experienced rapid rates of growth because of this. Their textile, steel, and automobile industries have shown considerable expansion in exports during the last two decades. In the meantime, the sunrise industries (including telecommunication, computer, aerospace, and weapons industries) and the services associated with them (investment banking, value-added networks, electronic publishing, and so forth) have shown remarkable growth in the advanced capitalist countries at the expense of the manufacturing activities.

Figure 24.1 bears out this argument rather dramatically in the case of the United States. U.S. manufacturing takes a downward turn in 1945, precisely at the moment that the United States assumes the role of a dominant superpower in world affairs. Subsequent to that, U.S. manufacturing industries had begun to invest massively abroad wherever economic conditions proved favorable (for example, lower land, labor, and residential costs) and political conditions more secure (in allied or client states). A commensurate rise in the services and information sectors during the same period suggests not only a rise of demand for these activities (as Colin Clarke predicted) but also the transformation of the United States from an exporter of mainly manufactured goods to an exporter of banking, insurance, shipping, high-technology, and information services.

In the United States, where productive possibilities typically run ahead of increases in consumer purchasing power, this necessitates ever-expanding marketing, advertising, and promotional activities to induce demand. The U.S. system of adjudication of social conflict through litigation has also necessitated a complex legal system and a huge legal establishment to operate it. By contrast, in Japan, where production and exports are far more important than domestic sales and where conflict is often adjudicated through the informal processes of interpersonal mediation, the relevant "information" professions are largely unnecessary to the operations of the industrial system.

The situation in the less-developed countries is even more confounded. Caught in the fusions and confusions of living simultaneously at several different stages of technological evolution and in different socioeconomic systems, the solutions they have adopted are often as inappropriate as the problems are felt and pressing. Before having fully reached the age of print and literacy, for example, most developing countries have had to face the age of satellites and computers. High levels of illiteracy among the masses are thus combined with high levels of education for elites tied to the global information and power networks. The contradictions of combined and uneven development have thus affected them more than the more-developed countries. Technological and social leaps are theoretically possible, but so are the intellectual confusions and social dislocations of having to deal with too much social imbalance and complexity too soon.

This new international division of labor in the world capitalist system and its consequences for the changing structure of employment should not be taken, therefore, as conclusive evidence for the rise of a new social system. The fundamental features of the world capitalist system have clearly remained unchanged. These include the legal rights of private property, the corporate domination of the economy, a social class structure flowing from the inequalities in the ownership of the means of production, a liberal political system that intervenes in the economy only at times of crisis to correct the economic imbalances, and a cultural environment supportive of the motivational patterns of capitalist growth and inequity. These fundamental features have continued to operate successfully at the centers and have even expanded into some metropolitan centers of the third world.

TECHNOCRATIC VERSUS COMMUNITARIAN SOCIETY

Our current Age of Technology clearly exhibits two contradictory tendencies — here identified as technocratic and communitarian societies. The technocratic society has been led off by the cybernetic revolution, but it is developing further by accelerating convergence of the print, telephony, broadcasting, cable, satellite, computer, and microprocessing technologies into what has come to be known as *informatics*. The rapidly emerging integrated services digital network (ISDN) simultaneously transmits sound, vision, and data linking global and local networks. Currently, the new technologies primarily serve the purposes of the highly centralized global and national technocracies such as the giant transnational corporations and the state military and civilian bureaucracies. They also serve a new communication elite labeled here as "the technologues." This elite is acting as the custodians and managers of the large bureaucratic machines that dominate our world today.

The technocratic society is first and foremost a global system. It is characterized by an international communication regime of information networking indispensable to the operation of its global transportation, banking, finance, and marketing activities. This global information network connects the corporate and government headquarters with their respective localized branches in a vast and complex network of centralized nodes of decision making. It provides services in airline reservation, electronic fund transfers, remote sensing and intelligence, marketing, advertising, transborder news and data flows, and so forth. The information society discourages, however, spontaneity by participation in its routinized systems of communication and control, innovation, and production; reduction of decision to their technical components; and fragmentation and delegation of decision-making powers to the technocratic elites.

A communication society is, of course, a far more difficult entity to define. There are clearly no historic precedents for it. With the possible exception of modern democracies, all human societies in the past have been based primarily on coercive rather than communicative methods of rule. The idea, therefore, represents merely a potential — a hope. But this is a hope that is not altogether Utopian; it is a historically grounded hope. Its central concept — communication — suggests an interactive process sharply in contrast to what goes on in the mass communication systems of the world today. These ideals represent human aspirations against a disturbing situation — replete with the conflicts of a nuclear race, enormous and widening inequalities among and within nations, and cultural homogenization and depersonalization. There is evidence to suggest that if these ideals fail to materialize, we might face serious political problems and tragedies. The rise of a variety of dogmatic and fundamentalist movements around the world, in both developed and developing countries, are currently giving vent to the frustrations of the common people against an incomprehensible and unjust world system. If these movements continue to gain momentum, they could once again turn the world into an arena of uncompromising racial, religious, and political conflict.

An "escape from freedom" (Fromm 1963) and a regression to the sanctity and security of tribal solidarity thus seems to be as likely an outcome of our own age of transition as the realization of its great democratic potentials. The new information technologies thus present a double-edged sword. On the one hand, they can eliminate the routine, repetitive tasks in production and administration; create greater leisure for cultural and political pluralism; facilitate access and participation in a new direct, "electronic democracy"; foster open learning systems through tele-education; and extend a variety of other social services to the remotest and most deprived sectors of the population. But on the other hand, they can also serve as instruments of a new totalitarian hegemony by reinforcing the surveillance powers of the state, expanding the gap between the information rich and poor, creating unemployment and underemployment through automation and robotics, and fostering excessive reliance on high technology in the problems of human conflict. The outcome clearly depends not on our stars but our choices.

CONCLUSION

The current debate on information society represents a recurrent pattern in the history of major technological breakthroughs. The Second Industrial Revolution, like the first, has found its celebrants among those who tend to assume technological determinist views of history. They tend, therefore, to underestimate the institutional fetters that stand in the way of spreading the full social benefits of the new technologies. They are the technological optimists. At the other extreme, however, we have the technological pessimists. The Luddites of the Information Revolution see in the new technological transformations the sinister designs of a new age of slavery. Both schools of thought tend to overestimate the powers of technologies in shaping our lives.

The new information technologies possess an additional trait that most other technologies of the past lacked. They feed on a renewable, self-regenerative, and exponentially growing resource. The more information we give, the more information we have. Information feeds on information and thus grows at an accelerating rate. But that is also a mixed blessing. The cultural backlash against "information overload" has led in many parts of the world to powerful social movements representing escapes from information. These movements recoil from complexity and call for simpler models and choices in facing reality. Because the current information revolution is global in scope, the backlash is also of global dimensions. The gaps in information largely correspond to gaps in income and power, and we may anticipate new populist revolts that fall back on the certitudes of the past to face the uncertainties of the future.

REFERENCES AND BIBLIOGRAPHY

Armstrong, Ben. 1979. *The Electronic Church.* Nashville: Thomas Nelson.

Bell, Daniel. 1973. *The Coming of the Post-Industrial Society: A Venture in Social Forecasting.* New York: Basic Books.

Blumler, Jay, and Elihu Katz. 1975. *The Uses of Mass Communication: Current Perspective on Gratification Research.* Beverly Hills: Sage.

Carey, James W. 1981. "Culture, Technology and Communications: An Annotated Bibliography." Unpublished doctoral dissertation. Champaign, Illinois: University of Illinois.

Eisenstein, Elizabeth L. 1979. *The Printing Press as an Agent of Change.* Vols. 1 & 2. Cambridge: Cambridge University Press.

Ferguson, Marilyn. 1981. *The Aquarian Conspiracy: Personal and Social Transformation in the 1980s.* New York: J. P. Tarcher.

Freud, Sigmund. 1919. *Totem and Taboo.* London: Macmillan.

Fromm, Eric. 1963. *Escape from Freedom.* New York: Holt, Rinehart & Winston.

Gouldner, Alvin W. 1979. *The Dialectic of Ideology and Technology.* Oxford: Oxford University Press.

Gouldner, Alvin W. 1979. *The Future of Intellectuals and the Rise of the New Class.* London: Macmillan.

Gouldner, Alvin W. 1980. *Two Marxisms.* Oxford: Oxford University Press.

Hamelink, Cees. J. 1983. *Cultural Autonomy in Global Communications: Planning National Information Policy.* New York: Longmans.

Hancock, Alan. 1981. *Communication Planning for Development: An Operational Framework.* Paris: UNESCO.

Head, Sydney. 1985. *World Broadcasting Systems: A Comparative Analysis.* Belmont, Cal.: Wadsworth.

Innis, Harold. 1950. *Empire and Communications.* Toronto: University of Toronto Press.

Innis, Harold. 1951. *The Bias of Communication.* Toronto: University of Toronto Press.

Jonscher, Charles. 1984. "Productivity and Growth of the Information Economy." In *Communication and Information Economics: New Perspectives,* edited by M. Jussawalla and H. Ebenfield. Amsterdam: North-Holland.

Lee, Jae-Kyoung. 1985. "Two Theories of Social Change: Jurgen Habermas and Peter Berger." Honolulu: Com. 650. Unpublished.

Machlup, Fritz. 1962. *The Production and Distribution of Knowledge in the United States.* Princeton: Princeton University Press.

Machlup, Fritz. 1980–84. *Knowledge: Its Creation, Distribution and Economic Significance.* Vols. 1–3. Princeton: Princeton University Press.

McLuhan, Marshall. 1962. *The Guttenberg Gallaxy: The Making of Typographic Man.* Toronto: University of Toronto Press.

McLuhan, Marshall. 1964. *Understanding Media: The Extensions of Man.* New York: McGraw-Hill.

Mortimer, Edward. 1982. *Faith and Power: The Politics of Islam.* New York: Vintage.

Mosco, Vinnie. 1982. *Pushbutton Fantasies.* Norwood, N.J.: Ablex.

Naisbitt, John. 1982. *Megatrends: Ten New Directions Transforming Our Lives.* New York: Warner.

Porat, Marc. 1977. *The Information Economy.* Washington, D.C.: U.S. Office of Telecommunications.

Porat, Marc. 1978. "Communication Policy in an Information Society." In *Communications for Tomorrow,* edited by G. O. Robinson. New York: Praeger.

Schiller, Herbert I. 1981. *Who Knows: Information in the Age of Fortune 500.* Norwood, N.J.: Ablex.

Schiller, Herbert I. 1985. *Information and the Crisis Economy.* Norwood, N.J.: Ablex.

Smythe, Dallas W. 1985. *Needs before Tools: The Illusion of Electronic Democracy.* Unpublished manuscript. International Communication Association, Honolulu.

Tehranian, Majid. 1980. "Communication and Revolution in Iran: The Passing of a Paradigm." *Iranian Studies* 13: 1–14.

Thompson, William Irwin. 1971. *At the Edge of History.* New York: Harper.

Thompson, William Irwin. 1985. *Pacific Shift.* San Francisco: Sierra Club Books.

Toffler, Alvin. 1970. *Future Shock.* New York: Bantam.

Toffler, Alvin. 1980. *The Third Wave.* New York: Bantam.

25

Social Implications of Information Technology

IAN MILES

Social life is a complex web of action, reaction, and counteraction. The feedback loops may be positive or negative so that although some activities find resonance through society, the echoes of others quickly die away or are smothered. These loops are often neglected by commentators. They fail to take account of social innovations that may offset problems associated with new technology. New social movements (for example, environmentalism) may lead to changes in the treatment of externalities, and thus the use and design of a technology, for example. Fears about the invasion of privacy may evoke a similar response with data-protection laws being passed in many countries. People may also change their behavior so as to compensate for the costs of change. Thus when we consider fears of the isolating aspects of telework and teleservices, it is as well to remember that similar fears were expressed concerning broadcast TV. Although TV has hit some other entertainment services hard, there has nevertheless been considerable expansion of some other forms of sociable leisure (for example, sports or entertaining at home).

It is hard for forecasters to correctly judge even the first phases of such cycles of action-reaction-counterreaction. Indeed, the forecasts themselves may be part of these cycles, efforts to influence the course of events even at the risk of disconfirming themselves. The discussion here cannot hope to trace through these cycles, but we shall contrast several views of their outcomes, by explicating the underlying world views that structure forecasts.

THREE VIEWS OF THE IMPLICATIONS OF IT

Many essays concerning the social implications of information technology (SIT) assert, stridently, that these implications take a particular form, that the broad outlines of the future with IT can be discerned fairly readily. However, the prophets' conclusions are often divergent. In consequence, there is now a large secondary literature concluding that the implications could be either centralizing, either deskilling or upgrading, either enhancing or threatening democracy, and so on, through a list of oppositions.

One thing is quite clear. A major technological change has far reaching social implications, and these are bound to be somewhat elusive for forecasters at the early stages of the change. Much uncertainty and many disagreements result. It would be possible to work through a long list of topics that has arisen in debates over SIT, assembling and documenting the arguments and conclusions, if any, in each. Given the vast proliferation of relevant evidence and of more or less relevant opinions, this approach would also be at best tedious, at worst downright confusing. To avoid this, this chapter will compare and contrast three distinct perspectives on SIT. The three such viewpoints that we shall distinguish, here labeled the continuity, transformation, and structural schools, are listed below.

Core assumptions of three perspectives on SIT are as follows:

Continuity. Sees information technology (IT) as part of long-term evolution of technical capabilities rather dismissive of claims of its revolutionary nature. SIT can be projected from experience with earlier generations of electronic devices. Main features of society liable to remain unchanged, unless as a result of political upheaval. Forecasts: typically short and medium term, based on tried extrapolation and conventional modeling approaches, and often restricted to employment and consumer market issues.

Transformation. Sees IT as a revolutionary development, contributing to as major a shift in civilization as those associated with the agricultural and industrial revolutions. IT follows from a complex of changes in values and institutions and can be identified as seeds of the future in some current experiments and social movements. Forecasts: typically long-term scenarios only loosely related to present, based on study of leading-edge developments, broad range of social and cultural topics treated.

Structural. Sees IT as the basis for a reorganization of industrial society — part of the core of a "new technological system," "long wave," and "growth paradigm." SIT generally related to the components of such a structural change, which can partly be deduced from historic analogies (for example, with electrification) and partly from studying changes in organizational structures. Forecasts: typically seek to combine elements of the two preceding approaches, but mainly concentrated on industrial and organizational change.

THE SOCIAL CONTEXT OF IT INNOVATION

Continuity and Competitiveness

For continuists, IT represents an incremental step on a long path of technological evolution. The key factors setting the pace and direction of innovation here are familiar ones: how far technological changes are matched to user needs and to the structure of factor costs and the availability of managerial, technical, and workforce skills. Case studies have related such factors to the innovation and diffusion of some ITs; and studies of national innovative performance provides considerable support for their fundamental significance.

The problem that the lagging countries face is how to avoid reductions in living standards in the face of these trends; the usual adjustment policies seem insufficient to create new employment opportunities, because they do not in themselves ensure the growth of dynamic new sectors. This has led to considerable interest in national innovation policies; but these are prominent in almost all countries, not just the laggards. It is remarkable how similar the broad trends here have been. Priority is given to R&D in IT, biotechnology and new materials, more effort is put into means of evaluating the direction and effectiveness of research and into the promotion of closer academic industry linkages and more public and industrial R&D in priority areas. The lagging countries do not seem to be at any particular advantage in pursuing such policies, even if their sense of urgency is greater.

Western Europe in general has specific concerns about technological innovation. A number of problems are raised (see Table 25.1). National markets are often too small for volume production and economies of scale (even, perhaps, for flexible manufacturing systems); national research capabilities are too limited to seriously address the whole range of priorities; entrepreneurship is inhibited by various obstacles (such as a lack of venture capital). Despite variations within Europe, these problems are widely conceded, and have promoted not only major national efforts (for example, Britain's Alvey Program for fifth-generation systems) but also efforts at collaboration (IT programs like ESPRIT, EUREKA, and RACE, and efforts to support venture capital and technological diffusion).

TABLE 25.1
A Schematic View of Regional Differences in
Conditions for Innovation

Japan	United States	Europe
Strictly coordinated export	"Market-pulled" innovation	Long tradition of scientific research
Politicoeconomic infrastructure with interweaving of state, banks and industry	Great personal mobility and competitiveness. Many new technology-based firms formed	Lack of entrepreneurship and the formation of new technology-based firms
Aggressive industrial policy, long-term public and private sector strategies	Legislation and education directed toward entrepreneurship	Emphasis on supporting traditional sector
Coordinated policy toward the acquisition of technology	Support for strategic sectors in connection with position as superpower (defense and aerospace)	Relative weakness in product development and marketing, in the commercial exploitation of new technologies
Strong emphasis on efficient mass production and on total quality control	Rapid growth of new industrial sectors based on radical technologies	Paucity of venture capital
Home market that demands innovation	High availability of venture capital, large home market that demands innovation	

Source: Rothwell and Zegfeld 1985.

Transformation and Attitude Change

Transformationists tend to put less stress on structures and strategies than on what they see as their underlying values and attitudes. Accordingly there has been considerable research into perceptions of the "impact" of IT at the workplace. Following the 1982 Versailles Summit, a major program of research into the public acceptance of new technologies was launched. This latter was particularly inspired by British concerns that public resistance to change was at the root of slow innovation.

Attitudes to work are a case in point. Despite the popular view that commitment to employment has declined immensely, it actually appears that having a job has become in some respects more central in people's lives (see Table 25.2). What has changed is the rewards people expected from work, and there are some signs of a mismatch between

TABLE 25.2
Workers' Perceived Effects of Technological Change, 1982

	United States	Germany	Sweden	Japan	Israel
More:					
Monotonous	22	25	25	41	—
Lonely	18	19	31	31	39
Of a psychological burden	—	35	40	62	56
Difficult	38	48	45	69	46
Dependent on others	38	38	44	30	51
Responsible	—	57	66	74	78
Interesting	74	61	74	59	72
Clean	42	52	53	51	61
Less physical strain	35	58	60	42	64

Source: Yuchtman-Yaar 1986.

Note: These are samples of workers reporting experiencing technological change; figures represent percentages agreeing that the condition "applies" or "partly applies."

aspirations and reality here. There is little support for a substantial shift to a set of new postindustrial values, and even less for attitudes as inhibiting technological progress.

As with other cross-national survey studies, there are some doubts about precisely what national differences indicate. Are they products of really diverse attitudes to technology or of other cultural differences? Nevertheless, there is a fairly strong message that worker attitudes to the use of IT are in general positive — and this also applies to those who have not had experience with IT directly.

Structures and Paradigms

A core assumption of the structuralist viewpoint is that many of our current uncertainties relate to being at a point of transition between structural regimes; we can see the stagnation and limits of old structures, but it is hard to assess the viability of newer models. New heartland technologies imply learning processes and organizational changes to capitalize on their potential; new areas of demand are needed to establish new patterns of growth.

Structuralist analysis typically attempts to identify key features of an emerging paradigm, most often from case studies of advanced sectors, and to outline the enabling and constraining factors around appropriate changes. Many of the features that are identified by commentators are ones seen as typical of Japanese styles of organization: just-in-time and quality-control systems in production, strong linkages within industrial sectors and between industries and state agencies, emphasis on the long term. Others are related more to perceived potentials of IT; flexible production systems leading to a proliferation of innovative small and medium-sized enterprises, emphasis on retraining to meet needs for technical skills and the design of systems to meet user needs, establishment of the infrastructure required to support new IT-based goods and services. So far this resembles a fusion of some continuist and transformationist arguments, but structuralists do place more stress on the role that intergroup relations play in national differences. Distinctive political economies condition the prospects for "catching up" and other innovation strategies.

Some commentators have argued that cultural and psychological factors have played a leading role in the creation of Japanese management styles, but others point to their evolution within a context of specific factor costs (shortages of materials and space, particular skill compositions) in postwar Japan. The latter view is more sanguine about the transfer of practices, although structuralists would argue that there is liable to be a lengthy process of rethinking the "common sense" of cost accounting in the context of new ITs, and the current linkages between financial and industrial sectors may inhibit management experiments with new work structures in Western Europe in particular.

Nevertheless, efforts to learn from Japanese management are widespread and it is likely that these will form part of an ongoing evolution toward new organizational structures in industry. It also seems likely that progress in the directions will be more rapid in societies where consensus-formation processes in management and government are better established, where trade unions are already organized on enterprise bases (and especially not on a craft basis, as in the United Kingdom), and where systems of worker participation and consultation can support loyalty to the enterprise and more support for plans for redeployment and retraining. Scandinavia and Germany seem relatively well placed in these respects.

At this point it seems worth noting that the Japanese model may itself be facing particular problems of structural change. Some commentators have suggested that Japanese culture may provide less support for radical innovation than for imitation and incremental improvement. Current consumer products and grand schemes such as that for integrated network services should be sufficient evidence to undermine these suggestions. More serious may be problems of adaptation of industrial structures. It has been argued that the IT market may decompose into a growing number of specialized niches in which there would be expanded opportunities to capitalize on non-Roman script and new geographical markets (especially Asia).

Structuralists, finally, also point to wider social changes associated with the consolidation of a new technology system. Although most of their analytic efforts have been centered on the policy-making and industrial structures, there is sufficient research and debate over the implications of IT for our ways in life in general to make it worthwhile to consider these issues in some detail. The next section is a first stab at doing so.

Formal Work

A vast range of specific applications of IT to different sectors of the economy are currently emerging. Table 25.3 lists those identified as most important for the next two or three decades. Forecasts of the implications of various applications for formal work are numerous, with estimates of future employment levels evoking much controversy. Studies of the use of IT in most established branches and sectors of the economy tend to forecast reductions in formal employment levels or jobless growth at best, with the exception of a few IT-based industries. Studies drawing on macroeconomic models tend to predict lower levels of job loss due to familiar compensatory effects, and some even suggest employment growth, at least for those countries that are able to innovate more rapidly. But three trends are widely agreed upon: (1) continuation of the long-term shift of dominance in employment levels from the primary to the secondary to the tertiary sectors; (2) continuation of the reduction in core manual and production occupations and relative increase in various ancillary, administrative, and professional jobs; and (3) continuation of the reduction in lifetime working hours. Issues such as centralization-decentralization, the roles of small firms and large corporations, and part-time and shift work are ones in which there is less agreement.

Thus, whereas new technology industries may be quick to realize the opportunities of IT for gains in capital and labor productivity and product innovation, more traditional sectors may be faced with less opportunity for profitable investment. This may lead to more efforts to intensify work and save costs by lowering working conditions, and to protectionist sentiment. Either constitutes a potentially repressive pattern of development, although the first would tend to evoke capital-labor conflict, the latter to be pursued by alliances of capital and labor in weak sectors and possible conflicts with other sectors, as well as in the international sphere.

TABLE 25.3
Key Applications of IT in Different Economic Sectors

Primary Sector 1: Agriculture	Remote sensing, communications systems, advanced portable instrumentation Simple robotics and automated/remote control systems Management aids, viewdata and database services, marketing intelligence systems
Primary Sector 2: Extraction and Mining	Remote sensing, remote and automated extraction from hostile areas Integration of extraction and finishing operations Management and distribution aids, expert systems
Secondary Sector 1: Construction/Utilities	Computer-aided design and prefabrication Enhanced instrumentation and power tools, simple robotics, metering Management and distribution systems
Secondary Sector 2: Manufacturing	Automated handling, manipulation, processing, testing, quality control, packaging, and dispatch Automated stockholding and warehousing; computer-aided planning and scheduling, drafting, and designing Integrated innersite communications
Tertiary Sector 1: Physical services (e.g., distribution)	Mobile communications, automated stockholding and warehousing Computer-aided planning and route scheduling, stock control and ordering systems Computer-aided fault diagnostics and repair
Tertiary Sector 2: Symbol-processing services (e.g., finance, broadcasting)	Office automation, expert systems for management and planning, electronic mail Transaction-clearing devices (ATM, EPOS, EFT), machine translation, advanced telecommunications systems, teleservices
Tertiary Sector 3: People-oriented services (e.g., health, education)	Office automation Expert systems for professional advice, machine translation and "intelligent" systems for lay use Teleservices, viewdata systems, advanced database search facilities

Source: Loosely based on Miles et al. 1985.

Note: Developments are liable to vary between intermediate and final demand-oriented branches of these sectors.

Changes in the type of formal work carried out in the typical hours contributed to the formal economy and in the types of education and training required are seen, especially by transformationists, as promoting changes in political interests and social values. Although work-leisure relations are not simple, it seems generally accepted that higher-level jobs tend to be associated with demand for more active, autonomous, and sophisticated leisure. A more dualistic pattern of employment, however, would find similar reflections in the sphere of leisure, and probably in national politics, too.

Housework

Private households have been steadily increasing their capital-intensity by accumulating over recent decades a wide range of consumer products. Consumer durables have increasingly made the home not merely a site of consumption and personal support, but also a site of informal production. To some extent this has shattered the vision of a postindustrial society in which consumption would shift toward services acquired from the formal economy. The continuity viewpoint sees little reason for the long-term trends in consumption patterns to change. The home will continue to evolve gradually, and levels of housework will be slightly reshaped in line with, for example, growing interest in do-it-yourself or specialized cookery. These trends might be disrupted, however, by dramatic changes in formal working hours or the relative prices of services and goods/self-services, but such changes are thought unlikely by continuity. IT tends to be used as a fashionable gimmick in household goods. Its serious applications are liable to remain few and people are unlikely to welcome high-tech solutions to everyday problems.

The transformationists, in contrast, see IT as liable to revolutionize housework and the home. They anticipate increased availability of free time for domestic work and shifts in values, which would encourage more sophisticated self-servicing. (Telework, too, should result both in increased time spent at home and in improved domestic computer-communications). Furthermore, IT is seen here as being productively incorporated into almost all forms of domestic equipment. As well as upgrading the quality, efficiency, and usefulness of individual household items, these stand-alone items are liable to be steadily integrated into interactive home systems in a process of home automation.

Transformationists believe that the continuity school's idea that people will largely reject the intrusion of "soulless" technology into their homes and everyday lives fails to recognize that processes of familiarization (of people) and simplification (of technology) will continue to march hand in hand.

Structuralists lean mostly toward the transformationist view of rapid change in and enhancement of household appliances. But they remain more skeptical of the degree of consumer enthusiasm for teleshopping and similar innovations and of whether there really is large untapped public demand for new information services and for technologies to apply to personal care.

A number of social issues are raised in this context. One concern frequently expressed is that the automated home will lead to greater social isolation — telework reduces social contacts at the workplace and teleservices do the same for activities like shopping. Although such concerns are probably overstated, it is not implausible that some groups are more vulnerable than others in specific contexts — for example, mothers with young children in northern Europe.

What about national differences? Several factors will be agreed upon across the three viewpoints. Consumer adoption of new technologies, unless they are simple modifications of existing facilities, tends to involve an extended learning process. Thus, experience with IT at work and in education may be important in facilitating innovation in the household economy; and thus innovation rates in these sectors will be rather important determinants of change. The availability of cheap formal services as alternatives to self-provisioning (for example, servants and laundries) and a cultural tradition of out-of-home activities (for example, catering) would be expected to slow the adoption of some sorts of domestic equipment. The United States and Japan have relatively high levels of private service-sector employment, Scandinavia and the United Kingdom low levels — growth in private-sector services has been particularly marked in the United States, whereas it has slowed down in Europe.

Leisure

As we have seen, the continuity viewpoint sees this sort of home automation as unlikely on any scale in at least the next few decades, whereas structural and transformational viewpoints expect progressively rapid developments. Continuists are quick to dismiss some trends as fads — witness the "bubbles" around videogames and home computers. The videotape recorder, enabling improved use of TV, but little in the way of a new leisure activity, is for them a more typical (and probably more enduring) domestic innovation. Transformationists, in addition, stress developments around computer systems and new information services. The wide-screen TV may be used with appropriate graphics software as electronic wallpaper, and this may be linked to new types of ambient music based on digital sampling devices and synthesizers. But TV screens will also be used to access computer communications networks — viewdata, bulletin boards, telegames (such as multiplayer role-playing adventures), and libraries (text, audio, and video). These networks will service leisure and entertainment requirements directly and also support improved access to existing services via telebooking, locating partners for sports, and the like. Finally, equipment for specific leisure activities (sport vehicles and clothing, exercise machinery, games, and toys) are liable to incorporate IT for monitoring performance and providing training advice, for closer simulation of reality, for convenience, and for sheer fun.

Social Participation

The three viewpoints differ (in ways that will by now be predictable) concerning these developments. Where welfare activities of various kinds are involved, continuists tend to anticipate steady process innovation within the formal services and a rather slow and sporadic uptake of new home- and IT-based education and medical services and systems. Transformationists, on the other hand, anticipate rapid process and product innovation, both pushed by technology and pulled by demand. They would, for example, stress the potential of teleservices to improve the quality of some parts of educational and medical systems, although many aspects of these activities clearly require close personal contact. Continuists are skeptical of the acceptability of such developments; structuralists point out their dependence on policy decisions and strategies by public service authorities, private competitors, subcontractors, and new entrants, and telecommunications systems providers. Quite clearly, major issues of public policy are involved and some of the actors are generally regarded as being rather slow to undertake radical innovations. However, ongoing social changes (for example, the aging of Western populations) and issues raised by the application of IT itself (for example, new requirements for training and retraining) may provide powerful incentives for experimentation.

IT can increase access to all sorts of public information dramatically, and some commentators see this as a major challenge for national political systems. Machine translation is widely heralded as a means of reducing problems associated with language barriers, but the broader implications of advanced machine translation capabilities have been seen as rather mixed by Gurstein (1985). In multicultural societies, individual language groups, despite gaining more access to national culture, may become more insular, putting less effort into mastering other languages and engaging in less informal contact with members of other groups. Pressure will grow on governments for translation into more tongues. Intercultural information flows should increase, but it is still likely that native speakers of those langauges that are (at first, at least) most economic to translate will be advantaged relative to others. And with machine translation applied to expert systems and other tradeable information services, fears about cultural imperialism may find a new focus.

CONCLUSION

This has been a whistle-stop tour of the SIT, and it would be inappropriate to draw many detailed conclusions for it. What is apparent is that there has been remarkably uneven development of research — if not of futurological speculation — and that this adds to the intrinsic difficulties associated with assessing the social features of a new technology system or information society. Although it is an established custom to call for more research at the end of such an essay — and the only qualification we would add in this case is that it should be more serious than much current analysis — it does seem particularly appropriate in this instance to draw attention to the need for social experiments. It is probable that, as structuralists argue, the implications of individual ITs are multiplicative and a grasp on the types of demand structure and ways of life that might evolve if home computers and broadband communications, mass information utilities, and so forth, are available cannot be gained by studying these in isolation.

The evaluation of experiments and experiences is an extremely important intelligence function for IT policy making, even if most initiatives to date are somewhat limited as models of information society. Nevertheless, our review here has highlighted a number of points that are worth immediate consideration. Innovation policy, for example, has been underlined as of central importance, and development of functions of marketing and assessment of user requirements loom large alongside more conventional aspects of R&D policy. The review could not escape some rather gloomy speculations about a widening, or at least persistence, of gaps in economic performance among industrial countries. International collaboration may be required both to facilitate innovation in these countries and to help them cover the costs of what adjustment is necessary.

REFERENCES AND BIBLIOGRAPHY

Arnold, Erik, and Ken Guy. 1986. *Parallel Convergence.* London: Frances Pinter.

Boden, Maggie. 1984. "Impacts of Artificial Intelligence." *Futures* 16 (1): 60–70.

Cameron, David R. 1978. "The Expansion of the Public Economy: A Comparative Analysis." *American Political Science Review* 72 (4): 1247–61.

Cole, Sam, Jay Gershuny, and Ian Miles. 1978. "Scenarios of World Development." *Futures* 10: 3–20.

Forrester, Tom, ed. 1985. *The Information Technology Revolution.* Oxford: Blackwell.

Freeman, Chris, and M. Jahoda, eds. 1978. *World Futures: The Great Debate.* London: Martin Robertson.

Freeman, Chris, and Carlotta Perez. 1984. "Long Waves and New Technology." Mimeo. Falmer Brighton: SPRU.

Gardiner, W. Lambert (Scot). 1980. "Public Acceptance of New Information Technology: The Role of Attributes." Gamma, University of Montreal/McGill University, Information Society Project, Paper 1–9.

Gurstein, Michael. 1985. "Social Impacts of Selected Artificial Intelligence Applications." *Futures* 17 (6): 652—71.

Hondrich, Karl Otto. 1984. "Value Changes in Western Society — The Last 30 Years." Paper presented to the Commission of European Communities' Seminar "Technology, Capital and Labour — Social and Cultural Aspects of Economic Change," Brussels.

Inose, Hiroshi, and John R. Pierce. 1984. *Information Technology and Civilization.* New York: Freeman.

McQuail, Denis. 1986. "Policy Perspectives for New Media in Europe." In *New Communication Technologies and the Public Interest,* edited by Marjorie Ferguson. London: Sage.

Miles, Ian. 1985. "The New Post-Industrial State." *Futures* 17 (6): 588–617.

NEDO. 1985. *IT Futures.* London: National Economic Development Office.

OECD. 1979. *Facing the Futures.* Paris: OECD.

Pavitt, K. 1979. "Technical Change: Prospects for Manufacturing Industry." Paper presented at EEC Workshop "Europe in Transition: The Challenge of the Future," Arc en Senans, France.

Perez, Carlotta. 1983. "Structural Change and Assimilation of New Technologies in the Economic and Social Systems." *Futures* 15 (5): 357–76.

Rothwell, Roy, and Walter Zegfeld. 1985. *Re-industrialization and Technology.* London: Longmans.

Rush, Howard, Ian Miles, Ken Guy, and John Bessant. 1986. *IT Futures Surveyed.* London: National Economic Development Organization (in press).

Schmidt, Manfred G. (1986). "Political Management of Mixed Economies." Paper presented at Symposium, "Industrial Societies after the Stagnation of the 1970s," Villa Borsig, Berlin.

Schuman, Gunda. 1984. "The Macro-and Micro-economic Social Impact of Advanced Computer Technology." *Futures* 16 (3): 185–260.

Soete, Luc. 1981. "A General Test of Technological Gap Trade Theory." *Review of World Economics* 117 (4).

Stephens, John D. 1979. *The Transition from Capitalism to Socialism.* London: Macmillan.

Vine, Richard D. 1985. *The Impact of Technological Change in the Industrial Democracies: Public Attitudes toward Information Technology.* Paris: Atlantic Institute for International Affairs.

Yuchtman-Yaer, Ephraim. 1986. "Economic Culture in Post-Industrial Society: Orientation Toward Growth, Technology, and Work." Paper presented at conference on "Industrial Societies after the Stagnation of the 1970s," Villa Borsig, Berlin.

26

Telecommunications Market Structure Changes: Expectations and Experiences

H. P. GASSMANN

COMPUTERS AND COMMUNICATIONS: COMCOM

Since the 1970s, we have witnessed a merging of two technologies that were separate before: computers and telecommunications. The driving force behind this merger is essentially microelectronics. Until 1975, computer and communications technologies were two distinct worlds; on the one hand, stand-alone large computers, mostly used for scientific and business data processing; on the other, the voice communications system, essentially based on electromechanical technology, both for switching and terminal equipment.

The computer industry grew as a competitive industry with one firm as an international market leader; the telecommunications industry had a market structure based on national or regional monopolies, with a cooperative, revenue-sharing system for international communications.

Two developments changed the situation:

1. The advent of transistors and then the microchip had as a consequence a gradual diminution of the cost and size of computers, while their power increased; this resulted in a rapidly growing number of minicomputers and then personal computers and the growing use of specialized computers also for telecommunication switching purposes. In parallel, as digital transmission began to replace analogue transmission, software became more and more important also for telecommunications.

2. The growing need for linking computers with data communications resulted in the emergence of data networks, such as
   Arpanet for research purposes, Tymnet and Telenet for business
   purposes in the United States, later Transpac, Datex, and other
   public networks in Europe, Japan, and Australia.

The driving human forces behind these changes were essentially
computer scientists and the computer department managers of large
firms, multinational corporations, banks, and airlines. It is they who
developed the concept of packet switching, whereas their conservative
telecommunications colleagues continued to prefer the line- or circuit-
switching approach. This resulted in a marked increase in the demand
for privately leased telecommunications lines, as well as for modems
needed to convert the digital into analogue signals or vice versa.

The pressures for institutional changes began to be felt in the early
1980s, as the dynamism of the computer hardware and software
developers increasingly contrasted with the more conservative
approach of telecommunications engineers.

The merger of two different technologies had as a consequence on
the organization level a clash of two corporate cultures. The computer
industry was marked by strong and growing competition, absence of
large-scale standardization, unregulated market structures, private
actors with easy access to capital markets, and relatively short
depreciation periods for equipment (five to ten years). The
telecommuni-cations services industry was characterized by little
competition, regulated or monopoly environment, strong tradition of
public service and infrastructure aspects (universal service), tradition
of standardization at national level and at international level for
interconnection purposes, often government ownership with restricted
access to capital markets, and long depreciation periods of equipment
(up to thirty years).

The merger of computer and communications technologies brings
important changes for these so far different corporate cultures; their
likely implications may be summarized as follows:

Computer Industry
more standardization as the computer-to computer-to terminal
   communications needs increase
the emergence of information networks at the user level
a growing dependence on telecommunications infrastructures

Telecommunications Industry
more competition, both at the national and international level

this might mean less standardization than at present, especially at
national level

there might be a danger that the established notion of universal service
might be eroded;

more competition might also mean a growing trend toward more
bypass, when large users might prefer to construct and manage their
own telecommunications systems, with consequent loss of revenue
for the public network.

STRUCTURAL CHANGES IN THE U.S. TELECOMMUNICATIONS MARKET

Since 1982, important changes occurred in market structure in some
countries, and discussion is going on in others on how to adapt their
structures to the merger of computer and telecommunications
technologies occurring in all of them.

The United States, the United Kingdom, and Japan have introduced
competition in the provision of telecommunications services, whereas
in other countries the traditional monopoly structure is still
prevailing.

Experience on the effects of these changes is still limited, and not
much can be said so far for the United Kingdom and Japan. For the
United States, there are diverging views on such effects.

It is difficult from outside the United States to understand two years
after divestiture in which direction the dust of deregulation is settling,
and there are continuing hopes, but also concerns.

First the hopes. Judge Harold H. Greene, who presided over the
consent decree of the AT&T divestiture in 1982, recently confirmed his
hopes in a bright future spurred by deregulation when he said in a
speech before the Brookings Institution in December 1985:

> Professor Rostow has observed that, since the days of Bismarck's
> first social legislation in 1883, the central domestic political
> question for the advanced industrial democracies has been
> this — how to build societies that reconcile efficiencies in a
> world of rapidly changing technology with the humane values
> in which Western culture is rooted. That is still the issue before
> us today.
>
> Many new telecommunications products have appeared in
> quantity on the retail shelves over the past two years. We can be
> certain that these innovations are becoming available now —
> rather than 10 or 15 years from now or 10 or 15 years earlier —
> because now there is competition, and because if one company
> does not supply these services, another will.

But consumer products are the least of it. It does not take a prophetic mind to predict that the nation that is able to develop the best, the most usefully sophisticated, the most cost-efficient tools of the Information Age will have the same advantages, now and in the future, that England enjoyed for a hundred years because it dominated in the development and use of tools of the textile and iron trades early in the nineteenth century.

That is where the newly emerging competitive environment in telecommunications comes in. Here again, the past year or two have witnessed far more dramatic developments than had occurred in the previous 10 or 20. We now see such technological breakthroughs as the use of fiber optics on a large scale; piggyback of data on voice; improved digital technology; message compression; voice-messaging systems; electronic mailboxes; and others. I do not believe that one would have to be much of a gambler to bet that the pace of these advances will accelerate sharply in the new climate.[1]

In the same vein, on the occasion of the Special Session on Telecommunications Policy of the Organization for Economic Cooperation and Development (OECD) Committee for Information, Computer, and Communications Policy (ICCP), Federal Communications Commission (FCC) Chairman Mark Fowler said in November 1985 in Paris:

Businessmen and consumers will seize opportunities that benefit them or that they can turn to their advantage whenever and wherever they can. Rapid changes underlying the industry are making possible a multitude of new ways to do business. That means business will be ahead of regulators and governments at every step of our journey into the unknown. The telephone business is not staid or predictable. In fact, it's no longer just the telephone business. To enjoy the fruits of the technological revolution, every country will have to recognize that placing extensive regulation on bold entrepreneurship works like heavy doses of pesticides. It kills the crops along with the pests.[2]

But there are also concerns that center on two main issues. These are whether or not universal service can be maintained in a competitive situation; and the fact that the average telephone user's bills have, on balance, been higher since the AT&T divestiture.

On the first theme, Judge Greene, in January 1986, indicated in an opinion to the Bell Operating Companies (BOCs) that he will not agree to remove business restrictions put on them by the 1982 AT&T divestiture agreement. The rationale for restrictions preventing BOCs from providing long-distance and information services was — and remains so far — that a monopoly provider of services can discriminate against competitors. Greene accused the postdivestiture BOCs of losing the commitment to local service that had been the forte of the old Bell System. After noticing that this system was imbued by a service mentality, Judge Greene said:

> By contrast, the regional companies, or some of them, indicate by their public statements, their advertisements, and their rush to diversification, combined with their relative lack of interest in basic telephone service itself, that an ascent into the ranks of conglomerate America rates far higher on their list of priorities than the provision of the best and least costly local telephone service to the American public.[3]

There is also widespread concern about the future of inexpensive universal service, especially threatened by the spectre of bypass. Large customers have increasing motives to bypass the existing universal telephone service at local level and to provide their telecommunications services themselves. The long-distance carrier access charges to use the local telephone networks are also the object of worries, especially by state public utilities commissions.

The Consumer Federation of America in a recent report on the status of residential telephone consumers two years after the breakup of AT&T concluded:

> Two years after divestiture, consumers face disturbing inequities in the distribution of benefits derived from increased competition and costs imposed by new pricing policies. Federal regulatory policies are accentuating this imbalance through reduced involvement in cost allocation problems. Without renewed efforts to distribute the benefits and costs of the Bell breakup equitably, the average consumer will remain a net loser in the post-divestiture.[4]

UNCERTAINTIES IN EUROPEAN COUNTRIES

Without doubt, the deregulation decisions in the United States, followed by the United Kingdom and Japan, have had their ripple effects in continental European countries. The question is often asked, If we do not follow this trend, will we fall back in our telecommunications-services quality and price, and may this ultimately affect overall economic performance? Table 26.1 shows the disparity in teledensity in various countries.

The answers are not given yet, but it may be interesting to note that neither in Scandinavian countries, nor Western European countries has there emerged so far strong political pressure to break up the telecommunications monopoly or to privatize it as it happened in the United Kingdom. The main reason for this conservative stance — so far — may be a generally held consensus that in infrastructures a state monopoly role is justified, because it is socially equitable and therefore best able to provide universal service, at the same rate in remote areas as in the cities. This opinion applies not only to PTTs but also to railways, gas, and electric companies and other service companies

TABLE 26.1
Telephone Lines per 100 Inhabitants (Ranked on the Basis of 1983 Data)

Sweden	60.22
Switzerland	47.75
Denmark	46.98
Canada	41.84
Finland	41.50
United States	40.91*
Iceland	39.47
Germany	38.26
Netherlands	37.95
New Zealand	37.89
Luxembourg	37.52
France	37.40
Australia	37.03
Norway	36.71
Japan	36.02
United Kingdom	34.75
Austria	33.75
Belgium	28.84
Greece	27.49
Italy	27.39
Spain	21.86
Ireland	17.49
Portugal	12.30
Turkey	3.48
OECD Average	34.81

*1982 data: 95 M main lines.

Source: International Telecommunications Union, "Yearbook of Common Carrier Telecommunications Statistics." 12th ed. and PTT annual reports.

providing transport infrastructures or utilities, and there was, and is, a strong tradition in many European countries to this notion of public service.

On the other hand, we witness a general search for modernization of telecommunications in Europe. In other words, answers are actively sought to the question, Can we maintain a PTT monopoly and at the same time be innovative in offering new services at attractive rates?

Sweden was the first country in the world to introduce cellular mobile radio, in 1981. The innovation record of Sweden's public telecommunications monopoly, Televerket, has always been very good, its tariffs are relatively low, and its customers by and large satisfied. Therefore, the question for other European countries with a public telecommunications monopoly is, What can be done to achieve similar results without liberalizing or privatizing?

In the Netherlands, a reorganization of the PTT has been almost completed, which resulted in a separation of the post and telecommunications activities — a step that was also first taken in the United Kingdom, when British Telecom was separated from the British Post Office in 1981. But this does not result in a privatization of the telecommunications company. Results to the end of 1985 for the United Kingdom are:

British Telecom (BT) has been privatized — share ownership now extends to 3.5 million people.

Mercury Communications Ltd. is now a competing carrier to BT; so in the United Kingdom a duopoly has been established, but with the requirement that both systems should be fully interconnected.

Two competing companies (Rascal Vodaphone and Cellnet) introduced cellular radios for mobile phones in 1985; their target is to serve 90 percent of the United Kingdom population by the end of 1989.

There has been a rapid growth of value-added network services, and by November 1985 there were 166 registered licensees.

A regulatory agency, the Office of Telecommunications (OFTEL) and the British Approval Board for Telecommunications (BABT) have been established as independent agencies.

Probable outcomes of telecommunication modernization in Europe might be:

1. In the field of telecommunications equipment, it is likely that a liberalization will take place and monopoly restrictions lifted. It may also be possible that lengthy and expensive approval procedures will be simplified, and perhaps testing of equipment in one EEC country will be recognized as valid for other EEC countries.

2. In the field of universal telecommunications service, it is unlikely now that competition will be introduced in European countries.
3. In the field of new telecommunications services, such as value-added services, some form of coexistence between monopoly providers and private service providers might well develop, or in other words, a situation of competition, albeit limited, may emerge.

CONCLUSION

The internal policy analyst has a fascinating future to watch in the developed countries' telecommunications scene. First, the moves toward modernization in various countries need to be monitored, analyzed, and compared. Second, the experiences of those countries having introduced competition need to be evaluated and also compared. Finally, across-countries comparisons need to be made and the performance of the various actors assessed. At this point, it is worth mentioning that revenues are linked with rates, tariffs, and charges (user, access, and others). This area has been found to be exceedingly complex in each country, so that it will be very difficult to arrive at meaningful rate comparisons among countries; probably the large international users, the telecommunications managers of multinational firms and banks are those best informed about such issues.

These will no doubt become more similar in the various countries during the next years, as some form of "geographic competition" among countries will develop. This might certainly benefit the large, multinational user; it is to be hoped that this across-country competition will benefit the average user as well, and that the notion of universal service will survive intact the upheavals the telecommunications industry is now undergoing.

NOTES

1. Harold H. Greene. 1985. Speech to Brookings Institution. Reprinted in *Communications Week,* January 20, 1986.

2. Mark Fowler. 1985. Speech to OECD, ICCP committee. Paris. November. Reprinted in *Communications Week,* January 20, 1986, p. 2.

3. Greene, speech.

4. Consumer Federation of America. 1986. *Divestiture Plus Three: Still Crazy After All These Years,* edited by M. N. Cooper and G. Kimmelman. Washington, D.C.

VI

INNOVATIONS AND FUTURE TRENDS

27

Emerging Technological Possibilities: ISDN and Its Impact on Interdependence, 1986–2016

DAN J. WEDEMEYER AND
RICHARD J. BARBER

INTRODUCTION

The world is entering an era that is operationalizing the forecasts of past telecommunications and computer designers. This new era will be characterized by both commonalities and wide differences. Commonalities will be found in hardware and software protocols and diversity will be enjoyed in the multiplicity of service offerings. For decades, professionals have been talking about the marriage of computers and communications; now these concepts are realities. A recent industry newsletter, Mitel's *Superswitch News* (1986, 8) states:

> ISDN is no longer just a concept, nor is it far down the road. The 1986–87 (ISDN) trials are not testing the concept — they are testing the implementation . . . by the end of the decade, most of the Fortune 1000 companies together with smaller organizations that recognize the importance of advanced telecommunications in winning a competitive edge, will be using ISDN routinely.

There is little doubt that advanced communications provides a competitive edge in trade. It is a necessary prerequisite. More important, perhaps, is integrated services digital network's (ISDN's) capacity to change structures of group work and individual relationships. Network organizations are replacing traditional hierarchical arrangements. Access to the organization will be through standard, physical interface using existing telephone wiring with an ISDN interface. In this regard, then, ISDN will combine the ubiquitous features of the voice network (e.g., multivendor, simplicity of use) with the richness and cohesion of data networks. Video services will soon follow.

ISDN is an imminent reality that holds great significance for the world community. In essence, it is the nervous system required for the design of a world brain. Executed well, the ISDN will link "intelligence" (both human and machine based) into highly efficient information exchange. Innovative applications of these advanced technologies could (and should) diffuse the benefits of service to less-developed and rural areas and stimulate both social and economic development.

Although ISDN seems most inevitable in highly developed countries and organizations, the "lack of telecommunication infrastructure in most developing countries could enable countries to bypass stages in development of the technology through which industrial countries have passed, and take full advantage of those (new) technologies" (Seo 1985, 99).

Although regulatory and technical considerations are obvious early concerns in ISDN development, the requirements of the end-users should be kept in perspective. Price and performance should be central to technical discussions if ISDN is ultimately to serve as a vehicle for interdependence. In the end, it is the user, not the carrier or manufacturer, who must be served by the network.

Whereas enormous worldwide efforts are required to make the complexities of ISDN a reality, the International Telecommunication Union's (ITU's) International Telegraph and Telephone Consultative Committee (CCITT) definition is quite simple. *The ISDN is an integrated services network that provides digital connections between user-network interfaces.* Agreement on how this is to be accomplished is currently engaging eleven CCITT study groups addressing nearly eighty complex social, technical, and economic questions and almost all major telecommunication and computer organizations worldwide. Major corporate players include:

North America: AT&T, GTE, Harris, IBM, ITT, Mitel, Northern Telecom, MCI, RCA, ROLM, SBS, TRT
Europe: CIT-Alcatel, L. M. Ericsson, GEC, Mitel, Philips, Plessey, Siemens, Thompson
Japan: Hitachi, Fujitsu, NEC, NTT.

These players, as well as the users of the new services, have a great deal at stake in the ultimate configuration and implementation of

ISDN. The features and capabilities will be of primary concern as the concept unfolds.

TYPES OF SERVICES

A host of services is provided within an ISDN. Generally, these fall into "enhanced telephone service," Group 4 facsimile, packet switching, voice and text mail as well as slow-scan video and videotex. Many of these services will be capable of being accessed at the same time or in conference configurations (e.g., a voice and data teleconference).

The ISDN concept is based on the idea of open-systems interconnections. It combines "the diversity of solutions found in private competition and a maximum of compatibility of the terminal equipment produced by various manufacturers in order that the greatest possible benefits for the customer can be achieved" (Schwarz-Schilling 1984).

CURRENT ISDN APPROACHES AND TRIALS

The move from analog systems to hybrid analog-digital to primarily digital, and on to the ISDN has been proceeding on a national basis in various ways at varying rates. This section provides a brief overview of how this evolution is taking place in several countries. It is anticipated that the underlying approaches by different countries will help to illustrate the complex nature of the topic.

West Germany

One of the more coherent examples of the move to ISDN is provided by West Germany. Through a highly centralized structure we can trace a logical progression.

In the Federal Republic of Germany, the Deutsche Bundespost is responsible for meeting current and future communication needs in what is seen as the coming information age. This age has been characterized as one in which "the value of information almost corresponds to that of the two classic factors of production: capital and labor" (Meierhofer 1986). Specifically, the Bundespost's objective is to offer services needed by customers in an economic and efficient manner; and to develop and introduce new forms of telecommunications on an economic basis.

Today, Germany's telecommunications services are provided over three networks. The first is the public telephone network with more than 24 million main stations. In addition to voice, this network is also utilized for data and facsimile, plus interactive videotex. The second is an integrated text and data network based on digital switching and transmission, providing telex, teletex, circuit, and packet-switched services, plus dedicated data circuits. Broadband networks make up the third system (Federal Republic of Germany 1986).

In 1979, a decision was made to digitalize the telephone network. A projected changeover will see an increasing number of subscribers linked to digital switches. Initially, most of these will be on analog lines, but increasingly by all digital connections. This digitalization of the network is expected to be complete by 2020. At that time it is envisioned that all 30 million subscribers would be linked by 64-kb/s digital connections. Speech, text, data, and pictures could then be offered through each subscriber line.

In preparation for ISDN, a pilot project was started in 1987 in Stuttgart and in Mannheim for about 400 subscribers in each city. The project's objective is to verify that all ISDN components, which will be based on CCITT recommendations, do, in fact, work together as expected. Successful trials will allow manufacturers to proceed in the necessary production of equipment to meet expected national demand.

Initial ISDN services on a commercial basis are expected to commence in 1988–1989. These will include telephony (enhanced), facsimile (group 4), teletex, access to the packet-switched public data network, various videotex and data services currently offered, and ISDN bearer service using 64-kb/s providing unrestricted information transfer for a wide range of user applications such as speech, data, image, text.

A second phase, expected to be implemented in 1990, will include telewriting, fixed-image transmission, and 7-KHz telephony.

Broadband services await the economical installation of systems based on fiber optics. A gradual integration is envisioned through the substitution of fiber optics for copper cables and the enhancement of exchanges with the necessary broadband switching capabilities. Radio and television programming will be distributed over a separate broadband network in 1992. The two systems could be integrated into an integrated broadband telecommunication network (Federal Republic of Germany 1984; Meierhofer, 1986).

France

France, too, has utilized its cohesive approach to telecommunications to its advantage in moving into the digital era.

France envisions a system of ISDN offering equal service to all subscribers. "Such equality is a fundamental principle of public service telecommunications and hence, of telecommunications in France" (Richardot and Prince 1986).

The French telecommunications system has experienced a period of rapid growth in the recent past and it now has some 23 million main telephone lines. This growth has been coupled with the installation of digital exchanges linking some 45 percent of all subscribers to digital local exchanges. By 1990, it is expected that 70 percent of all subscribers will be so connected. Additionally, due to recent installations, there are over 1.3 million videotex terminals in offices and homes in France.

Two trials are planned in France to test the ability of the existing systems to handle the new digital bit rates. The tests will also measure ISDN services and user reactions. During these trials users will also be encouraged to develop new services. The interrelationships between the engineer, the service provider, and the end user are major concerns. One trial will be in Paris, the other in the west of France, with about 300 subscribers. The Paris trial will link some 1,000 subscribers and will be based, in part, on the experiences of the smaller trial.

The French are also testing the ISDN concept via satellite. Currently, the Telecom I communication satellite is being used to provide digital point-to-point networks for French businesses. France's experience with their Telecom I satellite may provide some caution regarding demand for data circuits. The initial satellite design called for primarily digital transponders; the resultant use of the satellite, however, has been primarily analog (Schaub and Dunican, 1986).

Japan

Japan, through its major domestic carrier, Nippon Telegraph and Telephone (NTT), has stated its philosophy of providing fair and equal provision of a more economic, more convenient, and more diversified telecommunications services.

Japan, again, through NTT has moved rapidly in testing their concept of an ISDN. They refer to it as INS, or Information Network System.

The current INS trial involves 450 digital telephones, 1,050 nontelephone terminals, and 9,000 analog telephones. Switching nodes are connected by fiber optics. The Japanese have very ambitious plans for this new means of communication.

Plans for the future system include:

Telephone: Digital subscriber telephone
                  Digital public telephone
                  Digital voice storage service
Still picture: Digital interactive videotex
                  Digital telewriting service
Data: Message communication service
                  DDX circuit switching service
Computer: Multimedia communication service
                  Integrated centralized extension service
Broadband: Video conference and video telephone
                  Video circuit service
                  Video response system
                  High-quality video transmission
                  Ultra high-speed facsimile
                  Color facsimile communication services

In mid-1985, four networks were in service: (1) telephone — 44 million subscribers plus a facsimile "add on" of 18,000 subscribers, plus land and maritime-mobile; (2) a circuit-switched data network with 2,900 subscribers; (3) packet-switched data network with 7,900 subscribers; and (4) a Telex network with 34,000 subscribers.

The tasks seen in moving to INS include the integration of the various telephone and nontelephone networks into a "single, all-inclusive digital system. As a result, bit volume can be taken as a guideline for determining communications charges" (Uehara 1986).

The suggestion that users be assessed on a usage-measured basis is causing concern. Further complicating the formula is the consideration given to the concept that the distance factor is lessened through use of satellites and fiber optics. Obviously, the ultimate pricing structure of ISDN in Japan is of prime concern to users as well as providers. This concern must balance providers' needs for return on investment with the consumers' decision to utilize the wide range of service offerings.

Japan (NTT) has achieved a gradual integration of all data communications with telex, telegraphy, and, subsequently, facsimile by 1987. This will be made possible in part by a nationwide, end-to-end digital service now being put in place. By 1995, the nontelephone network is to be fully integrated into the INS. It is not clear at the moment at what point the broadband services will be integrated.

One focus of the current trials is to continue developing advanced communication technologies along with new communication services.

United States

The move toward an ISDN, or ISDNs, in the United States follows a familiar pattern of multiple approaches fostered by competing carriers and suppliers.

As an illustration, Pacific Bell, one of the seven regional Bell operating companies (RBOCs), formed by the breakup of AT&T, plans a three-phase evolution to a full-scale ISDN.

In 1986, Pacific Bell tested a number of analog and digital switches from different manufacturers to see how they work with one another. Advanced digital multiplexers and fiber-optic lines were used in these trials.

A transition phase will have the Pacific Bell network carrying a number of "ISDN-like services," including circuit-switched 56-kb/s data service. In this phase, attempts will be made to maintain and upgrade all Centrex's to handle future digital needs.

An intermediate ISDN phase is expected to continue into the 1990s. This will follow the resolution of the major standards issues, the supply of reasonably priced equipment, and a better understanding of user demand.

A mature ISDN phase, beginning around 1990, will depend in large part on the development of user applications and the spread of digital connectivity. A broadband switch and ISDN interface is envisioned to be introduced at this time, likely using fiber optics, which will by this time dominate all transport (Bandler 1986).

Another RBOC, Bell Atlantic, in 1984, found a great deal of confusion and a lack of information among consumers regarding this topic and began developing a demonstration of an ISDN.

This demonstration unit on interactive display in several cities is producing valuable information regarding customer reactions, mostly from large organizations. Such information will help plan their first ISDN trial in 1987 (Albers and Darr 1986).

A consensus is building that the Bell operating companies are focusing their attention on enhancing centrexes as an intermediate step toward ISDN. This move is seen by some as a way to preserve their monopolies against bypass carriers.

Working trials of ISDN are planned by most BOCs within the next two years.

CURRENT AND NEAR-TERM ISSUES

ISDN provides a convenient vehicle for the discussion of a wide range of concerns as the world's nations continue to recognize that the value of information is equivalent to the two classic factors of production: capital and labor. The manner and efficiency in which information resources are managed determine, to a great degree, the power base and quality of life within countries, organizations and individuals in the coming decades. It is, therefore, the focus of considerable discussion and debate. Current issues can be categorized as technical, economic, political, and social. This section will address all but the latter, which is reserved for a later section of this paper.

Technical Issues

In the long term, utility of ISDN will depend to a large extent on its technical capabilities. This involves:

the provision of adequate interworking capabilities with other networks so that the ISDN user can continue to communicate with all existing users of the network,

the spread of the new service over a wide geographic area so that customers can be rapidly connected to the evolving ISDN,

the emergence of international standards so that international communication can take place using common protocols,

the capacity of existing networks to handle high-speed data communication,

the ability of existing networks to shift to ISDN without causing interruptions in service,

the implementation of ISDN capacity in a time frame that allows major customers relatively equal treatment, and

the resolution of the interface question, while technical in nature, is perhaps more political.

In the next few years, much of the CCITT's work will focus on technical issues, especially standards, surrounding ISDN. Specifically, in the area of standards, a number of study groups will be integrating the concerns of the International Standards Organization's (ISO) Technical Committee 97 (TC97) with their own responsibilities in ISDN. At stake is a coordinated and consistent set of technical standards, which will make integration possible.

At the core of the Standards discussion is the seven-layered ISO protocol model (see Figure 27.1).

Political and Economic Issues

Political issues, both nationally and among major corporate players, are at the heart of ISDN debates. At the national level, various PTTs

FIGURE 27.1 — OSI Reference Model

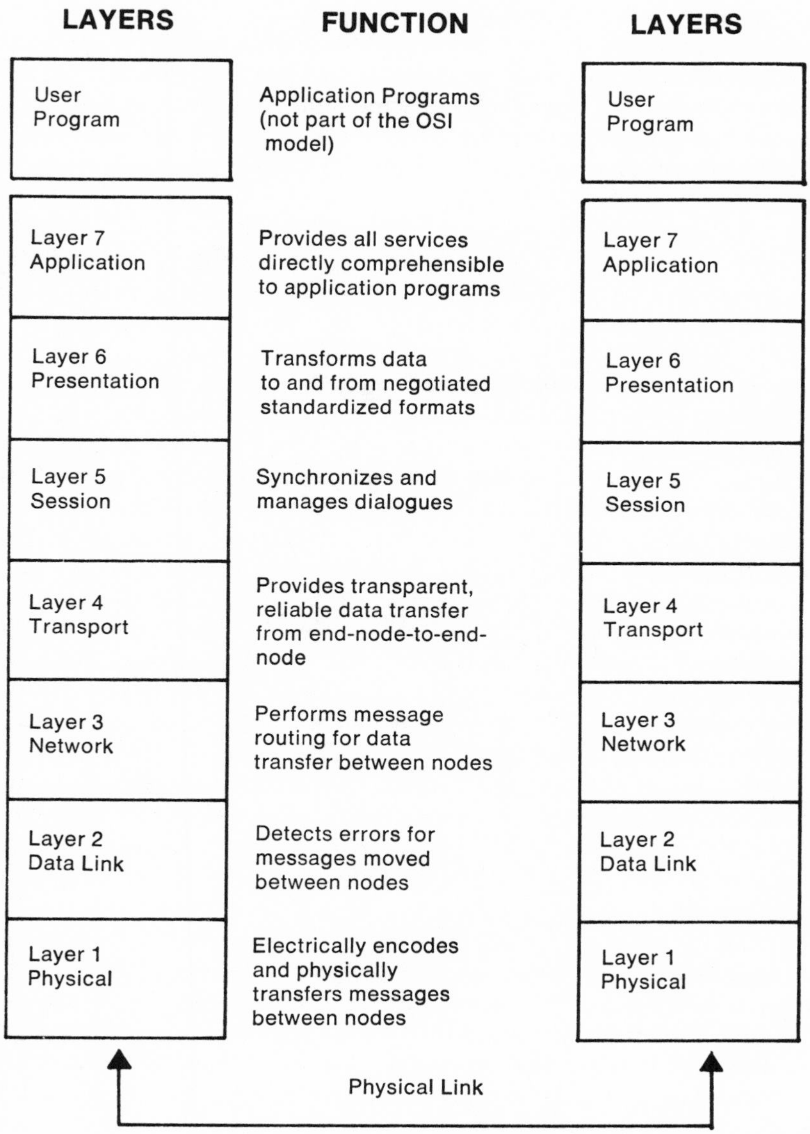

LAYERS	FUNCTION	LAYERS
User Program	Application Programs (not part of the OSI model)	User Program
Layer 7 Application	Provides all services directly comprehensible to application programs	Layer 7 Application
Layer 6 Presentation	Transforms data to and from negotiated standardized formats	Layer 6 Presentation
Layer 5 Session	Synchronizes and manages dialogues	Layer 5 Session
Layer 4 Transport	Provides transparent, reliable data transfer from end-node-to-end-node	Layer 4 Transport
Layer 3 Network	Performs message routing for data transfer between nodes	Layer 3 Network
Layer 2 Data Link	Detects errors for messages moved between nodes	Layer 2 Data Link
Layer 1 Physical	Electrically encodes and physically transfers messages between nodes	Layer 1 Physical

Physical Link

Source: Boeing Corporation. Technical and Office Protocols, November 1985, p. 2-2.

and, in the United States, the FCC and the Bell operating companies have very different policy agendas. The various regulatory approaches, while applicable to the past telecommunication environment, may have little applicability in an ISDN environment (Rutkowski 1985). At the core of many of these differences is the "privatization versus monopoly" issue. Proponents of privatization contend that ISDN user requirements can be best served by leaving the provision of services to the marketplace. The problem with this, opponents point out, is that it results in a number of ISDNs instead of a single public network. Individual corporations vying for market dominance in ISDN may seek advantages in proprietary systems, thus negating the possibility and economies of scale of a common ubiquitous system. It also has the risk of incompatibilities at the international level. The possibility of this occurring is greatest in the United States, where the FCC is pursuing a laissez-faire approach.

Multinational organizations seem ill disposed to await the provision of an ISDN for their use. At a recent ISDN conference it was noted that "Indeed, when we heard from representatives of the Bank of America and General Motors, it was obvious that both were proceeding with their own plans for proprietary world-wide networks, and weren't likely going to be influenced by an ISDN" (Stoffels 1985).

Another confounding variable in the United States is the basic/enhanced telecommunications services dichotomy. Decisions coming out of Computer Inquiry II set out this two-class service notion, which regulates basic services and opens all enhanced services to the competitive marketplace. At issue here is whether ISDN is truly an "enhanced service" or is, in the long term, just plain old telephone service (POTS). Computer Inquiry III has directly addressed this issue.

A THIRTY-YEAR SCENARIO, 1986–2016

Admittedly, forecasting alternatives for the future is an inexact science. Although straightforward trend analyses and extrapolations from the past have certain validities, they are inappropriate in settings involving the introduction of wholly new technologies and services. And the inclusion of sociocultural and political aspects further removes forecasting from rigorous "scientific methods." To be sure, there are ways of applying expertise to such forecasts, most notably through policy Delphi techniques in which a panel of experts is used to collectively explore issues and possible outcomes.

General Framework

In this case, the authors generated the scenario. The speculations perhaps reflect more on personal biases and logic patterns than on any well-grounded theory. Nevertheless, the scenario provides a good vehicle for further speculation and discussion and it is offered with that intent.

The general approach taken here suggests that there are three stages of change associated with ISDN. These three stages have scenes of ten years each and therefore project thirty years into the future, to 2016 (see Figure 27.2). The progression of each ten-year period moves from the near term, in which we are primarily concerned with the articulation and resolution of issues, to a second stage in which consequences will be experienced.

In Stage One, the issues are primarily seen as technical and regulatory in nature with economic and political overlappings. The issues of Stage One, as they begin to be addressed and resolved, will directly affect the national and global infrastructures in such ways as to alter the processes of human activities. Thus, Stage Two, 1996–2006, may be mainly characterized by changes experienced in the economic sphere. With the application of the new technology, the scale and scope of economic activity, including production, trade, and consumption, will be greatly expanded and altered.

Stage Three of this model is primarily concerned with the consequences of the changed economic activities. Thus, the period 2006–2016 envisions a number of significant sociocultural impacts, linked with both political and economic changes as well.

The basic premise restated in a simplified manner is that in three ten-year stages, the solution of technological issues will change the economic processes, which in turn will alter the sociocultural environment. ISDN and related technological developments are clearly not seen as "value-free" innovations. They have consequences in all spheres of human endeavors.

Stage One: Issues, 1986–1996

In the 1986–1996 period, the major technical-standards questions will be, for the most part, resolved, paving the way for the establishment of separate narrowband and wideband ISDNs. Private local area net interconnections via ISDN are also foreseen. Trial broadband (i.e., fully integrated ISDN systems) will be tested. Later in this period there are expected to be major developments in artificial intelligence some directly built into ISDN. New developments in

FIGURE 27.2 — General Framework, ISDN Scenario

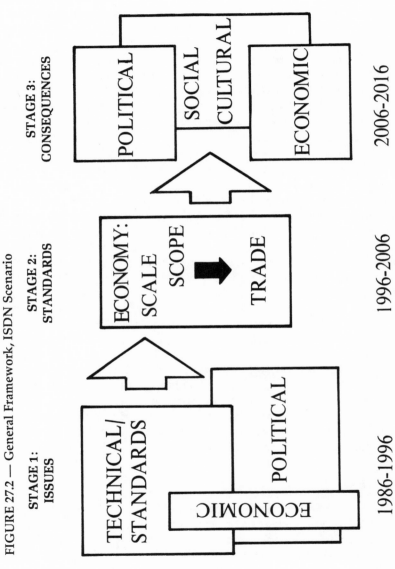

STAGE 1:
ISSUES

STAGE 2:
STANDARDS

STAGE 3:
CONSEQUENCES

TECHNICAL/
STANDARDS

ECONOMIC

POLITICAL

ECONOMY:
SCALE
SCOPE

TRADE

POLITICAL

SOCIAL
CULTURAL

ECONOMIC

1986-1996

1996-2006

2006-2016

multipurpose, generic, communication-intensive computer operating systems will be refined and compatible with ISDN's technical requirements. UNIX, for example, is already in mid-stages of development and generic protocol work is being carried out in projects such as Boeing's technical and office protocols (TOP) and manufacturer's automated protocol (MAP) at General Motors, the objective of these being standardized interfaces for end-to-end applications of all office and manufacturing information exchanges. Another development of particular note will be the artificially intelligent-based automatic language translator, which will facilitate day-to-day communication first for specialized lexicons and subsequently for all users of the ISDN.

Various multinational firms are seen to continue to develop their own private networks, basing them more and more on ISDN principles. National defense establishments, in the name of "secure circuits," will develop and utilize separate ISDN links.

With major shifts in the information industry and in other sectors, this ten-year scene will exhibit great structural unemployment. This will continue to be a major problem, especially as it affects third world countries that lack the depth to manage rapidly shifting employment opportunities and unemployment burdens. Education and training will be seen as the appropriate response to these problems, but will not be widely available until the mid-1990s.

The coming decade will continue to see a rapid rise in awareness among leaders *and* the populace of the global information society. With this will be a growing recognition of information as a primary social-economic resource.

Stage Two: Process, 1996–2006

The boundary between Stages One and Two is an artificial one, established primarily for the sake of conceptualization. It is not to be seen as a solid line or magical window. Change from 1986 to 2016 and beyond will be as change has always been: gradual, interrelated, and sometimes, as pivotal events occur, rapid and full of surprises.

In the technical realm we will see widespread use of fully integrated broadband ISDN. We will see the introduction and use of optical fiber switching to optimize the fiber networks, which have been widely implemented in the past decade.

At the same time, the world will be engaged in a "second wave" review of telecommunication transmission standards, taking into consideration the major technological developments of the last decade (1986–1996).

A freeing of the radio spectrum through the use of broadband (optical fiber-based) ISDN will lead to nontraditional use of communication satellites and the airwaves in general. Specifically, mobile-type technologies will become economically viable as broadband services are moved "off the air" and delivered via fiber.

As a selected few will receive more training for access and use of the system, the division between the "information haves" and the "information have-nots" will increase. This will occur within countries as well as between countries. Of course, knowing how to access a system without its availability will also be a factor and is a possible forerunner to information terrorism as individuals and groups begin to feel "shut out" of the system.

During this period, as information comes to be seen as a fundamental resource and commodity, new definitions or redefinitions of work, privacy, and property will be proposed. This, too, will have ramifications in Stage Three of the scenario.

Stage Three: Consequences, 2006–2016

The consequences of the new technological developments will be reflected in the ubiquitous use of artificial intelligence both within and at the ends of the network. The development of a "world brain" concept will emerge. Such a brain will be able to facilitate the management of complexity as well as monitor several aspects of the earth's environment. It will be key to personal quality of life as well as resource and crisis management.

Leading into this period could be a series of "information wars" — unfriendly electronic encounters brought on by conflicting desires to obtain, possess and control information and communication.

At the same time, acts of information or telecommunication terrorism could occur. Individual, social, and cultural information disenfranchisements could also result in additional barriers to full international telecommunication integration. The social and cultural consequences of ISDN in this third decade could prove to be negative unless managed well. Particular attention should be paid to "distributing the wealth" of information/telecommunication resources.

SUMMARY AND CONCLUSIONS

This has been a journey from the present to the future facilitated by concentrating on the manner by which we will share information via ISDN. We have examined ISDN's present issues and trials and envisioned a path of development from 1986–2016. The possibilities and problems of ISDN are evolutionary, but patterns of that evolution can be shaped early by concerns for full interdependence of stakeholders. Caution should be given to proprietary developments of the ISDN concept. People manage their environment by information; telecommunication networks facilitate this flow. We should not take lightly the development of the full ISDN concept.

REFERENCES AND BIBLIOGRAPHY

Albers, R. F., and J. W. Darr. 1986. "Bell Atlantic Takes ISDN One Step Further." *Telephony.* P. 28.

Bandler, Michael L. 1986. "Pacific Bell Foresees Three-Phase ISDN Evolution." *Telephony.* P. 44.

Belitsos, B. 1986. "Regional BOCs Focus on ISDN." *Communications International.* Pp. 46–49.

Beveridge, G. J., and S. S. Gorshe. 1986. "The Clear Channel Shortcut to ISDN." *Telephone Engineer & Management.* Pp. 63, 68.

Boeing. 1985. "Technical and Office Protocols."

British Telecom International. (n.d.). "The World of International Business Communications." Brochure.

Coit, K. T., and M. J. Maher. 1986. "Cost Considerations for ISDN Line Code Selection." *Telephony.* P. 62

Communications Engineering International. 1986. "ISDN — American Style." Pp. 58–61.

Communications Engineering International. 1986. "News Digest 2." P. 11.

Communications International. 1986. "CeBIT Launches with Urgent Call for ISDN Agreement."

Communications Systems Worldwide. 1986. "Conference Report: Europe Struggles to Cooperate." Pp. 43–44.

Connolly, R. D., C. A. Pleasance, and S. E. Zillman. 1986. "Why Use a Digital Access?" *Telephone Engineer & Management.* Pp. 98–99.

Daude, J. A. Bloc. 1986. "Alcatel EIO in the ISDN Environment." Conference Papers, CommunicAsia'86, InfotechAsia'86, Singapore Exhibition Services, Singapore. April 9–12. P. 10.52ff.

Dawson, F. 1986. "Making the Most of International Telecommunications." *Telecommunication Products & Technology.* Pp. 21–36.

Federal Republic of Germany. Federal Ministry of Posts and Telecommunications. 1984. "Development Strategy of the Deutsche Bundespost for the Public Telecommunications System in the Federal Republic of Germany." Brochure. Bonn.

Federal Republic of Germany. Federal Ministry of Posts and Telecommunications. (n.d.). "ISDN — The Deutsche Bundespost's Response to the Telecommunications Requirements of Tomorrow." Brochure. Bonn.

Gilhooly, Denis. 1986. "Comment: Order Out of Chaos." *Communications Engineering International.* P. 5.

Hudson, Malcolm. 1986. "The ISDN Revolution: Australia." *Asia-Pacific Broadcasting and Telecommunications.* Pp. 27–28.

IGI Consulting, Inc. "ISDN: Technologies, Services and Markets." Brochure.

Komiya, M. 1986. "Integrated Services Digital Networks in the United States and Japan: A Comparative Analysis of National Telecommunication Policies." *Pacific Telecommunications Council Conference Proceedings.* P. 22.

Lohse, E. 1984. "Progress in Information Systems and Use." *Pacific Telecommunications Council Conference Proceedings.* P. 179ff.

McPherson, G. T. 1986. "Communications in New Zealand: Coping with Rapid Expansion Using Front Edge Digital Technology." Conference papers, CommunicAsia'86, InfotechAsia'86, Singapore Exhibition Services, Singapore. April 9–12. Pp. 10.23ff.

Meierhofer, J. 1986. "ISDN — The Deutsche Bundespost's Response to the Telecommunication Requirements of Tomorrow." Conference papers, CommunicAsia'86, InfotechAsia'86, Singapore Exhibition Services, Singapore. April 9–12. Pp. 5.56ff.

Mitel Corporation. 1986. *Superswitch News.* Spring.

NEC (n.d.). "C&C Linking Nations and People." Brochure.

Northern Telecom. 1985. "Annual Report 1985: ISDN." Brochure.

Olsen, R. J. 1986. "The Digital Pacific — Evolution or Revolution?" *Pacific Telecommunications Council Conference Proceedings.* P. 199.

Plessey. (n.d.). "Plessey." Brochure.

Richardot, H., and B. Prince. 1986. "ISDN: Why and How It is Implemented in a Modern Telecommunication Network." Ministry of PTT France, Conference Papers, CommunicAsia'86, InfotechAsia'86, Singapore Exhibition Services, Singapore. April 9–12. Pp. 5.18ff.

Ruiterkamp, Wim. 1986. "Private Telephone Exchanges in the ISDN Environment." Conference Papers, CommunicAsia'86, InfotechAsia'86, Singapore Exhibition Services, Singapore. April 9–12. Pp. 10.60ff.

Rutkowski, A. M. 1985. *Integrated Services Digital Networks.* Deedham, MA: Artech House.

Schaub, T., and J. Dunicau. 1986. "From Scratch to Operation: The Telecom 1 Satellite." Conference Papers, CommunicAsia'86, InfotechAsia'86, Singapore Exhibition Services, Singapore. April 9–12.

Schwarz-Schilling, Christian. 1984. *ISDN — The Deutsche Bundespost's Response to the Telecommunication Requirements of Tomorrow.* Bonn, Germany: Federal Minister of Post and Telecommunication.

Seo, Jund Uck, Yong Son, and Sang Chul Lee. 1986. "Korean Strategies for a Digital World." *Pacific Telecommunications Council Conference Proceedings.* Pp. 26–30.

Siemens. (n.d.). "Public Communications Networks, Siemens Telecommunications: Ideas for the Future Became a Reality." *Siemens Aktiengesellschaft.* Brochure.

Siemens. (n.d.). "Digital Communications Equipment for Suburban and Rural Applications." Brochure.

Siemens. (n.d.). "Operator Service Systems OSS." *Siemens Aktiengesellschaft.* Brochure.

Sofrecom. (n.d.). "Local Network Characterization for ISDN." Brochure.

Sofrecom. (n.d.). "The French Telecommunications Consultant." Brochure.

Standard Elektrik Lorenz AG-ITT. (n.d.). "Systems 12 Digital Exchange: The Necessary Solution." Brochure.

Stoffels, Bob. 1985. "ISDN '85 Sends Mixed Signals." *Telephone Engineer and Management.* Pp. 108–9.

Taylor, M. 1986. "Enhanced Centrex Rivals PBXs." *Telecommunications Products & Technology.* Pp. 28–30.

Telecoms. (n.d.). "ISDN." Brochure.

Uehara, Toru. 1986. "Evolution of Domestic Telecommunications in Japan." *Pacific Telecommunications Council Conference Proceedings.* Pp. 9–17.

White, C. E. 1982. "Siemens in the USA: Charting a New Course." *Telecommunications.* P. 66.

White, C. E. 1986. "Users Face the Reality of Telecommunications." *Telecommunications.* Pp. 72–76.

28

INTELSAT and Separate Satellite Systems Issues

JOSEPH N. PELTON

We live in a changing world. This is particularly so in the world of high technology. In a survey of executives in new start-up venture-capital firms, it was found that 43 percent of those surveyed had a personal computer at their desks and that these were in use a significant percentage of the time. Let's take another example. It is today possible to transmit a single page of information across the Pacific Ocean some 50 million times faster than it was a couple of centuries ago. Whichever way one looks — satellites, computers, television, telematics, or robotics — the story is the same: innovation, change, and economic and social revolution, driven by new technologies.

Although the importance of communications to industrialized countries is often obvious in many ways, there is increasing evidence (reflected in studies commissioned by the International Telecommunication Union and the Organization of Economic Cooperation and Development) that telecommunications is also essential to the economic progress of developing countries. Cost-benefit ratios as high as 100 to 1 have been identified in such diverse parts of the world as Egypt, Kenya, and India. Examples are often as straightforward as the Indian farmer who walked with his ox seven days to pick up fertilizer from a supply depot, only to find the stocks exhausted — returning after a fourteen-day round trip empty-handed. Had he been able to walk even five kilometers to a telephone to make inquiries, most of the wasted effort could have been eliminated. On the island nation of Tonga it was found that export prices negotiated via satellite in the international competitive marketplace increased by as much as 30 percent, while import prices were also reduced by a similar amount as a result of international quotes and bids. The use of affordable telecommunications can lead to remarkable differences when used to establish import and export prices rather than relying only on the prices set by the first ship that steams into port.

INTELSAT: MYTHS AND REALITIES ABOUT
THE GLOBAL SATELLITE COOPERATIVE

Thus, if one accepts the overriding economic and social importance of telecommunications as being clear and well documented, let us now turn to INTELSAT and its particular role in international telecommunications development. In particular let's focus first on, what is INTELSAT? How has it changed the world of global telecommunications, at the national, regional, and international levels? And, perhaps most important, what changes does it promise for the future? It is impossible to answer these questions, however, without first clearly understanding what INTELSAT is. This is particularly true because there are many myths and misunderstandings about INTELSAT, how it operates, its organizational structure, its goals, and even the mechanisms by which INTELSAT's accountability to the world community is maintained.

First of all, INTELSAT is an intergovernmental international organization, established under two international treaties. The governments of 110 countries currently adhere to the INTELSAT agreements, whereas 110 designated signatories participate as the working members of INTELSAT. Although INTELSAT is operated on a commercial basis (which means that all members must pay for services received), it is also a nonprofit cooperative, and services are made available to all countries of the world on an open and nondiscriminatory basis. Thus, although INTELSAT has an official membership of 110 countries, it actually provides services to 170 different countries and territories around the world, including countries that are democracies, planned economies, monarchies, and every other form of government.

INTELSAT, indeed, does not have a monopoly on international telecommunications. Since the beginning, INTELSAT has had, and continues to have, serious competition from submarine cables — most recently in the form of highly cost-efficient fiber-optics cable systems. In addition, certain regional satellite systems have been established, but within the framework of the INTELSAT agreements; namely, for limited services within definable regions of the world, as reflected in the coordinations of the ARABSAT, EUTELSAT, and Southeast Asian PALAPA systems.

It has also been maintained that the INTELSAT structure is established so that only monopoly post, telegraph, and telecommunications (PTT) organizations can utilize the INTELSAT facilities and, thus, it serves to stifle competition or deregulation at the national level. Again, experience in both the United Kingdom and the United States has demonstrated that this is also an inaccurate characterization of the INTELSAT structure. The United Kingdom's government has authorized establishment of two organizations — namely, British Telecom International and Mercury — to access the INTELSAT system and to provide services to end-users in the United Kingdom. In the United States, the FCC has authorized international carriers who wish to provide either video services or digital business communications services from customer-premise or small earth terminals serving as urban gateways to own and operate such earth stations and to obtain the services from INTELSAT through the U.S. signatory on a "debundled" rate (that is, the space segment and earth station charges are separated from one another).

These changes at the national level, reflecting the goals of increasing competition and deregulation in those countries, have been accommodated with the INTELSAT system. In many ways, the INTELSAT system should perhaps be seen as equivalent to an international railway, upon which countries and commercial organizations can place their trains or boxcars, or even containerized packages, of information, which can be transported on a global basis. There are today, in effect, transoceanic satellite and cable "telecommunications railways," as represented by the INTELSAT system and by submarine cable systems. The question is, how many railways should be built before serious overinvestment occurs?

Overcapitalized telecommunications investment in the United States, in my view, could in the next decade be among the contributing factors in developing countries not being able to finance and capitalize needed new telecommunications projects.

INTELSAT AND U.S. DEREGULATION OF TELECOMMUNICATIONS: CONFLICT OR COMPATIBILITY?

The other members of INTELSAT, of course, respect the sovereign right of the United States to seek to move INTELSAT in new directions. The concern is that the United States has shown some inclination to move unilaterally to institute change, without some international negotiation and outside of the procedures established by the INTELSAT agreements. This is not a minor issue. More than seventy countries have placed letters and diplomatic notes on file with various agencies of the U.S. government with regard to their concerns about "unilateral" approval of so-called private satellite systems. Many of these countries have very clearly stated that if the United States wishes to change the structure of INTELSAT it should do so through the authorized procedures and not attempt to reinterpret independently the INTELSAT agreement so as to achieve a restructuring of INTELSAT on a de facto basis.

Recent studies of international U.S. trade policies have shown that the previous attempts by the United States to unilaterally redefine multilateral agreements in the transportation field have met with mixed success and even at times outright failure and embarrassment to U.S. policy makers. There is no particular reason to suspect that similar uncoordinated and unilateral initiatives in the telecommunications area might not lead to similar results. In fact, it may well be that RCA's recent decision to abandon its petition to modify the F-6 satellite to provide both domestic U.S. and international services to Europe reflects the lack of support for such systems by the authorized European telecommunication entities, as well as a business decision that recognizes that rapid growth potential does not exist at this time — given current growth of about 9 percent. This is significant, because the other private satellite system proposers (namely, ORION, ISI, Cygnus, and FINANCESAT) are small, inexperienced corporations that lack capital resources.

INTELSAT, in my view, is not only highly accountable to the international communications and information marketplace, but receptive to constructive proposals for change and innovation. The mechanism that has produced accountability — namely, the INTELSAT agreements — has also allowed INTELSAT to be an effective global common denominator, a bridge among all of the various countries of the world, regardless of the sophistication of the telecommunications and information infrastructure and regardless even of whether they are members of INTELSAT or not. In this respect, INTELSAT is unique among other international organizations, which, unlike INTELSAT, have frequently been marred by serious political bickering and a decision-making process that is often characterized by politics first and objective decision making on merits last.

First, it should be noted, for the sake of clarity, that there are no restrictions that limit the ability of the United States to encourage and to achieve new and effective means of deregulation and procompetitive policies concerning the use of access modes to the INTELSAT system. This can be accomplished on a strictly domestic basis, under the regulatory authority of the FCC, and consistent with the Communications Act of 1934 and the Comsat Act of 1964, as both have been amended. Indeed, U.S. policy decisions by the FCC have been accommodated by INTELSAT itself in terms of allowing a large number of new U.S. international carriers to access the INTELSAT satellite system for video and digital communications. This U.S.-initiated change is being accommodated in other parts of the world: European PTTs signing new operating agreements or letters of intent to operate with new U.S. entities. Such letters of agreement have been signed in the United Kingdom, West Germany, Switzerland, and elsewhere.

This shift toward international "service" competition in international telecommunications, plus increasingly sophisticated and earnest competition between INTELSAT and fiber-optic cable systems, could, without any further "facility competition," fundamentally change the scope, cost, and direction of international telecommunications. In this respect, U.S. policy makers need to consider what objectives have been or will be achieved under changes now approved and what are the "pros" and "cons" of pushing beyond the scope of changes already made.

INTELSAT AND INNOVATION FOR THE FUTURE

The ultimate success of INTELSAT, of course, will not hinge on the number of mechanisms available to achieve accountability or the protections provided in the INTELSAT agreements. The ultimate test will be, in fact, the international communications and information marketplace.

In short, will INTELSAT be able to expand the volume, scope, and flexibility of its service offerings to meet effectively emerging demands? Also, can and will INTELSAT keep users happy? In this respect, INTELSAT's record, by objective measures, would appear to be extremely impressive. The INTELSAT system has gone from 0 percent of the international overseas transoceanic telecom-munications market to approximately two-thirds of the global traffic demand in this area.

INTELSAT has also become the predominant supplier of international video relays on a transoceanic basis, even though new wideband fiber-optic systems should be able to provide strong and effective competition in this area. INTELSAT, for instance, in anticipation of future market demands, has recently approved and introduced a digital television service, which, within the next five years, should allow the provision of video services at significant rate reductions. In the meantime, different priority levels for video services are allowing cost reductions now. Equally important, television services can now be leased on a full-time basis for different time periods, ranging from one to seven years.

Also, for low-volume users, there are now part-time lease services, plus peak and off-peak occasional-use rates that allow users to tailor their distribution services to their specific needs. Digital signal processing of the future will allow multiple TV channels to be sent through a single transponder. There can also be a parallel reduction in the size and cost of earth stations that will receive such digital services.

On the horizon, INTELSAT expects to introduce, in the near future, electronic document-distribution services. This might ultimately lead to highly interactive INTELSAT-type data broadcast and distribution networks. Also, by the 1990s, INTELSAT will likely be providing high-definition television services. INTELSAT will also likely move even further toward diversification of a tariffing structure to allow tailored telecommunications and broadcasting needs to respond to new market demands.

Although it is in many ways clear and reasonable to compare INTELSAT's technological and service innovations record with that of domestic satellite systems (such as exist in the United States, Canada, Japan, Europe, and, indeed, a number of developing countries such as India, Indonesia, Mexico, and Brazil), the one area of significant difference between INTELSAT and such other systems should be particularly highlighted. INTELSAT, more than any other system in the world, has as its objective global interconnectivity.

It is the INTELSAT objective of achieving global interconnectivity that forces the INTELSAT space segment design, in terms of its use of frequency and power, to be less cost effective than domestic systems. It is, in fact, only due to such aspects as lifetime extensions and economies of scale and scope that INTELSAT transponder costs per year in orbit have been able to be maintained in surprisingly close proximity to domestic systems. The INTELSAT system, for instance, provides on a global basis some 1,700 earth–station-to-earth–station pathways. It is significant to note in this respect that half of these pathways (that is, in excess of 850 of them) provide INTELSAT with less than 10 percent of its revenues. Furthermore, it is equally significant that about 10 percent of the pathways represent approximately 50 percent of INTELSAT's revenues.

This aspect of INTELSAT is important in another way — in the conservation of the use of the orbital arc. INTELSAT's seventeen satellites from only seventeen orbital locations serve over 170 different countries and territories for international services. They also provide eight international television networks, twenty-seven domestic satellite systems, and an important element of mobile services to the world maritime community. In an era of satellite proliferation, the world's largest common-user satellite system is the most effective conservator of the geosynchronous orbital arc. This fact was especially noted and emphasized among the attendees of the World Administration Radio Conference on Orbital Locations (WARC/ORB 85), held in Geneva, Switzerland.

Not only will fiber-optic systems and new digital-processing techniques serve to push the cost of INTELSAT's services down, but the new integrated services digital networks (ISDN) standards should aid in maintaining the quality and integrity of future telecommunications services.

The need to provide effective interconnection to fiber-optics systems and domestic and regional satellite systems in the ISDN mode of operation will be, indeed, one of the great technical challenges of the 1980s and 1990s. It is, in many ways, remarkable, to me at least, that the INTELSAT system has been able to introduce a very high rate of technological innovation and continues to diversify service offerings responsive to the needs of highly sophisticated users (such as banks, oil companies, and other multinational enterprises), while at the same time continuing to be highly responsive to the needs of the third world and developing countries.

In this respect, INTELSAT has introduced, within the last few years, VISTA low-density thin-route communications service, the INTELSAT Assistance and Development Program (IADP), and during 1985 and 1986 it conducted Project SHARE (a rural test and demonstration program related to health and rural education for developing countries). We have also initiated a serious study of what we call the INTELSAT Development Fund, which will help in the financing, as well as in the design, of telecommunications systems in rural parts of the world, with such financing covering not only the ground segment but also terrestrial interconnect and terminal equipment as well.

INTELSAT AS A VIABLE CONCEPT FOR THE FUTURE

I would like to close by presenting a brief comparative analysis of government-controlled PTT entities, on the one hand, versus private enterprise (market-driven, competitive, and deregulated) on the other. It is often assumed that monopolies and government-controlled enterprises can best achieve such objectives as universal access to all users and the provision of subsidies for rural and isolated customers in the provision of basic and traditional telecommunications services like switched telephony. It is also widely assumed, however, that such entities may well tend to maintain rates at higher levels than are necessary, that the organizational structures of such institutions are very bureaucratic and slow to respond, and that they do not provide innovative and new services in a timely manner.

On the other hand, it is often assumed that private, unregulated, market-driven organizations are quick to respond to service innovation, that they depreciate obsolete equipment more rapidly, and that they introduce new facilities or services at the earliest possible date. In short, private organizations are typically seen as highly responsive to very sophisticated communications users who demand innovative services, flexibility, and service offerings.

INTELSAT has sufficient competition to innovate, introduce new technologies, and develop new services quickly. It is a nonprofit cooperative. It does not have a profit motive nor a "subsidy" requirement in a classic economic sense to retain prices at high levels. INTELSAT cannot retain excess revenues under the INTELSAT agreement, so again it only has motivation to grow, expand, and reduce the cost of its services. INTELSAT does not give special breaks in charges or services to any single set of users, because this is prohibited under Article V of the INTELSAT agreement. Therefore, all users — big, medium, and small — know they are being treated fairly and equitably. The cumulative effect of worldwide participation provides sufficient traffic volume to keep prices low for everyone.

CONCLUSIONS

In short, INTELSAT is a unique twentieth-century mechanism. It seems to combine social and valuable characteristics well-suited for high-technology commercial ventures requiring international collaboration, compatibility, and common capital investments. Such strengths that INTELSAT possesses, particularly in the form of effective North-South political, economic, and technical cooperation, should be built upon and improved in the 1980s and 1990s. The INTELSAT experience indeed seems to show a rare ability for "objective," technically based international cooperation, which should not be easily discarded for the promise of ill-defined benefits from a totally unregulated international telecommunications environment. The course that seems most promising is to improve INTELSAT's strengths, minimize its weaknesses, and encourage it to be innovative in response to a rapidly changing worldwide telecommunications market. This can be done with time, patience, and the willingness of all countries to empathize with the goals and objectives of their international telecommunications partners.

29

Satellite Communications: Technologies and Services

Toshio Sato

In November 1963, the first transpacific television reception experiment was conducted at the Ibaraki earth station via the Relay II satellite. The material transmitted from the Mojave station in California on this memorable day was the first news of the assassination of President Kennedy. This event made a deep impression on the Japanese people because of its political importance as well as its novel technology — television transmission via satellite. Since those days — only twenty-five years ago — enormous progress has been made. Nobody could imagine then that a tiny satellite could support the vast amount of telecommunications traffic we have today.

Although geostationary satellites are communications repeaters, they are at the same time celestial bodies governed by celestial mechanics:

1. *Solar Cell Degradation.* In the space environment, ionized particles may degrade the performance of semiconductor devices, including solar cells. Cosmic dust may also degrade the thermal radiation characteristics of the satellite surface and solar cell performance.
2. *Station Keeping.* Another important and decisive factor is the propellant required for keeping the satellite at the predetermined location in the geostationary orbit. When the propellant for maneuver has been depleted, the satellite is considered to have reached the end of its life, since it then loses the capability to serve some areas.
3. *Sun Interference and Eclipse.* Twice a year, at the autumnal and vernal equinoxes, solar interference occurs for several consecutive

days. At this time, the sun is located exactly in the direction of the earth station antenna beam. Because of the increased noise, a circuit may be out of service for five minutes a day at maximum. Total annual outage time may be about twenty-three minutes for a thirty-meter antenna at 4 GHz.

4. Another factor is the eclipse of the satellite. The earth blocks the satellite from the sunlight twice a year in the vernal and autumnal equinox seasons, lasting for forty-five days. In the eclipse, the solar panels can not generate electric power, and conventional batteries have to be provided for backup.

One of the most significant advantages of operating a satellite communications system may be the economy of scale. The history of INTELSAT space segment charge reductions clearly indicates the successful operation of the INTELSAT system. All such success has been achieved through the increasing amount of communications channels provided by newer generations of INTELSAT satellites.

The INTELSAT VI satellites will have the equivalent of some 80,000 telephone channels. This should be compared with the 240 of the first INTELSAT satellite, Early Bird. The consistent traffic growth has necessitated the growth of satellite capacity with each generation, and the enhanced capacity has stimulated the traffic demand in turn.

TREND TOWARD DEREGULATION

In March 1983, the Orion Satellite Corporation applied to the Federal Communications Commission (FCC) for permission to offer transponders for video networks, governmental organizations, and multinational corporations in the Atlantic Ocean region. Five other systems followed with similar objectives but with different approaches.

On November 28, 1984, President Reagan signed a presidential determination that separate satellite systems were "required in the national interest."

At the direction of the president, the Department of State and the Department of Commerce jointly informed the FCC of the president's decision and the criteria necessary to ensure that the United States meets its international obligations and to further U.S. telecommunications and foreign policy interests. The following are the two restrictions to be imposed on the alternative systems prior to final authorization by the commission: (1) each system is to be restricted to providing services through the sale or long-term lease of transponders or space segment capacity for communications not interconnected with public-switched message networks (except for emergency restoration service); and (2) one or more foreign authorities are to authorize use of each system and enter into consultation procedures with the United States party under Article XIV(d) of the INTELSAT agreement to ensure technical compatibility and to avoid significant economic harm.

In this vein, Orion, PanAmSat, and others have been conditionally authorized by the FCC to construct their satellites. However, the final authorization for the operation of these separate satellite systems will not be issued until the conditions as mentioned in (2) above are met.

RECENT DEVELOPMENTS IN THE INMARSAT SYSTEM

Traffic Growth and Services Offered

In 1979, INMARSAT came into being after a long period of preparation for the purpose of offering communications services to ships at sea. INMARSAT is an international organization formed by the Convention on the International Maritime Satellite Organization (INMARSAT).

The number of ships equipped with ship terminals or ship earth stations (SESs) has continued to increase dramatically since the commencement of operations in February 1982. The annual growth rate of the number of SESs in the past three years is almost 40 percent. Because of the remarkable traffic growth, saturation of satellite capacity is anticipated in the near future, especially in the Atlantic Ocean region.

The major services offered by INMARSAT now are telephone and telex. Data transmission at the speed of 1,200 and 2,400 bits per second (bps) is also offered over the telephone channel. High-speed data transmission of 56 kilobits per second (kb/s) is available at some SESs for seismic ships and oil rigs.

For the users, such as oil drilling platforms, very high-speed data (VHSD) service is being offered with a data rate of 1.0 megabits per second (MB/s).

Group call service using telex channels has begun, offering broadcast-type calls to all ships at sea, ships of the same nationality, ships of a specified fleet, and specific groups of ships.

Second-Generation Space Segment

INMARSAT needs the second-generation space segment from mid-1988. A contract was awarded to British Aerospace to construct at least three spacecraft. The second-generation space segment will consist of satellites capable of supporting 125 voice-grade channels. The full bandwidth allocated to the maritime mobile satellite service at WARC-79 will be used.

The transponder in the ship-to-shore direction will be divided into four channels in order to accommodate a variety of services. The channels provided are for Standard A SESs, smaller SESs (such as Standards B and C), data transmission from ships, and EPIRB (emergency position indicating radio beacon).

INMARSAT has been suffering from the frequency coordination with the INTELSAT system for the feeder link frequencies in the 4/6 GHz bands. The INMARSAT council decided to shift the feeder link from the existing bands to a set of new bands — 3,600–3,621 MHz and 6,425–6,441 MHz — which are adjacent to the bands used in the existing INTELSAT system.

However, in some countries, such as Japan, these bands may be subject to interference to and from terrestrial systems, which makes coordination difficult. Solutions for this are being sought.

Small-Size Ship Earth Stations

In order to satisfy the increasing demand for better communications quality and quantity, studies are under way on new SES standards, typical of which are Standards B and C.

Taking advantage of recent developments in digital techniques, SESs will be fully digitalized in the near future. By applying forward error correction (FEC), required satellite power could be reduced by about 5 db. This margin could be used to increase the number of satellite channels by a factor of three using the SES antenna of the same size as Standard A SES.

The resultant concept is the Standard B SES, offering the same voice quality as the existing Standard A SES. For small ships, it may be beneficial to have much smaller antennas. Studies are being made to develop a system using an antenna as small as 40 cm and a special voice-coding technique such as 7.2 kb/s residual excited linear predictive (RELP) coding.

Standard C SES could have an antenna as small as 15 cm to 20 cm for telex communications only. Such SESs would be suitable especially for transmission of navigational and/or meteorological information. This type of SES would play a very important role in the Future Global Maritime Distress and Safety System (FGMDSS), due to be implemented by the International Maritime Organization (IMO) as early as 1990.

RESULTS OF WARC-ORB

The first session of the World Administrative Radio Conference on the Use of the Geostationary-Satellite Orbit and the Planning of Space Services Utilizing IT (WARC-ORB-85) was held in Geneva in August and September 1985.

As a result of this conference, it was decided to adopt a report for submission to the second session of the conference, to be held in 1988. Major principles for the planning method adopted in the report are, among others:

The planning shall concern only the fixed satellite service in the bands 6/4 GHz, 14/11–12 GHz, and 20/30 GHz;

The planning methods shall guarantee in practice for all countries equitable access to the geostationary satellite orbit and the frequency bands allocated to the space services utilizing it;

No administrations are entitled to permanent priority in the use of particular frequencies and geostationary orbit;

The planning method shall take account of the requirements of administrations using multiadministration systems created by intergovernmental agreement;

The planning method should be able to accommodate multiservice and/or multiband satellite networks, without imposing undue constraints to planning; and

The planning method should ensure efficient and economical use of the geostationary orbit and frequency bands.

Next decided was the planning method, consisting of two parts — an allotment plan and improved procedures.

First, an allotment plan will permit each administration to satisfy requirements for national services from at least one orbital position, within a predetermined arc and predetermined band(s). The frequency bands in which an allotment plan is applied are part of the expansion bands, 300 MHz each in the 6/4 GHz and 500 MHz each in the 14/11–13 GHz bands allocated at WARC-79.

All ITU members will have at least one allotment consisting of an orbital position in a predetermined arc, a minimum bandwidth, and a service area. This plan is a rather rigid one, and the plan is established for a period of at least ten years.

Second, the improved procedures are a planning method based on the periodic multilateral planning meetings for gaining access to the geostationary orbit/spectrum resources. The approach will be a new and separate procedure to be added to the radio regulations. Details will be considered by the second session of the conference.

The overall aim of these improved procedures will be to guarantee for all countries equitable access to the orbit/spectrum resources in the relevant bands by means of multilateral coordination. The improved procedures will be mainly applied to the existing bands in the 6/4, 14/11–12, and 30/20 GHz bands.

A lot of work was required to finalize the planning before convening the second session of the conference in 1988. It was decided to direct the IFRB to develop a software package for the preparation of the allotment plan and to carry out appropriate planning exercises. The IFRB will make regular reports on the activities undertaken for the intersessional program. Comments from administrations will be taken into account.

Meetings for development and reviewing the computer programs will be convened by the IFRB. Account will be taken of technical expertise and computer software that may be available from administrations.

It is felt very difficult to implement the allotment plan, especially in the 14/11–13 GHz bands and for the hybrid satellite system using the C and K bands, satisfying the requirements of administrations in the 6/4 and 14/11–13 GHz bands simultaneously. Administrations will be urged to support the IFRB in order to establish practicable and usable planning methods.

KDD has developed a computer program called ORBIT-II for placing as many satellites in the geostationary orbit as interference to and from adjacent satellites allows. The program has been transferred to ITU and INTELSAT and is expected to be used for development and evaluating the planning methods in preparation for the second session of the WARC-ORB in 1988.

VII

TELECOMMUNICATIONS AND DEVELOPMENT

30

The Case of India

Vijay Menon

Dr. Vikram Sarabhai, Chairman of the Indian Space Research Organization (ISRO) saw the potential of space communication and its practical significance. "Developing nations such as India," he said, "have the possibility of effectively using space communications for national needs. Compared to advanced nations . . . they have indeed an advantage through not having an existing major investment in older technologies."

Thus, in 1955, India set up its first Experimental Satellite Communication Earth Station with assistance from the United Nations Development Program (UNDP). A decade later a center was established to provide training to earth station operators and technicians from developing countries. In 1969, work commenced on India's first Overseas Communications Earth Station at Arvi. A Memorandum of Understanding signed between ISRO and the National Aeronautical and Space Authority (NASA) of the United States in the same year resulted in the Satellite Instructional Television Experiment (SITE) in 1975–76.

Among the general objectives of SITE were:

to gain experience in the development, testing, and management of a satellite-based instructional television system, particularly in the rural areas;

to demonstrate the potential value of satellite broadcast television in the practical instruction of village inhabitants; and

to demonstrate the potential value of satellite technology in the rapid development of effective mass communication.

Among the specific objectives were:

to contribute to family planning;
to improve agricultural practices;
to contribute to general school and adult education;
to contribute to teacher training;
to improve other occupational skills; and
to improve health and hygiene.

Thus, from the very start, India's satellite program has been designed to contribute to the rural sector. The real impact of satellite technology has been felt in India since the launch of the Indian national satellite INSAT-1.

HOW INSAT IS USED TO REACH INDIAN VILLAGES

The INSAT system is a joint venture of the Department of Space, the Posts and Telegraphs Department of the Ministry of Communications, the Indian Meteorological Department of the Ministry of Civil Aviation, and All India Radio and Doordarshan of the Ministry of Information and Broadcasting. INSAT was conceived of as an aid for achieving certain basic national objectives: socioeconomic uplift of the masses; education; information and dissemination; and national integration.

INSAT is a multipurpose satellite system and is used by various agencies as:

All India radio for networking for news and radio programming distribution;
Posts and Telegraphs Department for telecommunications traffic;
Indian Meteorological Department for meteorological data collection and dissemination, disaster warning systems, and so forth; and
Doordarshan for TV networking and TV direct reception.

As of January 31, 1986, INSAT-1B had completed twenty-nine months in orbit and over twenty-seven months of operational service. As of February 1986, thirty-seven telecommunications terminals were in the INSAT-1B network and some 3,956 two-way, voice, or equivalent long-distance telecommunications circuits were loaded on sixty-seven routes.

The initial set of 100 disaster warning system (DWS) receivers had been installed in selected coastal areas. These can receive warning messages originating from the Area Cyclone Center, Madras, via satellite.

The initial set of 100 data collection platforms (DCPs) for automatic collection and transmission of meteorological data from remote locations had been installed.

By the end of December 1985, 173 TV stations in the country, out of 179, were in the INSAT-1B TV network. Fifteen hundred direct reception sets (DRSs) had been installed in various parts of the country. Also, ninety-three All India Radio Stations were in the INSAT-1B network.

The major objective of the INSAT-1B system is to provide television service to the remote rural and backward areas of the country where developmental effort requires mass media support. Eighteen districts in six states in India (Andhra Pradesh, Bihar, Gujarat, Maharashtra, Orissa, and Uttar Pradesh) have been selected on the basis of the backwardness of the area, the availability of suitable physical and developmental infrastructure, and the utilization of existing television program production facilities.

In the six selected states the INSAT facilities are used for the following:

educational programs for about forty-five minutes to each of six selected states in the country between 8:15 A.M. and 12:45 P.M. on a time-shared basis;
to provide area-specific programs for about forty minutes in the evening to each of the selected six states between 5:20 P.M. and 9:00 P.M. on a time-shared basis;
programs of national importance from 9:00 P.M. onward;
programs for the universities from 3:00 P.M. to 4:00 P.M.; and
programs of informative value and entertainment.

Immediate Coverage by INSAT

In the first phase in two states, Orissa and Andhra Pradesh, rural communities in 800 villages received programs directly from INSAT with the help of DRSs besides the VHF sets covered by transmitters at Hyderabad and Jabalpur. In addition, VHF sets covered by the terrestrial transmitter at Nagpur (Maharashtra) are also getting programs.

In the second phase (for example, from August 1984), terrestrial transmitters have been installed at Rajkot (Gujarat), Ranchi (Bihar), and Gorakphur (Uttar Pradesh). The programs fed through satellite are received by 300 DRSs in each state as well as VHF sets in the selected districts.

Instructional Objectives

The instructional objectives on INSAT television cover the areas of agricultural productivity, health and hygiene, family welfare, formal and nonformal education, national integration, and so forth. In accordance with the objectives, the thrust of the area specific programs are:

to provide developmental instructions in support of extension methodologies in the field of agricultural productivity;

to stimulate participation and involvement in extension activities that will directly benefit the rural people, particularly the weaker and the underprivileged sections;

to provide instructions for better public health and hygiene, including messages on family welfare;

to move away from a curriculum-oriented approach and emphasize direct teaching. The aim is to improve the quality of education in classrooms as well as through teacher-training programs;

to emphasize science education in order to promote scientific temper;

to help promote social justice; and

to stimulate public interest on news and current affairs, games and sports, and other important events.

In 1985, the installation of a large number of high-power transmitters (HPTS) and low-power transmitters (LPTS) for the relay of TV programs (for example, 180 transmitters in all) increased the reach of Doordarshan to about 70 percent of the total population. Under the DRS scheme, about 2,000 villages receive programs directly from the satellite with the help of a rugged TV set augmented by a 12-foot diameter, parabolic, chicken-mesh antenna and a front-end converter.

IMPACT OF INSAT ON RURAL SOCIETY

It is not quite three years since INSAT-1B became operational. Provision has been made for a team of social scientists to work in close cooperation with program producers and for a continuous feedback system to provide data on viewer attention, comprehension, and retention of program content. Nevertheless, few reports have been published, and it is rather early for conclusive findings on the impact of INSAT on rural society in India. However, the findings and conclusions on the impact of satellite usage, especially of TV transmission, drawn from the Satellite Instructional Television Experiment (SITE) can be usefully projected, as the INSAT program has its origins in SITE and Satellite Telecommunications Project (STEP).

India was the first developing country to use space science for "community" broadcasting through the SITE, which took place in 1975. SITE was a one-year experiment in educational broadcasting coordinated from the Space Applications Center in Ahmedabad. Five thousand villages all over India were equipped with their own direct reception antenna (dish aerial) and community television sets. Programs were transmitted for about four hours a day — one and a half hours for schools in the morning and two and a half hours for adult villagers in the evenings. As well as the educational programs, SITE villages received for the first time national and international news.

SITE was viewed as a technological triumph, although doubts were raised about its educational value. Educational broadcasting to remote rural areas is one of the most popular arguments advanced in favor of communication satellites.

IMPACT OF TELECOMMUNICATION AND INFORMATION TECHNOLOGIES ON INDIA'S ECONOMIC DEVELOPMENT AND SOCIAL CHANGE

Dr. Robert T. Filep, an eminent U.S. educational media expert who was associated with SITE, had this to say on the use of modern technology by India:

India cannot afford not to spend on space if it wants to provide telecommunications facilities quickly and cheaply to the rural and remote areas. And satellites provide the most cost effective way of achieving this today for a country like India whose terrestrial communications network is not so extensively developed. As for returns on investment in space technology, just one major crop saved by means of information derived through remote sensing from space or meteorological forecasting through net satellites will pay back all the money spent on the entire program.

The government of India, going by recent policy pronouncements and by its seventh five-year plan, accepts the fact that telecommunications and informational technologies will provide the momentum for growth.

In 1979–80, the last year of the fifth plan, the electronics sector achieved a production of approximately $685 million. Against this background of modest achievement, the sixth plan was drawn up. A compound growth rate of a little over 20 percent was planned with the terminal-year production at $1,630 million. During these five years (1980–85), the industry has grown an average annual rate of 28 percent. The growth achieved during 1984 was 37 percent over 1983.

Thus, the electronics industry has been growing consistently at a much higher rate than the average growth rate in gross national product, as also the overall industrial growth rate. The encouraging growth achieved in the past and the new directions in the policy framework being adopted for the industrial sector in general and the electronics sector in particular have encouraged the Department of Electronics to draw up an ambitious plan for the next five years. The industry is planned to grow at an average annual growth rate of 35 percent in 1985–90.

In the electronics sector, a package of policies was announced on March 21, 1985. This came on the heels of the telecommunications policy announced in March 1984 and the computer policy in November 1984. These policies have had an encouraging response from the industry. A large number of entrepreneurs from India as well as abroad have been encouraged to invest in the industry. It has achieved a growth rate of over 32 percent in 1985–86.

The Department of Electronics has initiated activities for the collection, compilation, and analysis of the socioeconomic data for the government. For this purpose, it is acquiring four supercomputers for compiling and creating data bases on the socioeconomic activities. It is also providing a system by which the data collecting agencies will not only provide information but will also have a mechanism of interacting with the system to monitor the economic progress of the region. The Department of Electronics through the National Informatics Center is developing a government informatics network to promote computerization of socioeconomic data from the district level onward. For providing computer access for the technical people and also for the commercial community, the Computer Maintenance Corporation Limited is promoting a computer network project, INDONET. It proposes to provide a variety of computer services to the commercial and technical communities at large.

Recognizing that such use requires a certain level of indigenous computer-manufacturing activities to sustain the tempo of computerization, the government has announced a new rationalized computer policy to broaden the production base and a large number of incentives have been provided. In the area of computer systems, a growth of 28 percent has been achieved in 1985–86.

Although it is difficult at this stage to assess the social, economic, and cultural consequences of these massive investments in communication technologies, we can note some broad trends. On the economic front, the new communication technologies are likely to contribute to a qualitative change in production processes. Information will increasingly become one of the key resources in the production, distribution, and service process. Take the example of computers. The computer industry is expected to register a five-fold increase in its turnover to $10,000 million in the seventh five-year plan period. This indicates the likely growth pattern in the coming years.

Further, as economic activity will increasingly be service oriented, this will provide greater employment opportunities. With the expansion of the electronic sector, manufacturing of electronic goods and equipment would require an expanded labor force. This would add still more job opportunities in production processes. More such opportunities will open up with the spread of new technologies in various economic, social, and cultural operations.

The job opportunities would bring about significant changes in economic and social status of the people. This trend is already evident in the country. *India Today*, a leading Indian news magazine, reporting on the decade 1975–85, said:

India's new middle class is a broadening band of something like 10 to 15 percent of the country's population that, at around 100 million, is more than the total population of most developed countries. In no more than a decade, they have shed the earlier image of being a financially squeezed section of the population and suddenly taken centerstage, made their demands felt, forced the government to shift its economic priorities and change its tax policy, and become the most visible sign of a rapidly progressing economy.

Ten years ago the political rhetoric centered on abolishing poverty. Today it looks forward to the twenty-first century. Then, it was a question of reining in monopoly capital. Now the government talks of industrial modernization and opening up the economy.

Ten years ago, India was still the first country that came to anyone's lips when he or she talked of poverty. The government's statistics say that only 37 percent of the population is now below the poverty line against 50 percent not so long ago. And in another five years it will be no more than 26 percent. Even if some allowance is made for exaggerated claims, there can be little doubt that poverty is in fact on the decline in most pockets.

Telecommunication and information technologies cannot take all the credit for economic and social development in

India but they are clearly playing a critical role in the country's progress.

The debate regarding the desirability of investing in the new technologies continues. There are those who believe that contrary to claims concerning their potential for enabling interaction and participation they are more likely to strengthen the structures of which they are the products.

It is argued that the assumptions underlying the proposal to use communication satellites are wrong, that satellites cannot provide solutions to problems that are primarily political, economic, and sociological, and that if satellites are used as an alternative to painful structural reforms, they are more likely to consolidate and perpetuate those conditions that in the first place produced those problems. But discussion and debate are characteristic of India.

REFERENCES

Filep, Robert T. 1976. Evaluation of SITE program submitted to the Indian Space Research Organization. Ahmedabad: ISRO.
India Today. 1986. "India during the Decade 1975–1985." *India Today.* April.

31

The Case of China

SU SHAO-ZHI

Since the 1950s, the speedy development of science and technology on a world scale has caused the surge of a new tide of scientific and technological revolutions.

China is a socialist country belonging to the third world. Because it is a big country, its development is uneven. It has launched satellites and rockets, and at the same time it has ox carts in certain parts of the countryside. As for the level of development, generally speaking, we may say that it is more developed than some less-developed countries (LDCs). Regarding our agriculture, we are self-sufficient in food grains and cotton and a small part is exported. Regarding industries, it has established independent and fairly complete industrial systems. Relatively speaking, we have the ability to absorb and digest investment and sophisticated technologies from foreign countries. But as for the impact on China's march toward modernization, the scientific and technological revolution represents both an opportunity and a challenge. There are two possibilities: one is that China takes advantage of this opportunity in good time and makes full use of the latest achievements in science and technology to develop its own economy and narrow the economic and technological gap between itself and the developed countries. The other possibility is that if China fails to deal with the technology properly or simply gives no attention to it, the gap between China and the developed countries of the world will grow and China will be left further behind. It should strive for the first possibility and avoid the second.

Since the end of the Cultural Revolution, China unswervingly shifted the focus of all its work to the drive for socialist construction, and made every effort to enhance the building of a socialist society with material progress and an advanced culture and ideology.

During the period of Sixth Five-Year Plan (1981–1985), China implemented three strategic and historic changes:

1. China's strategy for economic and social development has changed from a lopsided pursuit of increased output and output value, in heavy industry, to emphasis on the need for the balanced development of agriculture, light industry and heavy industry, and for all around economic, scientific, technological, educational, cultural, and social development, with a focus on the achievement of better economic returns.
2. The stagnant economic structure characterized by excessive and rigid control has been replaced by a vigorous new one appropriate to the planned development of a commodity economy based on public ownership.
3. As for China's economic relations with other countries, a closed and semiclosed economy has given way to an open economy characterized by positive use of international exchange.

The difficulties faced now are: (1) China is short of competent personnel in science and technology, especially what is called X personnel (that means a person who is both a specialist of computers and of other various specialized fields); (2) China lacks the ability to create a relevant infrastructure including communication, transportation, and storage; (3) China lacks enough organizations and economic framework to utilize and diffuse new science and technology. In the Seventh Five-Year Plan (1986–1990), China emphasizes the promotion of science and education by continuing to attach strategic importance to the advance of science and technology and to the exploitation of intellectual resources.

A striking feature of the Seventh Five-Year Plan is the importance it places on developing science and technology, so as to provide a more solid base on which to build the economy. To attain this end, China must pay enough attention to three things. First, it is essential for it to ensure that the whole nation understands the strategic importance of science and technology and has a sense of urgency about speeding up their developments. Scientific research institutions and research departments within universities and colleges shall be further oriented toward economic development. They shall form new economic associations with production units to integrate scientific research with production through different measures. China will conscientiously apply the patent law to protect the rights of inventors and stimulate the creativity of scientists, engineers, and workers.

Second, to apply and develop science and technology from China's conditions: Although it is a developing country that is several decades less developed than the advanced countries, it has established independent and fairly complete industrial and national economic systems, and what is more, many of our technologies are already matured under current conditions. It is now possible for China to catch up with the developed countries in certain fields and directly enter into a new era characterized by the application of computers, biological engineering, laser technique, and fiber optics by skipping over certain conventional stages of industrial development and by adopting advanced scientific and technological achievements from foreign countries. China already has many traditional industries, basic industries, and quite a number of capital-intensive industries, so it must now develop intermediate technologies and move toward further industrialization. And it will make every effort to adopt new techniques to remake traditional industries, and to enhance the study of applied science and basic science.

Third, scientific and technological progress and the success of modernization both depend on the training of competent personnel and the advance of education. It is China's consistent long-term strategy to attach great importance to education. It will establish a system for offering advance studies to scientific and technological workers and improve it systematically. It will strive for greater successes in the research and development of new and high technologies.

While implementing the policy of invigorating the domestic economy and opening to the outside world and energetically promoting the development of science and technology, China must be sober minded and pay attention to the following:

1. While working hard to build a socialist society that is advanced materially, China attaches due importance to promoting cultural and ideological progress. It firmly resists the corrosion of any decadent ideology, and absolutely will not allow its socialist society to be reduced to a pathological society.
2. In carrying out economic construction and introducing foreign investment and advanced technology, China must guard against environmental pollution and preserve ecological balance.
3. China shall hold in check the excessive growth of population and overcome defects of excessive urbanization. It will not only strictly carry out the family planning program, but will promote late marriage, late and fewer births, and eugenics so that China's population will be kept under 1.2 billion by the year 2000. It shall also prevent excessive urbanization by developing industrial and

commercial enterprises in the rural areas; for example, by encouraging the peasants to remain in the rural areas while engaging in industrial and other undertakings.

Obviously, the newly emerging scientific and technological revolution will help China to reach its targets set for the turn of the century. All in all, it will facilitate earlier fulfillment of the general task, which is to achieve modernization and build China into a socialist country with a high level of democracy and culture.

32

Computer-Aided Learning for Development

Hajime Oniki

The human capital formed through education is the most important infrastructure for economic and social development. Computer-aided instruction (CAI) can significantly accelerate education in certain, if not all, areas crucial for development.

The economic development of Japan during the postwar period was made possible by the presence of human capital, which had been built through a nationwide system of compulsory and higher education during the prewar period extending for more than 100 years. The importance of education for development was recognized after the war, and many countries enjoyed sustained economic growth as a result of having devoted a large amount of human and nonhuman resources to education.

CAI is a means of increasing the efficiency of education, as paper and pencil, blackboard, or textbook are. Typically, it is a personal computer equipped with an application program called a courseware. The major characteristic of CAI lies in its ability to "teach" students through conversational interactions. CAI was initiated more than twenty years ago in the United States and is now widely used in the United States and the United Kingdom — where it is known as computer-aided learning (CAL) — as primary and supplementary means for instruction in both elementary and higher education. To what extent it can replace human teachers is controversial now. In many countries, including Japan, however, the government is funding research to produce efficient courseware.

It is clear that not all educational activities needed for the development of a nation can be supplied by CAI. Education, school or other, forms a personality, including behavior patterns, value judgments, psychological reactions, knowledge, and skills. In many cases, this can be done only through repeated personal interaction between students and teachers, which cannot be achieved by a programmed machine, at least with the technology available now.

It is also true, however, that there are some educational activities for which CAI is useful. Basically, they are those in which the object of education can be fully represented, and the process of instruction can be fully controlled, by a computer. An example is teaching arithmetic to youngsters. Some people believe that CAI is more effective than human teachers.

Because education is a necessary condition for development, and education consumes a large amount of resources, effective CAI may accelerate the development of a nation significantly. One can think of, for instance, the amount of money and the length of time needed to train teachers.

INTERNATIONAL COOPERATION TO PROMOTE THE USE OF CAI

Whether or not CAI is more cost-effective than human teachers depends on the usefulness of the CAI system and its price relative to the wage rate of teachers. Currently, the price of hardware and software for CAI is still high even in developed countries. It is expected, however, that the price of hardware will fall rapidly because of technical progress and mass production; the price of a personal computer will be comparable to that of a television set in the near future.

The major obstacle to wide use of CAI is the cost of software (courseware) and its quality. To produce good courseware, it is necessary to combine the knowledge of good teachers and that of good programmers, although a machine with programs called CAI languages may be substituted for the latter. A great deal of research has been done in the United States and the United Kingdom, but there is still a lot to be done before CAI is widely adopted. The recent development of artificial intelligence and expert systems, both in theory and applications, will be useful to the development of CAI.

Developing countries will benefit greatly if they can use a good CAI system soon after it becomes available. It can save the money and the time needed to supply teachers for education. However, importing and implementing a CAI system is not like buying a tape recorder, because the former is an extremely complicated system. To evaluate CAI systems and to select a good one requires a lot of expertise. Usually, the system has to be tailored according to the needs; for example, the software may have to be adjusted to hardware, and the (human) language used in the system may have to be translated into another. In addition, there has to be somebody who can teach others how to use the system and who can do maintenance work. All of these will become a burden to developing countries when they intend to import CAI systems. International cooperation should be considered to lessen it.

At this point, let me describe the situation in Japan. Although a respectable amount of research and experimentation to produce good CAI systems has been conducted, there is virtually no CAI system being used in Japan. A few months ago, a newspaper article alarmed us by reporting that Japan was far behind Singapore in the adoption of CAI for elementary education, and the Japanese Ministry of Education started a committee of experts to explore ways to introduce CAI to elementary education. Few teachers in the elementary and the secondary schools in Japan, however, have shown an interest in using CAI.

On the other hand, elementary and secondary education in Japan, most of which is supported by public funds, is currently being challenged by small, private schools called *juku*. I expect that, in the near future when relatively inexpensive CAI systems become available, *juku* will start adopting them rapidly. The public schools in Japan will then move forward to introduce CAI in order to remain competitive with *juku*.

Based on this observation, I foresee that in the near future a possibility of mutually beneficial cooperation between developing countries and Japan for the use of CAI will emerge. It is desirable for us to prepare for cooperation now, and I offer the following recommendations to that end:

1. An international information center (database) of CAI systems should be formed in order to facilitate transfers and exchanges of CAI systems; registration of courseware, evaluation of courseware, collection of technical information about CAIs, transactions in coursewares, and the like would be the major tasks of the center; and
2. An international group of experts should be formed to assist translation, implementation, and maintenance of CAI systems.

33

The Role of Industrial Nations in Building Communications Infrastructure for Developing Countries

Iwane Takahara

It is fair to say that the telecommunications system is to a state what the nervous system is to a human being. As such, the telecommunications system has taken on vital importance as an aspect of the infrastructure that is indispensable to the economic development of a country.

At the Nippon Electric Company (NEC), the term *new telecommuncations technology* is defined as technology for exchanging information through the integration of computers and communications, or C&C for short. Indeed, we believe that only the C&C system can process and communicate large amounts of complex data and is therefore an indispensable tool for the realization of an information age.

The C&C system requires an extensive network of highly sophisticated equipment, and many countries are not yet technologically prepared to undertake the construction of such a system. Experienced manufacturers in industrial nations can lend a helping hand to these countries, from the planning stage to the installation and maintenance of such systems. Because the construction of a telecommunications network requires large sums of money, the receiving countries sometimes need some kind of assistance from the supplying country, and this is often provided on a governmental basis.

JAPANESE ROLES IN THE DEVELOPMENT OF TELECOMMUNICATION

Under such circumstances, one role to be played by industrial nations is to extend wide-ranging economic and cultural assistance in ways designed to support self-help efforts of these countries for the development and self-sufficiency of their economies. I would like to stress, however, that technology transfer and the training of managerial and technical personnel in these countries should be given top priority.

With this in mind, the Japanese government and private corporations have been actively involved in helping these countries improve their communications technology by sending specialists and by inviting many engineers to come to Japan for training.

In 1958, shortly after Japan resumed export after the war, the NEC established a manufacturing firm in Taiwan in a joint venture with a local partner. In the ensuing years, this company has developed its own technological resources, by dint of which it has grown into one of Taiwan's leading electronics companies. It is now exporting telephone switching systems and telephones to the world market.

In 1974, NEC set up a joint venture in Malaysia, and this company has since been manufacturing telecommunications equipment. In 1980, this company landed a contract for the construction of a nationwide communications network based on a digital switching system. The digital switching system embodies state-of-the-art technology, which will become the core of communication technology, and we are extending technological assistance to the company through a new plant constructed for that purpose.

In China, too, NEC is transferring technology in the areas of hardware and software in an effort to help that country build an up-to-date infrastructure for communications. In the area of hardware, we are cooperating with our Chinese partners in the manufacture of microwave communications systems and personal computers, and in the area of software, we established in 1982 a Sino-Japanese Software Center in a joint venture with the Chinese Ministry of Electronics Industry. This center aims at training software personnel in China and has already graduated more than 1,000 trainees, some of whom have acquired enough knowledge to act as instructors. The center has also been producing its own high-quality products.

In addition, we are extending technological assistance for the production of computer software in Singapore and Taiwan and communications software in Brazil and New Zealand.

It will be extremely gratifying to us if our technological cooperation proves to be instrumental in generating growth in these countries.

CHALLENGES POSED BY THE INFORMATION AGE

One factor that is going to play a key role in realizing this kind of human-oriented technology, which will continue to depend very much on human labor, is software. Software performs the function of instructing computers on what actions to take and what information to process and how. What we can achieve by our C&C systems depends on our software.

Software must be designed to meet the requirements peculiar to a given country. To ensure efficient operation of an information system, the design of software compatible with the language and business customs of the country is a necessity.

Because software is the culmination of sustained intellectual and scientific pursuit, newcomers cannot acquire the necessary production knowhow overnight. Cooperation in the development of the software industries of developing countries will, therefore, certainly go a long way toward accelerating the industrialization of their economies. It is an economic imperative for developing countries with a large population to redouble their efforts for the development of the software industry. In this area, the industrial nations also have a vital role to play.

CONCLUSION

We are firmly convinced that bilateral and multilateral cooperation for the development of such communication and data-processing systems will eventually lead to peace and prosperity in the world. We therefore feel that it is the role of those of us engaged in the development of C&C systems to work toward higher economic and social development throughout the world. To build cooperative relationships among people of the world with diverse economic, cultural, and ethnic backgrounds on the basis of mutual understanding, nothing is more important than personal exchange.

If an automatic interpretation telephone system becomes a reality, through the development of very large-scale integration technology and software, communication between different languages will be dramatically improved, and many obstacles standing in the way of cooperation and solidarity among countries will be effectively removed, paving the way for a durable peace in the world.

In this area, industrial nations have an extremely important role to play, and such communication systems would help the industrial nations and developing countries deepen their understanding of one another's people and culture and forge stronger relationships.

VIII

CONCLUSIONS AND RECOMMENDATIONS

34

Multinational Firms and Global Information Industry Development

KENT E. CALDER

For the long-range potential of the informatics revolution to be fully realized, for nations of the South as well as the North, two conditions must be met. First of all, the power of markets must be harnessed to stimulate innovation, especially in the area of information services. Second, the power of markets — together with the force of policy, where global consensus is possible — must again be utilized to promote the diffusion of new products and services on a global basis.

Assuring a vigorous, market-oriented innovation mechanism for the global information industry is preeminently an issue for relations among the advanced nations. Above all, it is a question for the United States and Japan, albeit in a multilateral context. Over the past five years, U.S. and Japanese firms, together with a few major European producers, have steadily lengthened their global lead in key sectors of information industry research and product development.

Recent patterns of U.S.-Japanese high-technology trade are rooted in national political and economic structure. Japan has made some significant technological breakthroughs of which U.S. citizens could profitably take note. But they are mainly in such areas as production technology, miniaturization, and energy efficiency. The United States remains clearly and significantly ahead of Japan in such areas as advanced circuitry, software, and large-scale switching equipment.

Many attribute the striking, yet complementary, differences in U.S. and Japanese research and production capabilities to culture. But structural analysis appears far more persuasive. Both innovation and production in U.S. high-tech industries are increasingly driven by the needs of military industry, with the tendency becoming stronger as defense procurement budgets increase and as warfare itself becomes more electronics intensive. Since the early 1980s, this bias of U.S. electroncs and information processing toward defense has intensified sharply under the dual impact of rising defense spending and intense competition in nonmilitary sectors with Japan. The net effect of this development is to intensify the traditional bias of U.S. electronics toward production of technically advanced products in relatively small quantities, rather than to aggressively mass produce for consumer markets.

The market incentives operating in Japanese firms are strikingly different. Because their market is overwhelmingly civilian and particularly consumer oriented, the incentive is to develop durable products that can be produced cheaply and in quantity. As U.S. producers become ever more oriented toward military markets, Japanese dominance of consumer applications becomes increasingly commanding.

Political forces, of course, cannot always recognize economic optimality, nor do they always permit it. Following the January 1, 1984, American Telephone and Telegraph Company (AT&T) breakup, a surge of demand for customer-premises telecommunications equipment in the United States, combined with misaligned exchange rates, triggered a sharp 30 percent increase in U.S. telecommunications imports during 1984, to $4.2 billion. This pattern continued into 1985, although growth in imports has recently become more moderate. The overwhelming share of these imports, as of U.S. electronics imports more generally, have been from Japan. Yet U.S. exports to Japan for a long period did not increase nearly so rapidly.

Aside from the rising trade imbalance and the symbolic impact it generates, important structural changes in the political economy of the U.S. information industry are also underway and profoundly affect prospects for free trade in electronics an information processing. One is the decline in the efficacy of military spinoff for the U.S. civilian electronics industry, which is intensifying U.S. frustration on trade issues as well. Another is the steady geographic dispersion of these sectors as they grow, making them a major force in an increasing number of congressional districts. These changes undermine prospects for free trade and generate pressures such as the recent Section 301 actions against Japanese firms in integrated circuits.

Offsetting internal developments within the U.S. domestic electronics industry that intensify protectionist prospects are the rapidly proliferating cross-national sourcing and research relationships between Japanese and Western firms in such areas as value-added networks (VANs), software, and data-base development. Strengthening the policy framework supporting such ventures would appear to be a crucial element in furthering free trade. Improved market access opportunities for foreign imports into Japan, of course, is also crucial. As the United States and Japan have both recently reaffirmed, strong protection for intellectual property rights is another indispensable element in stimulating global innovation in information processing, while also helping to improve the bilateral climate for U.S.-Japanese trade relations.

Whatever the political complications, it is clear that multinationals of the industrialized world must think seriously about third world markets, especially in the more basic telecommunications equipment areas. The global telecommunications equipment market may approach $90 billion by 1989, with the developing nations representing a sizeable proportion of this. With 71 percent of global population, 17 percent of global GNP, and only 7 percent of the existing stock of telephones (not to mention more sophisticated equipment and services) in these nations, it is clear that significant underinvestment in telecommunications services has occurred. If economic development is to proceed, and if North-South gaps are not to widen precipitously, there will need to be rapid acceleration of third world telecommunications-related spending. In one nation alone, the People's Republic of China, the number of telephones is expected to grow by 28 million within less than a generation — from the 5 million phones of 1985 to around 33 million by the year 2000. The expenditure for this project alone may well exceed U.S. $30 billion.

The critical problems for the major multinationals in assisting third world telecommunications development will inevitably center on finding a way to reconcile their commercial interests and overall market orientation with the statism of most developing nations. Throughout the world — North as well as South — telecommunications services have been traditionally regarded as a public good, the distribution of which had profound welfare and national-security implications for society at large. As a consequence, telecommunications development has traditionally been supervised by public post, telegraph, and telecommunications monopolies, a pattern that is just beginning to change even in the major Organization for Economic Cooperation and Development nations. Private telecommunications-sector investment in developing nations by foreign multinationals has frequently been a prime target of local nationalizations, particularly in Latin America. Intellectual property rights proprietary to multinationals have also at times not been properly protected.

Involvement by multinationals in third world information-industry development will inevitably be influenced by the position of local governments on such questions as intellectual property rights, local ownership requirements, and safeguards against nationalization. The stronger the global regimes that are created by multilateral agreement in these areas, the more active Western corporate involvement in third world development will likely be.

In the short run, the bias of third world telecommunications and information-sector demand will no doubt continue to be toward basic telecommunications infrastructure and hardware. Foreign exchange may often be a problem, with foreign firms forced to deal at times through compensation arrangements with local governments. Accordingly, the trading company — particularly the specialized trader conversant with market requirements and capable of after-service and training — may well be a vital element in telecommunications-trade transactions. In this regard, the establishment of Nippon Telegraph and Telephone International in October 1985, is likely to have positive implications for third world development. With an organization combining engineering and technical expertise with the financing and marketing knowhow of ten Japanese general-trading companies, this new entity should have real strengths in the planning and installation of telecommunications networks in third world nations as it gains international experience.

As was noted earlier, there are substantial and rapidly intensifying complementarities in the structure of high-technology industry in the United States and Japan, as well as, to a lesser degree, between the industries of these two nations and their counterparts elsewhere in the world. Transpacific joint ventures, and other forms of cooperative interaction, are rapidly increasing as corporate recognition of these complementarities grows. In an era of rising protectionist sentiment, corporate relationships transcending national boundaries are ever more essential in preserving the fabric of free trade. Recently, binational ventures to aid economic development in the third world, such as the joint Mitsubishi-Westinghouse nuclear energy projects, as well as several projects in telecommunications, have emerged. Encouraging such projects could be a valuable means of harnessing, through market forces, the capacity of advanced nations to aid the developing countries in their struggle to attain affluence and technical advancement.

35

Conclusions from TIDE I

SOGO OKAMURA

Rapid progress is being made in the area of information and communications as systems technology, supported by microelectronics components technology, is coming out with new products and services with increasing speed, thereby continuously posing challenges to existing scientific knowledge, rendering established industries obsolete, and forcing societies to rethink their structures, systems, and values.

Progress in information and communications technology can be expected to accelerate because the industry itself is developing the hardware and software that increase its research and development capability. The convergence of historically separate industries in communications, computers and components, also helps to overcome technological barriers and to push technology beyond its current limits.

The new information technologies have brought about productivity gains and increases in industrial and business efficiency in a wide area of applications, thus presenting a bright prospect for new economic growth and wealth creation. Needless to say, there are some negative aspects as well. But their impact, thus far, has mainly been felt in industrial countries, which still represent the overwhelming part of the world's GNP, but house only a fraction of today's world population.

In the developing world, the newly industrialized countries are undertaking great efforts to catch up with the North by devoting substantial financial and human resources to developments in the information and communication sector. These efforts have already reached a stage exceeding some countries in the North.

A large number of other developing countries are trying to become part of the worldwide network of suppliers and subsuppliers, using the most advanced communications systems to stay in close contact with the global market for information technology. In the least developed countries, radios and TV sets are common products already, and telephones are being increasingly installed to link farspread regions with little transportation infrastructure, and thus contribute to nation building. The point was also made that telecommunications are unevenly distributed across the world.

The South is an extremely heterogeneous group of developing countries, affected by and benefitting from information technology to varying degree. Some developing countries have reached technological competence comparable, or even superior, to those in certain parts of the North.

Assuming that accelerated progress in information technology will continue to come mainly from the United States, Europe, and Japan, and diffuse from these to the newly industrialized countries and to the other less developed countries, and assuming that the former group of countries will increasingly benefit more from this progress than developing countries, the gap between the more and the less advanced countries may widen further. This is evidently an undesirable direction, opposed to our shared goal of an interdependent world; because growing disparities cannot be accepted for humanitarian reasons, they will limit international trade prospects, and they could lead to regional and global destabilization, thus endangering world peace. It is the common interest of the world to bridge the gaps in information technology between developing and developed countries.

It is therefore of utmost importance to look at today's and tomorrow's technological achievements in the telecommunication and information areas to see to what extent the countries of the South can benefit from them in terms of their economic and social development, and what steps should be taken by both the North and the South to facilitate development, particularly through the transfer of technology. It is in this context that the first of the three symposia entitled TIDE 2000 (Telecommunications, Information, and Interdependent Economies) is devoted to the impact of information technologies on interdependence between the North and the South.

36

Conclusions from TIDE II

MARY G. F. BITTERMAN

Information and communication technologies can have major beneficial effects on society and, like all major technical advances, are an integral part in the evolution of the economic and social systems of industrialized and industrializing nations. Just as technological change affects our political, economic, and social structures, so does technological change itself depend on the performance of our economy, on the functioning of our social systems, and, most important, on the capacity of our societies both to generate and to absorb new ideas.

At its second conference, held in Honolulu, TIDE 2000 highlighted the implications of advanced information and communication technologies for the economy, for society, and for international relations.

Information and communication technologies are a major new force in the development of our economies and societies. The implications of this new force are so pervasive, so diverse, so radical, and so profound that almost no human action, no industrial and other economic activity, and no social organization will remain untouched by them.

Consideration of the first experiences and successes, the still unexplored opportunities, and the risks and uncertainties involved leaves no doubt that the dramatic changes brought about by the new information technologies will have effects that are not only domestic but international, as well.

Helping opportunities associated with the new technologies to materialize, rendering adjustment costs politically and socially acceptable, and containing the risks attending the progressive introduction and application of advanced information and communication technologies are the responsibility and challenge of government, industry, labor, and society as a whole.

To enhance the acceptability of new information technologies at the domestic level, there is a need to protect privacy, to strike a responsible balance between data protection and freedom of information, to promote structural adjustment, to provide for education and training, and to ensure that the new technological resources are utilized in the most cost-efficient manner.

Despite sound domestic policies, differences in political, economic, social, and cultural conditions may lead to uneven distribution within and among countries of the benefits and costs stemming from the progressive use of advanced information technologies. Such conditions should not result in policy responses that would tend to undermine the further development of the open multilateral system of trade, investment, and finance.

Increased international interdependence demands policy approaches that take into account the international implications of domestic policies. Closer international cooperation in dealing with the opportunities and risks of advanced information and communication technologies is required. Improvements in the "rules of the game" are needed in such areas as trade in services, international investment, technology, standards, transborder data flow, and intellectual property rights.

The activities of relevant international organizations in dealing with the new information technologies should be strengthened and avenues should be explored to facilitate cooperation among such organizations. Consideration should be given to practical and effective measures to increase public awareness and understanding of trends in and international implications of the development of new information and communication technologies.

Index

information technology: applications in different economic sectors, 228–30; benefits to airline industry from, 77–78; changing attitudes of work force toward, 79–80; and communications technology defined, 9–10; contradictory developments of, 218–20; data-protection problems raised by, 178–81; deregulatory trends in (by country), 25–32; economic analysis of deregulation of, 21–25; education and training in, 57, 59, 63, 80, 200–4, 208, 259; effect on services activities, 128–32 (table); global competition over markets for, 32–34; impact on banking and financial services, 102–3, 109–11; impact on economic growth and employment, 12–15, 21; impact on India, 285–88; impact on international relations, 15–17, 40–45; impact on society, 10–12, 199, 222–33; legal issues raised by, 43–44, 193–96; policy issues, 18, 51–52; rules of competition being changed by, 127–28; six fundamental themes in environment of, 125–26; social science interpretations of, 209–10; three social implications of, 223–28; TIDE 2000 conferences on, 3–8, 193, 306, 307; trade interdependence fostered by, 132–34; typology of workers in, 214 (table). *See also* communications; informatics; telecommunications; telematics

information trade: barriers to, 4, 7, 11, 17, 24, 66–67, 79, 80, 87, 92, 95, 99, 143–44, 145, 147–48, 153, 186, 195; four stages of interdependence in, 132–33; imbalance and Japan, 55–56; new rules for, 194–95; property rights as barrier to, 187–91. *See also* transborder data flow

INMARSAT (International Maritime Satellite Organization), 274–75

INSAT (Indian national satellite), 282–85

INSEAD, 4

Instinet (financial network), 87

integrated services digital network. *See* ISDN

intellectual property rights, 3, 8, 51, 67, 144, 145, 173, 174, 186, 190, 193–94, 303, 304; as barrier to trade, 187–91; Paris Convention on the protection of, 195; variety of laws providing for, 183–85; WIPO, 145, 146, 173, 174, 192n.1, 195

INTELSAT, 24, 25, 32, 34, 58–59, 146, 150, 152, 275, 277; Assistance and Development Program (IADP), 270; and deregulation in U.S., 266–68; Development Fund, 270; future prospects, 270–71, 273, 274; innovations in, 268–70; origin and operations, 265–66

interdependence in information technology, 132–45; four stages of cooperation, 132–33; international corporate, 138–42; revolt against, 142–45

Intergovernmental Bureau for Informatics, 68, 167, 176

International Consultative Commission on Transborder Data Flow Policies, 68

international corporate arrangements (ICAs), 138–42, 149nn.2, 3, 5

International Maritime Organization (IMO), 275

International Services Organization (ISO), 140, 145, 146

International Standards Organization (ISO), 254, 255

International Telecommunication Union (ITU), 7, 56, 68, 137, 138, 140, 144, 145, 146, 181, 248, 264, 276, 277

ISDN (integrated services digital network), 29, 41, 57, 64, 71, 125, 126, 133n, 137, 142, 149n.9, 218, 247–61, 270; defined, 248; in Germany and France, 249–51; in Japan, 251–52; long-term technical capabilities, 254; privatization vs. monopoly of, 256; three stages of change associated with, 257–60; types of services, 249; in U.S., 253

ISI (private satellite system), 267

Israel, 7, 146; attitudes toward technological change in, 226 (table)

About the Editors and Contributors

EDITORS

MEHEROO JUSSAWALLA is a Research Economist with the Institute of Culture and Communication at the East-West Center in Honolulu, Hawaii. She is the author of *Communications Economics and Development* and *Communication and Information Economics: New Perspectives,* co-compiler of *Telecommunications Economics and International Regulatory Policy: An Annotated Bibliography* (Greenwood Press, 1986) and *The Calculus of International Communications,* and has written numerous related articles.

TADAYUKI OKUMA is a senior research fellow in the Japan Institute of International Affairs and a member of the Japanese Committee for TIDE 2000.

TOSHIHIRO ARAKI is with the Division of North American Affairs in the Japanese Ministry of Foreign Affairs and a member of the Japanese Committee for TIDE 2000.

CONTRIBUTORS

JONATHAN D. ARONSON, School of International Relations, University of Southern California, Los Angeles

RICHARD J. BARBER, Executive Director, Pacific Telecommunications Council, Honolulu

ROGER BENJAMIN, Department of Political Science, University of Minnesota, Minneapolis

MARY G. F. BITTERMAN, Director, Institute of Culture & Communication, East-West Center, Honolulu

YALE M. BRAUNSTEIN, Professor of Economics, School of Library and Information Studies, University of California at Berkeley

ARTHUR A. BUSHKIN, Principal, ATKEARNEY Management Associates, Alexandria, Va.

KENT E. CALDER, Associate Professor, Woodrow Wilson School of International Affairs, Princeton University, Princeton, N.J.

JEAN-PIERRE CHAMOUX, Chairman, Droit et Informatique, Paris

STEPHEN DWORAK, Graduate Student, Department of Economics, University of Hawaii at Manoa

JAN FREESE, Director General, The Federation of Swedish Industries, Stockholm

H. P. GASSMANN, Head, Division of Information, Computer and Communication Policy, OECD, Paris

KLAUS W. GREWLICH, Director, Auswartiges Amt, Bonn

MICHAEL D. KIRBY, President, Court of Appeals, Supreme Court, Sydney, Australia

RAYMOND J. KROMMENACKER, Counsellor, GATT, Geneva, Switzerland

VIJAY MENON, Secretary General, Asian Mass Communication Research and Information Centre (AMIC), Singapore

HANSJURG MEY, University of Bern, Institut fur Informatik und angewandte Mathematik, Bern, Switzerland

WOLFGANG MICHALSKI, Head of Advisory Unit to the Secretary General on Multidisciplinary Issues, OECD, Paris

IAN MILES, Senior Fellow, Science Policy Research Unit, University of Sussex, U.K.

KAZUO OGURA, Bureau of Economic Affairs, Ministry of Foreign Affairs, Government of Japan, Tokyo

SOGO OKAMURA, Professor of Engineering, University of Tokyo

HAJIME ONIKI, Professor, The Institute of Social and Economic Research, Osaka University, Osaka, Japan

JOSEPH N. PELTON, Director, Strategic Policy Formulation, INTELSAT, Washington, D.C.

GÉRARD POGOREL, Director of Enseignment Superieur, France Telecom, Paris

NEIL PRIMROSE, Space Telecommunications and Postal Policy Division, Department of Communications, Belconnen, Australia

EDWARD J. REGAN, Vice President, Manufacturers Hanover Trust, New York

WALTHER RICHTER, IBM Haus, Vienna

PETER ROBINSON, Special Advisor, International Informatics, International Relations, Government of Canada, Ottawa

TOSHIO SATO, Director, Transmission Department, Kokushai Denshin Denwa, Tokyo

SUZANNE R. SETTLE, Office of International Affairs, NTIA Department of Commerce, Washington, D.C.

SU SHAO-ZHI, Director, Research Institute of Marxism-Leninism-Mao Zedong Thought, Chinese Academy of Social Sciences, Beijing

MARCELLUS SNOW, Professor of Economics, University of Hawaii, Honolulu

JOAN E. SPERO, Senior Vice President, International Corporate Affairs, American Express Company, New York

IWANE TAKAHARA, Senior Vice President, Director, Nippon Electronics Corporation, Tokyo

MAJID TEHRANIAN, Professor of Communication, University of Hawaii, Honolulu

DAN J. WEDEMEYER, Associate Professor of Communication, University of Hawaii, Honolulu

MASAKATSU YONEZAWA, Deputy Director General, Communications Policy Bureau, Ministry of Posts and Telecommunications, Tokyo